Studies in Child Development

In Search of Promise

STUDIES IN CHILD DEVELOPMENT

The National Children's Bureau

In Search of Promise

A Long-term, National Study of Able Children and Their Families

E. M. HITCHFIELD
Deputy Principal of Northampton College of Education
Formerly Senior Research Officer
National Children's Bureau

LONGMAN
in association with
THE NATIONAL CHILDREN'S BUREAU

LONGMAN GROUP LIMITED
London
Associated companies, branches and representatives throughout the world

© *National Children's Bureau* 1973

First Published 1973

ISBN 0 582 36516 3

*Printed in Great Britain by
William Clowes & Sons Limited
London, Colchester and Beccles*

Contents

Foreword

In Search of Promise marks a significant stage in the association of the National Children's Bureau with Longman as publishers of the *Studies in Child Development* series.

In 1966 *Four Years On* (now in its third impression) appeared as the first book in this distinguished series; and this year *In Search of Promise* is the twenty-first volume to be published. It is clear that these publications are accepted as works of the highest professional standards and they have exerted a significant and important influence both in this country and in America.

As a publishing venture this series has been based on a real appreciation of the aims and achievements of the Bureau since it was formed. In particular, the series reflects the scholarship and approach of the Bureau's director, Dr Mia Kellmer Pringle.

This volume not only brings *Studies in Child Development* to the maturity of twenty-one publications, but also stands as evidence of the wisdom of extending and developing the range of the Bureau's research and other activities since it was first formed.

In this study a group of children was identified as 'gifted' on multiple criteria. Then they were interviewed and assessed in many ways which included the Wechsler Intelligence Scale for Children. The results show the need to consult parents, teachers and the children themselves if a balanced judgment about 'giftedness' is to be made.

It is interesting to note the reservations made as to the role of creativity (with special reference to the American scene). This signposts the need for further research and study at a time when teachers of English in particular tend to overstate and overwork this concept in secondary schools in Britain.

For a publisher it is interesting to note that the ownership of books, access to them, and research or reference are all associated with the cleverest children. Equally encouraging to us is the fact that with very few exceptions teachers are identifying 'gifted' pupils and are providing for them. At the same time the study concludes that there is no evidence

ix

to support the case for segregating the clever ones from the rest of the school population—rather the contrary.

Educational research today rightly tends to concentrate on failure, on juvenile delinquency and on underprivilege. Elizabeth Hitchfield's volume provides a valuable and objective study which turns our attention to positive considerations of achievement. I am not qualified to comment on the techniques employed in the study, but no one will dispute the author's scholarship, nor question the importance of her conclusions.

Happily *In Search of Promise* provides me with an opportunity to pay tribute to all concerned with the work of the Bureau in the year of its tenth birthday. Longman (250 years old in 1974!) are indeed proud to have their imprint associated with the National Children's Bureau. I hope there will be further anniversaries to celebrate together.

June 1973   J. R. C. YGLESIAS,
                                                        Joint Managing Director
                                                              Longman Group

Acknowledgements

The Leverhulme Trust is to be thanked for its generous financial sponsorship which enabled this study to be carried out.

Tribute must be paid again, as in other National Child Development Study reports, to the co-operation of local authority staffs in England, Scotland and Wales, in particular to the teachers, school medical officers, health visitors and school welfare officers who undertook the initial interviewing, testing and examining of the whole cohort. This study depended on the material they provided in the two major surveys.

The parents and children deserve special gratitude for their co-operation in long interviews; these enjoyable, individual encounters will not be forgotten.

The initiator of the project, Dr Mia Kellmer Pringle, gave support and guidance throughout. Many members of her staff at the National Children's Bureau were called on at different times for advice and assistance which were generously given.

Miss G. Kidgell assisted with the interviewing of the children and Miss M. Donald and Miss H. Houghton with the interviewing of the parents.

Miss J. Bowles and Mrs J. James gave valuable assistance with the recording and analysis of the data.

Members of the Froebel Institute helped with marking and assessing, and offered most welcome comments and suggestions.

The final manuscript owes much to the interest of Miss M. Brearley who gave constructive help at each stage of the writing.

E.M.H.

Part I

Purpose and framework of the study

The National Children's Bureau is carrying out a longitudinal study of a group of children selected nationally. The work is a continuation of that started by the large-scale Perinatal Mortality Survey which took as its subjects all babies born in England, Scotland and Wales during the week 3 to 9 March 1958. Comprehensive information has already been obtained on the children at ages 7 and 11 concerning their physical growth and health, emotional and social adjustment, educational attainments and home background. This has provided valuable descriptive and normative material which can act as a standard of reference against which teachers, doctors and psychologists can compare individual children. It has also provided the background data for the intensive study of small subgroups of special or exceptional children. The results of two such studies have already been published: *Born Illegitimate* (1971) and *Growing up Adopted* (1972).

The present book records a study of a specially selected group of 'gifted' children. There has been no previous investigation in this country of the development of 'gifted' children on a national scale. 'Gifted' in this study has been interpreted in the widest possible sense so as to include not only those of high general ability but also those outstanding in any one of a range of specific abilities, e.g. mathematics, art, music, sport. A special feature of the sample has been the deliberate inclusion of a substantial proportion of children from social classes IV and V to counteract the usual under-representation of these groups.[1]

The purpose of the project was to study this nationally representative group of gifted children and to compare their development with that of their peers, not only at one point in time, but also over a period of time longitudinally. This combines the results of survey techniques appropriate to large-scale population studies with a more intensive, detailed case study approach. The views of parents, teachers and the children themselves were sought in relation to physical, social, emotional and educational aspects of development.

It is acknowledged that this study did not select all the children in

[1] See p. 14 for clarification of these groups.

1

the cohort who could be described as 'gifted', it did not even sample all the possible categories of 'giftedness' that could have been defined from the available data. The information that follows is about a small group of children who could be said, at the time they were selected to represent the achievements, circumstances and views of their peers, to be showing 'promise'.

1. Sources of information and comparison

Who is 'gifted'?

The first task in the project was to identify the group of children who were to be called 'gifted'. This was not easy, there being no absolute criteria on which to judge. The term is used sometimes to denote those of high general ability and sometimes those outstanding in one special ability. Moreover the words 'high' and 'outstanding' can be defined in whatever proportion the user decides, referring to the top 1 per cent, 5 per cent or even 20 per cent of any group on any dimension chosen for assessment. The decision about criteria in each case needs to be made in relation to the population and the type of data available from which the gifted are to be drawn.

A summary of the large-scale surveys on the whole birthday week gives the background from which this study's gifted children were chosen.

Background and source of 'gifted' sample

THE PERINATAL MORTALITY SURVEY

Information was gathered on virtually every baby born in England, Scotland and Wales in 1958 during the week 3 to 9 March. This group of children—numbering some 17,000 births in all—thus makes a completely representative cross-section. The term 'cohort' has been coined for such groups and it will be used to refer to them as well as the phrase 'the whole birth week'. The Perinatal Survey sponsored by the National Birthday Trust Fund, was designed to study the administration of British maternity services and investigate the causes of perinatal death, i.e. stillbirths and deaths in the first week of life (Butler and Bonham, 1963; Butler and Alberman, 1969).

An unparalleled amount of sociological, obstetric and medical information was collected concerning the mother and the course of her pregnancy and labour. These data, as well as detailed information on the baby, were amassed at the time of delivery by the birth attendant, usually a midwife, from antenatal and labour records, and a record was made of the infant's weight, progress and any illnesses in the first weeks of life. The sociological data were collected in an interview with the mother herself shortly after birth.

The results of the survey brought into sharp focus the increased perinatal mortality risk associated with certain clearly identified antenatal, social and obstetric conditions. For example, the risk of a perinatal death when a mother was having her fifth or subsequent baby was 50 per cent greater than average. Similarly, increased risk was associated with unskilled occupational status (30 per cent greater than average); maternal age over 40 (100 per cent greater); severe toxaemia in the mother (over 180 per cent greater); and smoking of ten or more cigarettes daily after the fourth month of pregnancy (35 per cent greater). The identification of these and other high risk groups led to more concentration of medical resources upon those mothers in greatest need.

This 1958 cohort of children is unique for a number of reasons: it is a representative national group, selected only by date of birth; the very high proportion of returns (an estimated 98 per cent of all babies born in the week) virtually eliminated the possibility of bias; and the comprehensive nature of the perinatal data still remains unrivalled anywhere in the world for a national cohort.

THE NATIONAL CHILD DEVELOPMENT STUDY (1958 COHORT)

In 1965 (and in 1969) it proved possible to trace and study again the children who as babies had been the survivors in the Perinatal Mortality Survey. This longitudinal, follow-up investigation is called the National Child Development Study (1958 cohort).

At each follow-up, information on the children is gathered from four main sources: first from schools by means of a detailed assessment schedule, completed by head teachers and class teachers; this provides a comprehensive picture of each pupil's attainments, behaviour and adjustment in school as well as information about the school itself and questions such as the contact between school and home. Secondly, each mother, and sometimes the father too, is interviewed by an officer of the local authority, usually a health visitor, to obtain detailed information about the home environment as well as about the child's development and behaviour. Thirdly, the school health service undertakes a special medical examination, including measuring height and weight, objective tests and clinical assessments of vision, speech and hearing, investigations of motor co-ordination and laterality, as well as a full clinical examination. Fourthly, the child himself is given a number of attainment and other tests.

The major findings of the study of the 7-year-olds have been published (Pringle, Butler and Davie, 1966; Davie, Butler and Goldstein, 1972).

The material gathered when the children were 11 years old is at present being analysed while plans are under way to re-examine the cohort before the majority of the pupils leave school.

The growth and development of the children will continue to be studied at least until they have reached adulthood because the project provides an unrivalled opportunity to find answers to many important questions, neither known nor easy to discover by any other means.

The data collected from schools in the 1965 survey provided the information from which the gifted children were identified. Norms from all three surveys provide the standards against which the special group was evaluated.

2. Aims, design and presentation

General aims

The plan was:

1. to collect data that would enable the gifted children to be described in terms of intelligence, educational achievement, social and emotional adjustment;
2. to compare their performance with that of their peers;
3. to find out if there were improvement or deterioration in the achievements and circumstances of subgroups and individuals over a period of time;
4. to determine whether the gifted had any special scholastic or developmental problems arising from or linked with their exceptional talents;
5. to collect all such information as would be of value in future studies of these children when they become adolescent and adult, e.g. their current dominant interests and hopes regarding careers which might indicate specific fields where eminence will be achieved.

General considerations

Most studies, since the classic work of Terman began in 1921, have followed his lead by taking children with IQs over 140 as gifted, but occasionally this line of demarcation has been questioned. For one thing, high all-round ability as measured by IQ tests might exclude those children who are specialists in one area, e.g. exceptional in a physical skill like swimming or skating, or in an academic subject like mathematics or an aesthetic one like art. Further criticisms suggest that selection on IQ alone picks out the obedient and conforming pupils who do well at what teachers ask of them and therefore are highly esteemed. This is said to miss some exceptional children who do not conform and do not excel in school-type tests, but who are gifted by reason of their originality and flair in situations which leave room for more self-initiation of activity than most classrooms allow. Terman himself reported, after a follow-up of his high IQ group in their middle age, that though they had on the whole done better than a control group in terms of success and adjustment there seemed to be no 'geniuses', no 'great' men or women emerging in any one field. Perhaps, even at the age of 40, it is too soon to bestow the title of greatness, and someone may emerge yet as the genius of Terman's group. It could also be true that, by selecting on IQ alone, he may have missed the quintessence he sought.

Another problem to be considered was that of social class. In Terman's study, 'the proportion of fathers belonging to the professional or semiprofessional classes is more than four times that in the general population; comparatively few are drawn from the ranks of semi-skilled or unskilled labour' (Burt, 1962a). Burt's own London survey in the 1920s and Parkyn's New Zealand survey in 1948 indicated similar imbalance in social background and many other studies that have selected children on scholastic or intelligence tests show this discrepancy between the children of non-manual and manual workers. Much more attention has been drawn to this point in recent years; the studies of Jackson (1964), Douglas (1964), Floud et al. (1957), Bernstein (1960), Lawton (1968) and Pringle (1966) among others have highlighted the educational problems of children of manual workers in our community. It was decided to include in the present study additional numbers of children from social occupation groups IV and V.

At the time of the selection of the gifted children the examination of the whole cohort at 11 years was being undertaken. To give additional information on those who might be considered gifted would have placed too much of a burden on teachers, who were already giving generously of their time by completing very detailed assessment schedules for all the children in the cohort. Therefore it was decided to make the selection from the data already available on the 7-year-old children. This had the added advantage that one could examine to what extent those children who were showing considerable promise at the early age of 7 were still continuing to do so at 11 years of age.

The design of the investigation

SELECTION PROCEDURES

The total sample of gifted children was selected by means of three criteria, namely the Goodenough Draw-a-man test score, high attainment in reading and number work, and parents' recommendation. No intelligence test was given to the children at 7 therefore IQ as a criterion was not available to the study even if it had been thought desirable.

Full details of the criteria are given below. [The final sample is given in Table A2.3.][1]

[1] Appendices are not included in this volume. Copies have been deposited with the National Lending Library (see 'Presentation of the material', p. 12 below). In the following text, references to appendices are shown in square brackets, and tables included in them are referred to with the prefix A, e.g. [Table A2.3] indicating the third table in Appendix II.

CRITERION 1

Goodenough Draw-a-man test scores (Harris 1963) were obtained when the children were 7 years of age.
Three groups were selected on the basis of this criterion.

Group 1

54 children: obtained a score of 44 or over, the top 0·4 per cent of the cohort distribution

Group 2

51 children: one in seven random sample of those who obtained scores between 37 and 43

Group 3

16 children: one in three in social classes IV and V with scores between 37 and 43 after Group 2 had been selected

It is important to mention that even on this non-verbal test social classes IV and V were under-represented in the higher scores. Therefore, as stated in the introduction a compensatory weighting was made.

CRITERION 2

School attainment in reading and arithmetic as assessed by teachers and measured by tests when the children were 7 years of age.

Group 4

47 children: maximum ratings from teachers and full scores on tests

Group 5

59 children: sample of one in seven from 414 children with high teacher ratings and high scores on tests

Group 6

22 children: half of the remaining children in social classes IV and V after Group 5 was selected
This group was the second example of compensatory social class weighting.

CRITERION 3

Parents' identification: a letter (Appendix 1a) was published in several magazines and the national press asking parents and teachers to write to the National Children's Bureau if they had a 'gifted' child born in the sample week. This, and an announcement in a talk on BBC radio by the Bureau's Director, brought 103 names of children eligible for consideration.

Group 7
56 children: selected from parents' letters [Tables A2.1, A2.2].

FINAL SAMPLE
Not all the children selected were able to take part in the study. The following table shows the number of boys and girls, totalling 238, who were actually interviewed. Ten children qualified on more than one criterion, in order to simplify the table they were categorised by giving priority to Group 7, Group 4 and Group 1 in that order.

Table 2.1. Numbers of children interviewed in three selection groups

Criterion	Boys	Girls	Total
1. Draw-a-man test	38	47	85
2. Attainment	50	50	100
3. Parents' recommendation	37	16	53
	125	113	238

[Fuller details in Table A 2.3]

It will be seen that nine more girls than boys were selected on the Draw-a-man Test. Harris (1963) reported that the sex difference between mean scores on the test favoured girls at each year of age by about one half-year growth.

In attainment the numbers were equal, but in the letters from parents' group there were twice as many boys as girls. This reflected the general pattern from the whole batch of replies. This might mean that the incidence of 'giftedness' is higher among boys than girls or that from parents' point of view boys are more readily recognised as gifted, or perhaps more highly valued if they show ability, than girls.

There were 61 boys and 66 girls whose fathers' occupations were non-manual, and 64 boys and 47 girls whose fathers' occupations were manual. The larger number of boys in the manual group was recommended by parents; twice as many parents in the manual social class group answered the letter in the press and magazines.

Interviewing procedures
It was decided to have only one interviewing session for each child, and in order to make this less exhausting the interviews and test battery were designed in such a way as not to occupy more than 3 hours for any one child.

Two educational psychologists shared the testing and interviewing of the children and two experienced interviewers saw their parents. For the most part, Chief Education Officers and Chief Medical Officers generously provided accommodation for interviewing in town and city centres and children and their parents travelled to meet the study workers. In some cases head teachers offered accommodation in their schools, and in others parents welcomed the interviewers to their homes and provided two rooms, despite some family inconvenience. Families made a tremendous effort to attend, making arrangements for younger members to be cared for, travelling long and sometimes inconvenient distances, taking days from work, etc. It was gratifying that 75 fathers accompanied mothers and 14 fathers came alone to the interview. It was one of the aims of the survey to include the contribution of fathers as much as possible.

The interviews were carried out between the middle of February and the end of July 1969, when the children were aged between 10 years 11 months and 11 years 4 months.

THE CHILDREN'S INTERVIEW

[A full list and description of the tests and other measures of assessment is provided in Appendix 2.]

The aim was to select a set of varied items that would challenge each child in general and in specific areas of knowledge or behaviour. It was an opportunity to be innovatory as well as repetitive of earlier studies of the 'gifted'. Where material was specially designed for the study it was tested on pilot groups of 10- to 11-year-olds, the same school year group as the study group children. The final battery of items was tried out on twenty highly intelligent boys and girls to ensure its feasibility in terms of time and intrinsic interest to the children. Three hours sounds a long time, but the children proved able to sustain their efforts over this period. Precautions were taken to minimise fatigue, the tests and questions were short and varied, breaks were provided according to the time and length each child seemed to need, food and drink were supplied, and finally, if anything was proving too difficult or fatiguing it was soon discontinued.

Tests and assessments

1. THE WECHSLER INTELLIGENCE SCALE FOR CHILDREN

An estimate of general intelligence seemed essential. The Wechsler Intelligence Scale for Children (shortened form) was chosen in preference to the Revised Stanford-Binet Test because it contains verbal and non-verbal scales. Phillips and Bannon (1968) demonstrated that though the Revised Stanford-Binet Test correlated highly with academic achievement at the age of 11, it was greatly influenced by those verbal abilities which distinguish social classes. We wanted the children from the manual social class to have every opportunity to show their abilities.

In addition, the shortened Wechsler scale is quicker to administer than the Stanford-Binet. The test was usually given at the end of the session as it dealt with commonly known test-type material rather than the newer and unexpected questions in the interview schedule and divergent thinking items.

2. PROPOSITIONAL LOGIC

The results of Lovell and Shields (1967) in their use of Piaget-type tests were interesting in that these obviously stretched the most able children. It was not possible to include the same ones in this study because of the time and the apparatus required. However, a test of propositional logic which deals verbally with the relationships of the sixteen binomial propositions in which Piaget categorises his work on thinking, had recently been developed in conjunction with the New British Intelligence Scale, so this was included in the battery of tests.

3. INFORMATION

A test of information was included to determine the direction of the children's abilities, examining four areas of knowledge, namely science, geography, history and the arts. As well as this the children were asked the difficult questions, 'What is science?' 'What is history?' (also geography, mathematics, art, poetry) to see what conceptual levels of thought they could bring to the definition of different subject areas.

4. SOCIAL REASONING

Five questions, taken from the New British Intelligence Scale of Social Reasoning, were asked, examining some of the children's concepts of responsibility, rules, equality, authority and causality.

5. DIVERGENT THINKING

It seemed imperative to include some tests of divergent thinking in view of the recent interest in and research on tests of this type. They were chosen with reference to certain subject areas with the hope of throwing further light on the direction of children's abilities and interests. Drawing (circles test), mathematics, science (verbal fluency test), word appreciation and music were represented.

6. BARRON-WELSH ART SCALE

This scale was given as it had been shown to be useful in differentiating artists from non-artists and research scientists from other scientists among adults. It was also claimed to be related to personality traits in respect of conformity and nonconformity.

7. SENTENCE COMPLETION TEST

A short sentence completion test was devised to give further information about attitudes to school and home.

8. INTERVIEW SCHEDULE

The schedule covered five areas of information: school, teachers, interests, self and friends. The questions were framed to be as open-ended as possible to allow children to elaborate in their own style if and when they could.

Material available from the second follow-up of the whole birth cohort at the age of 11

1. Verbal and Non-verbal Reasoning Test.[1]
2. Reading Test.[1]
3. Mathematics Test.[1]
4. An essay: on interests, home life and work, written after the children had been asked to imagine they were now 25 years old.
5. (a) Teacher's assessments of general knowledge, number work, use of books, oral ability (all on a five-point scale).
(b) Teacher's responses to the specific questions detailed in Chapter 5.
6. Stott's Social Adjustment Guide completed by teachers.

In addition all the interview and assessment schedules, obtained in the two earlier major studies described in the previous chapter, were available for this investigation. Thus it draws on data collected and available in precoded form, at the time of birth and then again at the age of 7 years.

Interview with one or both parents

The interviews with the parents took about 2 hours and covered information about their child's schooling, interests and hobbies, friends, personal qualities and general behaviour. The parents were also asked about their expectations and hopes regarding their child's future, further education and employment. This was coupled with questions about their own educational achievements.

Fathers were asked to complete a seven-point rating scale on the personality of their child: this consisted of items from Terman's 'Ratings on Physical, Mental, Social and Moral Traits' form. This was to give fathers a chance to take part in the study even if they could not attend the interview, for it could be completed at home and returned by post.

Presentation of the material

The results of the study are presented as far as possible in non-technical language, and the tables have been made uncomplicated and kept to a

[1] National Foundation for Educational Research Tests.

minimum. The results are shown in the form of percentages to the nearest whole number [Levels of significance are shown in the relevant appendix.]

Those differences mentioned in the text, for example between sex, social class, IQs above or under 130, have been tested and found to be statistically significant. (Because of the size of the sample, only p 0·01 or less was accepted as significant.) Where such differences are described as tending to be in a certain direction, it means that there was a statistically significant trend in that particular direction.

A complete set of all the tables referred to in the text together with a statistical note can be obtained at cost price from: The Supplementary Publications Scheme, National Lending Library for Science and Technology, Walton, Boston Spa, Yorkshire, LS23 7BQ quoting reference number . . ..

A set is also deposited in the Bureau's library for free consultation. The text has been written in such a way as to include all the essential information. Tables not in this volume are referred to in square brackets, with Appendix number.

Definition and relevance of social class

In everyday usage, 'class' tends to have overtones of social prejudice. Frequently it implies also a value judgment, its connotation being influenced by one's view of society in general and one's political persuasion in particular. Used in this way, the term refers to a person's standing, and even 'worth', in a society which, while becoming egalitarian in some respects, is still organised to a considerable extent on hierarchical lines. Here the term 'social class' is not used in this way but as an entirely neutral description for the occupational group of the children's fathers, mothers or grandfathers, as the case may be.

The classification most frequently used in Britain is that adopted for census purposes by the Registrar General (1966). Occupational groups are divided into five categories: social class I consists of occupations requiring very high professional qualifications, usually a university degree or its equivalent; II includes such occupations as school teacher or manager in industry; III is by far the largest single group (containing more than half of the population) and is usually subdivided into non-manual and manual sections (occupations such as shop assistant and clerical workers are placed in the former and all skilled manual occupations in the latter); IV consists almost exclusively of semi-skilled, and V of unskilled manual occupations.

Thus generally, social classes I, II and III non-manual cover 'white collar' jobs and these groups will be described as 'middle-class'; whereas the other three groups, almost exclusively of a manual nature, will be referred to as 'working-class'. A summary of these classifications is shown in Table 2.2 together with the proportions of children in the

National Child Development Study whose fathers fall into each group.

The reason for using social class as a yardstick rises out of its convenience as an indirect measure of what might be termed a family's 'lifestyle'. Hence it embodies a wide variety of environmental influences which affect a child's development and, furthermore, reflects to some extent the influence of hereditary factors. For example, children of professional workers are taller and show higher educational achievements than those of unskilled manual workers, which is likely to be due to the combined effects of 'nature' and 'nurture', rather than to the influence of one or other alone.

Table 2.2. Classification of occupations

Social class	Group	Nat. Child Devel. Study (%)
I	Higher professional	5
II	Other professional and technical	14
III	Other non-manual occupations	10 ⎫ 54
III	Skilled manual	44 ⎭
IV	Semi-skilled manual	17
V	Unskilled manual	6
	No male head of household	3

Part II
Results

The large-scale surveys of the whole birth week and the special study of the gifted children yielded a vast amount of data. This was analysed, first to describe the gifted in comparison and contrast with the whole cohort; secondly to describe them as a group, using the special material collected from them; thirdly to compare and contrast subgroups within the gifted group (particularly in relation to sex, social class and IQ); lastly to present some individual case histories to illuminate the uniqueness of individual children.

3. The years between seven and eleven
A comparison of the 'gifted' with the whole cohort

Social class distribution
The first difference of importance to note between the specially selected group and the whole cohort is that of social class distribution. The gifted group is skewed in the middle-class direction. Three times as many children from social classes IV and V were included by compensatory weighting on two criteria, but their numbers were still 20 per cent below the proportion represented in the whole cohort. At the other end of the scale, twice the proportion of children from social classes I and II appeared in the gifted sample as in the whole birth-week group.

Table 3.1. Social class distribution

Registrar General's Social Class classification	Whole cohort (%)	'Gifted' group (%)
I	5	12
II	14	28
III	54	40
IV	17	13
V	6	5
No male head of household	3	2

School achievements
One of the aims of this study was to see how this special group of children fared in school. This can be done by looking at their results on attainment tests and teachers' ratings. Comparison can be made between the gifted and the whole cohort at ages 7 and 11. (Twenty-two of the gifted children who did not take part in both large-scale surveys have been omitted in this section.)

READING ABILITY AT 7 YEARS OF AGE

Table 3.2. indicates that, even allowing for those specially selected because of high attainment, the gifted group was doing well at 7 years

16

of age, three-quarters of them being placed in the top 30 per cent of the whole cohort. The difference between boys and girls was highly significant in the whole cohort, but not in the gifted group.

Table 3.2. Teachers' ratings of children's reading ability at seven years of age

Descriptive categories for rating	Whole cohort			'Gifted' group		
	Boys (%)	Girls (%)	Total B + G (%)	Boys (%)	Girls (%)	Total B + G (%)
1. Avid reader; reads fluently and widely in relation to his age	5	9	7	39	45	42
2. Above average ability, comprehends well what he reads	21	30	25	36	34	35
3. Average reader	43	44	44	19	16	18
4. Poor reader	28	16	22	6	5	6
5. Non-reader, or recognises very few words	3	1	2	0	0	0

Table 3.3. Teachers' ratings of children's reading ability at 11 years of age

Descriptive categories for rating	Whole cohort			'Gifted' group		
	Boys (%)	Girls (%)	Total B + G (%)	Boys (%)	Girls (%)	Total B + G (%)
1. Exceptional; Reads very widely for pleasure and information. (Approx. top 5% of age group)	4	6	5	18	25	22
2. Above average; turns to books very readily. (Approx. 25% of age group)	22	29	26	43	55	49
3. Average. Skill and comprehension satisfactory for school requirements. (Approx. middle 40% of age group)	45	48	47	37	21	29
4. Below average. Still learning the skill of reading; not inclined to turn spontaneously to books for pleasure and information. (Approx. 25% of age group)	25	16	21	1	0	1
5. Very poor or non-reader; recognises few words; very limited use of books because of poor skill. (Approx. 5% of age group)	4	2	3	1	0	1

Table 3.4. Teachers' ratings of children's mathematical ability at 7 and 11 years of age[1]

Descriptive categories for rating	Whole cohort at 7 years			'Gifted' group at 7 years			Whole cohort at 11 years			'Gifted' group at 11 years		
	B (%)	G (%)	B & G (%)	B (%)	G (%)	B & G (%)	B (%)	G (%)	B & G (%)	B (%)	G (%)	B & G (%)
1. Extremely good facility with number and/or other mathematical concepts; grasps new processes very quickly; shows insight and understanding	4	2	3	38	31	35	4	4	4	25	17	21
2. Understanding of number work well developed; grasps new processes without difficulty	18	16	17	30	37	34	20	21	21	47	57	52
3. Average ability in this sphere	42	45	44	28	26	27	36	39	38	24	22	23
4. Rather slow to understand new processes. Rather poor facility with numbers, although able to do some things by rote	32	33	33	4	5	5	33	31	32	4	5	5
5. Little, if any ability in this sphere; shows virtually no understanding at all	4	3	4	0	0	0	6	4	5	0	0	0

[1] It will be noted that in Mathematics and General Knowledge the results of the 7 and 11-year-old surveys are represented in one table because the same descriptive categories were used.

READING ABILITY AT 11 YEARS OF AGE (Table 3.3)

The descriptions in the rating scale were altered in the second follow-up to take into account the development of skill and interest in reading that takes place in the junior school. Teachers were asked to rate 'use of books', instead of 'reading ability'.

Although nearly three-quarters of the gifted group were rated in the top two categories, showing that they were still an above average group, there was a considerable drop in the number of children placed in category one. The girls in the gifted group were rated significantly higher than the boys.

MATHEMATICAL ABILITY AT 7 AND 11 YEARS OF AGE (Table 3.4)

The results were similar to those in reading in that the majority of the gifted group rated above average at 7 and 11, but numbers dropped in category 1 on the second follow-up. The same proportion of boys and girls proved above average, but more boys appeared in category 1.

There was found to be a significant overall tendency for the boys to receive higher ratings than the girls at 7 in the survey group (11,000 *Seven Year Olds*, 1966), but this did not apply to the gifted group.

ORAL ABILITY AT 7 YEARS OF AGE (Table 3.5)

Eighty per cent of the gifted group were rated as above average as compared with 25 per cent of the survey group. This difference was of importance considering that some children were selected on a non-verbal test. In the whole cohort the girls were rated significantly higher than boys, but the difference was not consistent at all levels of oral ability, the girls were not significantly better in the gifted group.

ORAL ABILITY AT 11 YEARS OF AGE (Table 3.6)

The greater complexity of language of junior school children led to an alteration of rating descriptions on the second follow-up. Again the pattern was repeated, with the gifted group having two-thirds rated above average, and again the numbers fell from category 1. This time more girls changed positions than boys, so that while they were equal in proportion if the top two categories were added, there were fewer girls in the top 5 per cent category. This did not happen where the other language ability, i.e. reading, was concerned; perhaps the gifted group contained more quiet girls who enjoyed the solitary pleasure of reading.

AWARENESS OF THE WORLD AROUND (GENERAL KNOWLEDGE) (Table 3.7)

In the whole cohort at 7 the boys were rated significantly more highly than the girls especially at the upper end of the scale. This held markedly

Table 3.5. Teachers' ratings of oral ability at 7 years

Descriptive categories for rating	Whole cohort			'Gifted' group		
	B (%)	G (%)	B + G (%)	B (%)	G (%)	B + G (%)
1. In conversation expresses himself well	10	13	12	38	40	39
2. In conversation or oral lessons, has good vocabulary and variety of phrases in relation to his age	14	15	15	33	39	36
3. Average oral ability for his age	51	55	53	25	19	22
4. Below average oral ability; tends to use simple word groupings	21	15	18	3	3	3
5. Markedly poor oral ability	5	2	3	1	0	1

Table 3.6. Teachers' ratings of oral ability at 11 years

Descriptive categories for rating	Whole cohort			'Gifted' group		
	B (%)	G (%)	B + G (%)	B (%)	G (%)	B + G (%)
1. Exceptionally good for his age; shows extensive vocabulary and complex sentence formation	2	3	3	20	13	17
2. Above average; has very good vocabulary and expresses himself well orally	18	23	21	38	53	45
3. Average for his age; expresses himself satisfactorily in conversation and oral lessons	54	55	55	41	33	37
4. Below average; rather limited in vocabulary, tending to use simple phraseology	23	17	20	1	1	1
5. Very limited oral ability for his age	3	1	2	0	0	0

Table 3.7. Teachers' ratings of General Knowledge

Descriptive categories for rating	Whole cohort at 7 yrs			'Gifted' group at 7 yrs			Whole cohort at 11 yrs			'Gifted' group at 11 yrs		
	B (%)	G (%)	B&G (%)	B (%)	G (%)	B&G (%)	B (%)	G (%)	B&G (%)	B (%)	G (%)	B&G (%)
1. Exceptionally well informed for his age	3	2	3	32	24	28	40	2	3	23	9	16
2. Good background of general knowledge	23	17	20	40	41	40	24	21	23	51	66	57
3. Average in this respect	45	53	49	25	29	27	43	46	45	25	19	22
4. Rather limited knowledge	25	24	25	4	6	5	25	27	26	1	7	4
5. Largely ignorant of the world around him; (lack of general knowledge is a substantial handicap in school)	5	4	4	0	0	0	4	3	4	0	0	0

for the gifted group at 11, in category 1, and elsewhere the familiar pattern emerged showing three quarters of the gifted group rated above average compared with one quarter of the cohort.

COMMENTS ON THE TEACHERS' RATINGS OF ATTAINMENT

It is obvious that the gifted children as a group were being identified by their teachers as above average. A recurring drop in position from category 1 to 2 on all aspects appeared in the second follow-up. This could be due to a number of factors: (1) the natural regression effect—a trend towards the mean in the comparison of scores or grades over a period of time; (2) 62 per cent of the gifted had at least one rating in category 1 at 7 years and this large proportion could only change in one direction: (3) the first ratings were done by infant school teachers and the second by junior school teachers and these two professional groups might judge on different criteria because of the difference in age of their pupils. It is perhaps a more difficult and complex task to judge children after six years of schooling than after only two. The drop from 12 per cent in category 1 in oral ability at 7 to 3 per cent at 11 years in the results of the whole cohort showed that either the altered rating-descriptions changed the teachers' perceptions considerably, or perhaps less opportunity presented itself in junior than in infant schools for children to reveal their powers of speech.

Primary school teachers have become sensitized to the grammar school—borderline grammar—secondary modern school distinctions. There is still some necessity for this in an education system which requires selection for secondary education at 11. There are no comparable pressures from the system to force teachers to make judgements about children in the top 5 per cent of their age group, and as there is no necessity for doing so the standards by which it might be done are not part of current teacher thought. The interim results on the whole cohort at eleven point to this problem, particularly in general knowledge and oral ability where standardized tests are not available to aid assessment. But even in mathematics in this study, the top two categories which should contain 30 per cent of the age group were somewhat short. The gifted group shared the underestimation problem with the whole cohort. However, it may be that those children who did exceptionally well at 7 were not the ones doing exceptionally well at 11.

The increases and decreases in ratings between 7 and 11 years of age were analysed in the gifted group to see if one sex, social class or IQ group were discriminated against, but no difference was significant.

Social adjustment at 7 and 11 years of age

Another measure that teachers used in the two surveys was the Bristol Social Adjustment Guide (Stott, 1963). The Guide consists of a large number of descriptions of behaviour, and a teacher is asked to underline those which best fit each child. It is then possible, by summing the coded score for deviance from normal behaviour and adjustment, to give an indication of whether a child is 'stable' (score 0–9), 'unsettled' (score 10–19) or 'maladjusted' (score over 20). (Stott, 1963; Chazan, 1968).

The proportions of children found to be 'stable', 'unsettled' and 'maladjusted' in the whole cohort at 7 were, 67, 21 and 12 per cent. The interim results of the 11-year-old survey showed a similar distribution. The gifted group compared very favourably on both surveys for 88 and 86 per cent of the children rated 'stable' and only 3 and 7 per cent 'maladjusted' [Table A3.1, A3.2].

The overall pattern in the whole cohort had more boys than girls and more working-class than middle-class children showing extremes of behaviour. Although the number of boys in the gifted group rated as 'maladjusted' increased from three to ten in the two surveys the differences between the sexes, social classes and IQ groupings were not significant.

As well as the teachers' ratings on adjustment at 7 years of age, parents were asked for some details too (Pringle, Butler and Davie, 1966). They were asked to rate their child as 'normally active, inactive or over-active' and as 'having difficulty in settling down to anything—frequently, sometimes or never'. On both these counts, the gifted children appeared in smaller proportions in the extreme categories. No evidence in this group supported the idea, sometimes put forward, of excessive activity and restlessness among able children. However, they seemed to be at a disadvantage where 'worrying' was concerned. The parents were asked if their child 'worried about many things frequently, sometimes or never'. The gifted group were significantly more frequent worriers than their peers. The result is interesting considering that 92 per cent of these children were said by their parents to have settled within a month of starting school, as against 71 per cent in the whole cohort. Perhaps this indicates that the gifted children revealed worries at home which they managed to conceal in school.

The 'gifted' compared with the cohort at birth

The results of the Perinatal Mortality Survey (Butler and Bonham, 1963) demonstrated that disorders of maturation, adverse social factors and high birth order increased the risk of stillbirth or neonatal death. In the first follow-up of these children at 7 years (Davie, Butler and Goldstein, 1972) these adverse sociobiological factors showed their effect on the development of the surviving children. The evidence showed that both shortened and prolonged pregnancies had the effect of depressing intellectual functioning and educational performance of the children at 7. The effect of birth factors was concluded to be small but important. Social adjustment, as measured by the Bristol Social

Adjustment Guide, was also affected adversely by length of gestation, the late-born children and those light in weight in relation to gestation period being most affected. Birth order, particularly first children from large families and those with two or more younger siblings also presented a greater risk.

It was expected that the gifted group would be favoured in respect of birth factors. There were not more 'only' children at 7, but there was a significant trend for the gifted to come higher up in birth order than the whole cohort. The gifted were heavier at birth, and though there were the same proportion of mothers under 20 as in the cohort, significantly more mothers were over 40.

Although individual cases of adverse birth factors were associated with unsettledness and maladjustment in children from the gifted group, no significant pattern of difficulty emerged.

By definition children with serious mental handicaps were eliminated from the able group, but physical handicaps were represented amongst them in similar proportion to the whole cohort, e.g. in the incidence of fits, congenital heart disorder, cleft palate, asthma, visual and auditory disorders. It was heartening to find such children doing well enough to be included in our special group.

Summary

1. Despite the inclusion of children selected by criteria not specially biased by scholastic performance and the special weighting being given to social classes IV and V, the distribution of the gifted sample clearly skewed towards the middle class.
2. Approximately three-quarters of the gifted group were rated in the top 30 per cent of the cohort by their teachers on reading ability, mathematical ability, oral ability and general knowledge both at 7 and 11 years of age.
3. Increases and decreases in ratings between 7 and 11 years did not discriminate against any one sex, social class or IQ group among the gifted.
4. The gifted group was shown to be more stable and less unsettled and maladjusted than the birthweek children as a whole, both at 7 and 11 years of age.
5. Parents revealed a tendency to 'worry' in the gifted group at 7, but they settled down more quickly in school. Did they cover up their feelings in the school situation, or did their ability to show early attainment deflect teachers' attention from their affective responses?
6. The proportion of gifted children with serious physical handicaps proved no smaller than in the whole cohort.

4. The 'gifted' group special study

Results of tests given at the individual interviews

1. Results of the intelligence test

The most valid and reliable test among those given to the children was the Wechsler Intelligence Scale. This showed that the sample of children was above average in general ability. The mean for the boys' full scale was IQ 131, for girls IQ 126, which indicated a significant difference between the boys' and girls' means [Table A4.1]. This bias of the Wechsler test in favour of boys has been commented on previously by Guilford (1967) and Brittain (1968). There was not such a large difference on the verbal scale, but it was highly significant on the performance scale. Full scale IQs of 130 and over identify children in the top 3 per cent of the general population: 58 per cent of the gifted boys but only 36 per cent of the girls reached that level.

Of the children identified as 'gifted' by different criteria, in terms of IQ [Tables A4.2, A4.4] the boys had higher scores than the girls. This was somewhat unexpected from the Draw-a-man results which at the outset appeared to favour girls. A trend test carried out on the Draw-a-man and IQ results showed no significant difference between them for boys, girls, or boys and girls together [Table A4.3]. Therefore, the high Draw-a-man scores at 7 were not useful long-term predictors of IQ scores at 11 for this group of above average children. This confirmed earlier work with the same test in the same age range (Pringle and Pickup, 1963). However, if high Draw-a-man scores had not been taken into account, 5 boys (out of 35) and 6 girls (out of 16) would have been missed from the group that had full scale IQ scores above 140: 7 boys (out of 38) and 7 girls (out of 25) would have been lost in the 130–140 IQ group.

There were 9 boys and 1 girl with IQs over 140 selected from parents' letters who were also not eligible on their Draw-a-man or attainment results. Similarly 11 boys and 3 girls in the 130–140 IQ group would otherwise not have been in the sample. In all, 21 per cent of the children who had IQs over 130 would not have been in the study had the letters from parents not been requested.

25

It was expected that the attainment criterion would yield the largest number of children with high intelligence quotients because it was composed of standardised test results and teachers' ratings which are known to correlate highly with measured intelligence. This was satisfactory for the boys, but the girls performed less well than anticipated. However, the bias of the Wechsler Scale, already noted, and previous work demonstrated that at 7 years of age girls were relatively more advanced than boys, particularly verbally (Pringle, Butler and Davie, 1966) but that boys improved throughout the primary stage and began to overtake girls by 11 especially in some subjects, e.g. mathematics.

A statistical comparison of the intelligence test results of the three criteria of selection groups is available in the appendix [Table A4.4]. It makes clear the fact that the Draw-a-man group 3 was significantly lower than the rest.

IQ AND SOCIAL OCCUPATION GROUPS

The efforts to increase the numbers of working-class children in the final sample resulted in there being 53 per cent in the non-manual and 47 per cent in the manual categories. Whether boys and girls were examined separately or together, those in the non-manual group tended to have higher full scale and verbal scale IQ scores [Tables A4.5, A4.6]. This was not the case on the performance scale where the evidence showed no significant differences between the groups. These results were the same whether the extra children in social classes IV and V who were selected on Draw-a-man group 3, or attainment group 6, were included or excluded in the calculations. This would appear to vindicate the choice of the Wechsler test for this study.

It has already been mentioned that the biggest response to the appeal in the Press for gifted children in the cohort came from parents in manual occupations, especially those with sons (p. 9). The children who were finally seen as a result of their parents' recommendation, performed as well on the intelligence test as the best of the Draw-a-man and attainment groups. Twenty-four out of twenty-seven working-class children referred by their parents would not have been in the sample if the latter had been selected only on data from the 7-year-old survey: ten of them had IQs over 130.

2. Logic test results [Table A4.7]

This test correlated more highly with the verbal than the non-verbal intelligence scales. Children in the non-manual occupation groups had a significant advantage over the others. The test confirmed the findings of Lovell and Shields (1968) that even for the brightest primary school children problems that involved abstract conditional propositions were largely beyond their level of thought. Only three boys with IQs of 131,

149 and 152, were able to deal with all sixteen binomial propositions, the first was considered gifted in mathematics by his parents, the other two were very good all-rounders.

3. Information test results

These tests correlated significantly with the verbal and non-verbal intelligence scales, but the manual group children did less well than the rest. The individual subject tests showed that the boys were significantly better than the girls on science and geography, but not on history or arts items.

4. Social reasoning test results

The test correlated significantly with the intelligence test scales. A significant difference between the manual and non-manual occupation groups showed the latter obtaining higher scores. The scores of boys and girls were not differentiated.

5. Divergent thinking tests [Table A4.8]

One of the points of controversy that arises in current discussions when the word 'creativity' is used is whether it is an ability separate and distinct from general intelligence. Guilford (1959a), Torrance (1963), Getzels and Jackson (1962) and Wallach and Kogan (1965) present evidence to support the claim that it is. English psychologists are not so confident, although Burt (1962b) and Vernon (1969) support the use of tests that encourage subjects' spontaneous divergent responses as well as the traditional, 'correct answer' convergent tests. They point to evidence which suggests that these are still largely correlated with a main general factor and not more highly correlated with each other as might be expected.

The conclusion seems to be that more evidence is needed on divergent type tests. It is easy to agree that these should be included in any test battery, but choice presents a difficult problem. There are, as yet, no standardised tests of 'creativity', though there is a published battery by Torrance consisting of verbal and non-verbal items. Researchers seem on the whole to select from these according to their own preference and sometimes to include others of their own making. This is what was done in this study.

As the direction of children's intellectual interests was thought to be important, tests allowing for freedom of response in drawing, use of words, mathematics, science and music were selected, but it was realised that the assumption that the tests would in fact test underlying abilities clearly defined by this subject grouping had to be tentative. Vernon (1969) warned against making such easy assumptions, but there was some support for the venture in the work of Lovell and Shields (1967) which reported that 'creativity' tests tended to split up into specific elements after a major factor had been removed.

The test in music was not included in the results. Children refused this test more often than any other; it proved difficult to score on criteria comparable to the other tests and, with the exception of a few interesting individual responses, seemed disappointing. A musician who assisted in investigating the marking possibilities commented: 'The results are evidence of a deprivation of musical experience and a conditioned response to the lowest common denominator in "everyday" musical statements.'

It was interesting how the children's answers were tied to their visual perception of the instruments; very few ignored the spatial arrangements of the chime bars. The most disappointing result was the number of children who played the opening bars of a popular tune, totally unaware of the pitch discrepancy although they successfully reproduced the opening rhythm. These impressions need only be connected with the children's low evaluation of music as a school subject to show that there could have been many reasons for the poor results as well as the fact that the test itself could have been inappropriate.

In the final calculations of the remaining creativity items fluency (how many answers were given in a set time) and uniqueness (how many answers were given only by 1 or 5 per cent of all the children) scores were selected to represent the divergent aspects of the tests. The results did not show significant differences between boys and girls so they were put together in the final analysis.

There were significant trends with the Full Scale IQ results for every creativity test [Table A4.7].

The 'drawing on circles' test was least connected with verbal ability and, as expected, had lower significance trends but the strength of the relationship with the IQ scores cannot be ignored.

The same table showed that the circles test indicated no significant trend with social class, but the words test had a highly significant trend with social class. This was not unexpected as it was clearly the one to draw on verbal educational ability.

The creativity items showed largely positive and for the most part significant correlations with other tests. It was unexpected that the Barron-Welsh test would be the exception as it claimed to identify artistic ability and nonconformity and it was anticipated that it would relate to measures of creativity.

The conclusion drawn from the results suggested that the intelligence test measured many abilities, including those labelled 'divergent'. The higher the children's IQs the higher were their divergent thinking scores. The variation in scores on convergent and divergent tests in this group of children may yield interesting information on individuals, but it gives no support to the idea that intelligence and creativity are separate factors in intellectual ability [Table A4.8]. These results are in line with other British results (Vernon, 1969; Haddon and Lytton, 1968; Burt, 1962b). (A 'principal component factor analysis' is available.)

6. The Barron–Welsh Test

This test did not correlate significantly with any other; neither did high scores identify those children with special talent in art as judged by their parents and teachers or the children's choice of art as a favourite subject or home interest; nor did the results coincide when matched against estimates of the children's conformity/nonconformity at school or at home.

An artist who examined the children's drawings-on-circles test for artistic elements such as composition, skill in handling tone, rendering of atmosphere, etc., identified a group who 'might have or might develop some degree of artistic ability'. This group was not significantly different from the rest on Barron–Welsh scores.

It remains to be seen whether the test will predict some special facet of the children at a later date. Most previous work on the test was done with adult subjects who had already revealed their occupational bias.

Summary

1. Boys in the gifted group obtained significantly higher intelligence test scores than girls on each criterion of selection.
2. Each criterion of selection identified a number of children in the top 3 per cent of the IQ range who would have been omitted from the gifted group had it not been used.
3. The Draw-a-man test subgroup 3 had significantly lower intelligence scores than other selection subgroups.
4. Parents were as effective in identifying intelligent children as other methods used.
5. Middle-class children tended to have higher full scale and verbal scale intelligence quotients than working-class children, but not in their performance scale quotients. Thus middle-class children had a distinct advantage in any largely verbal test.
6. There was no support in this study for the claim that intelligence and creativity are separate factors in intellectual ability. (For further consideration of this point see Chapter 9.)

5. The teachers and their views

No data was collected from teachers specially for the gifted study. Their views on the children were obtained from the material available from the second follow-up on all the birthweek children when they were 11 years old, i.e. ratings on a five-point scale for general knowledge, mathematics, use of books and oral ability; Stott's social adjustment guide; answers to five open questions:

1. compared with other children of this age does he/she reveal *outstanding* ability in any area, e.g. writing stories, chess, modelling, music, science, sport, etc?
2. what do you consider the child's most favourable qualities of personality and character?
3. what do you regard as his/her most serious weakness or drawback of personality or character?
4. what do you consider he is likely to achieve academically at secondary school and/or in further education?
5. what *kind* of job or career do you feel might best suit his abilities or aptitudes?

It was possible to abstract a general picture of the gifted group and the individuals in it from the above information together with the results from the standardised tests of reading and mathematics and the special assessment procedures used.

Teachers' ratings and IQ test result

It has already been shown that the gifted group of children were performing very favourably at school when compared with the whole cohort. In their teachers' estimates 40 per cent of the gifted had at least one rating which indicated that they were in the top 5 per cent of their age group; statistically 15 per cent would be expected from such a sample of a normal population. A further 50 per cent of the children had at least one rating which indicated that they were above average, i.e. in the top 6–30 per cent of their age group. In the light of the junior teachers' conservative use of the extreme categories in the rating scale for the cohort, it can be claimed that the able children represented in the gifted group were not suffering from any special underestimation by their teachers.

The overall teachers' ratings when matched against the IQ scores obtained in the individual interviews showed a highly significant trend as expected [Table A5.1]. The girls tended to be rated more highly than boys on the whole, but the same percentage of boys as girls received at least one high rating (top 5 per cent) suggesting that the girls were considered steadier and the boys more erratic over the four subject areas. This point received some support from the reading and mathematics test results where the boys and girls in the whole cohort showed no significant difference in mean scores but the boys tended to do better and worse than the girls at the extremes of the distributions while the girls settled in a smaller scatter around the mean [Table A5.2, A5.3].

It was thought, because of the general tendency for the proportions in the high ratings to fall in the 11- compared with the 7-year-old survey, that perhaps the most able children in the gifted group (IQ over 130) would show more changes of position, particularly downwards. But this was not so; 20 per cent of the children at 11 obtained at least one higher rating, 45 per cent made no change in position and 35 per cent had at least one drop in place. The proportions in the two groups above and below IQ 130 were almost identical, and that proved true of both boys and girls.

The teachers' ratings of individual subject areas compared with test results all showed highly significant trends, i.e. mathematics rating with its test, use of books with the reading test, general knowledge with the information test. These results were all to be expected as previous work on teachers' judgments of children had shown high correlation with test results. Nevertheless it was necessary to check our results to confirm in as many ways as possible that the more able children, as defined in this study, were not as a group achieving too little or being underestimated by their teachers.

Outstanding ability in any area

The question on 'outstanding ability' was inserted to find out which children were perhaps gifted in their teachers' judgment in subjects other than those assessed on the ratings and in specific ways other than having high intelligence. Fifty per cent of the boys and 60 per cent of the girls were included in response to the question, and half of them had two or more subjects mentioned. The teachers did not focus only on academic subjects (though the examples given with the question helped this). The teachers did not concentrate only on the very high IQ children; as many with IQs below 130 were thought to be outstanding in some way as those above 130.

It can be inferred that the teachers were using high standards of judgment, probably taking the number of children as outstanding in any field as less than the top 5 per cent of the age group. Forty-five children were rated as having 'extremely good facility' in mathematics and came in the top 5 per cent of the 11-year-old population in this respect, thirty-five children were placed in the top 5 per cent for general knowledge and eighty-three were in the top 5 per cent on use of books, yet these numbers do not appear again in answer to the 'outstanding' question.

Table 5.1. Teachers' nomination of those with 'outstanding ability'

Subject	Number of times mentioned	
	Boys	Girls
English	4	12
Writing stories	9	22
Poetry	3	5
Oral work	2	2
Drama	2	2
Modern languages	1	1
History	1	2
Art	19	16
Craftwork	13	9
Music	5	13
Mathematics	4	3
Science	4	0
Chess	4	1
General knowledge	2	0
Good all round	3	3

The parents were rather more optimistic about their children, thinking 77 per cent of them exceptionally good at something compared with the teachers' 55 per cent, but there was a two-thirds agreement on individual children showing that they were judging more on common than on differing standards. The children's answers fell neatly in between their parents and teachers, 64 per cent considering themselves exceptionally good at something, showing perhaps that they drew on both sources for the criteria by which they judged themselves.

Personality descriptions of the children [Appendix IIIa]

Personality is difficult to assess, but must be considered because the concept takes into account the all-roundedness or integration of a person (giving some general picture of his functioning) together with physical, social, emotional, intellectual and moral factors.

Previous literature suggested that highly intelligent children fared well when rated on other non-intellectual dimensions (Terman, 1925).

Research carried out on maladjusted children has shown that the gifted as a group do not avoid the behavioural and nervous difficulties others are prone to, although they are no more or less represented in the population (Lewis, 1943; Pringle, 1970). Some work has suggested that the most able of all, i.e. IQ 150 and over, have special difficulties because of their extreme deviation from the average (Burns, 1949; Witty, 1951; Burt, 1968). In several studies, underachievement has been found to be related to personality factors in bright children (Gowan, 1955; Passow and Goldberg, 1963).

There are many ways in which to measure personality; it was decided in this study to use open-ended questions directed to teachers, parents and children. It seemed important to obtain as wide a range of response as possible both in extent and variety to see if any new ideas on gifted children needed to be explored and how far previous research and current concepts were influencing the parents' and teachers' judgments.

What had the teachers to say of their pupils when given the opportunity to comment on the most favourable qualities and most serious weaknesses of their personalities and characters?

Not all the teachers availed themselves of the opportunity to comment freely on the children they were assessing, but 90 per cent did. Previous research (Warburton, 1961) had shown that teachers tended to use an introvert-extravert dimension when describing children so the comments were categorised, putting all those that described outgoing dynamic qualities into the 'extrovert' category; the quiet, shy, withdrawing type into the 'introvert', and the conforming character qualities which were somewhere between the two into a 'reliable' category. (A full list of words used by the teachers is given in Appendix IIIa.)

The children with IQs of 130 and over were significantly more often extrovert according to their teachers; the under 130 IQ more often introvert, while the 'reliable' group was distributed evenly above and below IQ 130. This finding was supported by earlier work (Jones, 1960; Savage, 1966) which demonstrated the intellectual superiority of extraverted children in the primary school age range.

It was thought that teachers who saw the more intelligent children as extrovert would tend to consider these children more favourably when it came to choosing who were exceptionally good or outstanding in any way at school, but there was no evidence to support this idea. The introverts were just as likely to be seen as exceptional as their more outgoing peers.

Conflict with authority

The comments on the children's 'most serious weaknesses or drawbacks of personality or character' were examined to see if there were any clustering of words around a particular IQ group. Highly 'creative' children have been judged as unusually competitive, resentful of adult authority and criticism and often exhibitionist in their behaviour

(Torrance, 1965a). The only significance that could be found in our study was in a difference between boys and girls, the boys being reported more often in conflict with authority. There were no within-group or between-group differences on sex or IQ in the number of times characteristics of withdrawal were mentioned.

It was a possibility that the very able children, being more outgoing and noticeable, would have more adverse comments made about them than the rest. Again, there was no evidence to support the idea; the adverse comments appeared in all IQ groups in about the same proportions.

These results should be noted because they showed that the teachers were neither favouring nor condemning the most able. They certainly seemed to be the most outgoing and busy children, but, fortunately, teachers perceived and valued the abilities of the shy, withdrawn ones, too.

Underachievement

One of the problems often raised when considering gifted children is that of under achievement. It is a source of anxiety for both parents and teachers if children of exceptional general ability are not able to use it in the classroom, yet concern about a particular child is sometimes unnecessary.

Expectations that a child with an IQ as high as 140 (in the top 0.5 per cent of the population) should score at that level in a number of different subjects frequently arise, but the probabilities of his doing so are very small indeed. Something like three in a thousand children with IQs of 140 score as high on one attainment test, and perhaps only one of those also as high in a second attainment test. This depends, of course, on how closely the tests are related (Ogilvie, 1973). It raises the problem of what is to be categorized as underachievement, and how far below a measure of general ability (such as an IQ score) an attainment score is accepted as satisfactory.

Research workers use different criteria: Lewis (1941) selected 'children whose educational ages are one year or more lower than their mental ages'; Gowan (1957) chose performance which placed the student more than a full standard deviation below his ability standing in the same group explaining that 'we may call gifted children (IQ 130 and above) underachievers when they fall in the middle third in scholastic achievement in grades and severe underachievers when they fall in the lowest third'; Pringle (1970) related underachievement or underfunctioning, 'solely to the capacity of the individual pupil', and distinguished this from backwardness which 'relates educational attainments to chronological age and hence the level of work reached by the majority of a child's contemporaries'.

In the gifted group of this study an examination of the teachers' ratings of children with IQs over 130 was made, and any boys or girls with two or more only 'average' ratings (in the middle 40 per cent of the age group) had their case studies inspected to see how they might be underfunctioning.

ONE GIRL 'UNDERACHIEVER'

There was only one girl of IQ 130 rated average in both general knowledge and oral work. She was thought to be outstanding in mathematics and needlework by her teachers and they predicted that she would obtain a general school certificate and the professional qualifications required for teaching. She was described by them as 'a pleasing personality, diligent and determined; very particular about her personal appearance'. However, on the debit side she 'blushes frequently and is very self-conscious'.

Her parents considered her gifted in needlework; they were ambitious for her and wanted her to go to grammar school to get 'a good job and certificates'. They found her 'shy and nervous, not a good mixer; her eyes too easily fill with tears; she is moody and oversensitive at the moment'.

The girl herself revealed no special personal anxieties; she said, when asked what kind of a person she thought she was: 'My mother says I don't go out enough.' She was tall and mature for her age, well into her adolescent growth spurt at 11; perhaps she was acknowledging this when she wrote, 'I sometimes wish ... I was older than I am.' Her main interests were reading and needlework, she designed and made some of her own clothes and helped other children make their costumes for a school play. Her greatest worry was, 'thinking I may not be good enough to be a teacher'. However, she was above average in the standardised reading test (top 15 per cent) and the mathematics test (top 13 per cent).

There would seem no cause for special concern over this child who was identified as 'gifted' on her high Goodenough man drawing and as an extra member of social class IV. Her shyness and reserve would account for her not standing out from the group in oral work, and her not joining in readily would probably lead to an underestimation of general knowledge gained by avid reading. Although her particular interests kept her indoors more than usual for a child of her age, she found life satisfying and her talents encouraged and appreciated.

BOYS WITH IQ OF 140 'UNDERACHIEVING'

1. MARTIN (IQ 140, social class III manual) was included in the study because his mother wrote to the Bureau about him (group 7). She said: 'I won't go into every detail but all his teachers have said he has a fantastic general knowledge, but the main thing that Martin is interested in is nature. He spends hours just watching anything from a water snail to a horse.'

His teachers rate him as only average (middle 40 per cent) in general knowledge, use of books and oral ability, and below average (bottom 6–30 per cent) in mathematics. Nevertheless he was described as 'cheerful and friendly', outstanding at 'natural history and knowledge of animals'. It was predicted that he would do CSE and go into forestry or farming. Test results suggested that Martin's ability was perhaps being underestimated. He scored in the top 20 per cent on the reading test and top 30 per cent on the mathematics test, but it was doubtful that he would exert himself all the time in subjects that were not connected with his dominant interest in life. He was seen as 'a small, gentle, quiet and thoughtful boy' at his interview. He was not unhappy about school and was very appreciative of his teachers, but on the whole he saw education as a necessity rather than an aid to his development. Life was more important out of school because he had friends older than himself who shared his deep country interests. He thought he got too little natural science in school and complained that in art he had to do fantasy drawings and paintings when he would rather do representative work connected with his observations of plants and animals.

His parents did not push him educationally, in some ways almost the reverse. They were strongly opposed to a grammar school education. His mother said: 'It worries me sometimes, he might have that sort of brain—he's geared into things—but he's not academically clever. I do sometimes have a horrible feeling he might pass the "eleven-plus" by some odd fluke. He'd be miserable. I think he'd worry terribly that he was being pushed further than he was capable of going. I'd rather he went to the secondary modern than scrape along at the bottom of the grammar.'

Martin attended a small village school quite a distance from home. He thought he was not much liked by some children because he found bullying and fighting distasteful. He had a wide vocabulary and confident verbal fluency but poor diction. He considered himself 'a bit soft, you know. My sister, she always gets round me. If I want to go out somewhere she starts to cry and I nearly always end up kissing her. And kids, if their ball goes into the river or something and I've got a spare one, I usually lend it to them. I'm a bit small and I'd like to get a bit fatter. I wish I could shoot a bit better and work a bit harder; I'm about average. I don't want to drop any lower, but I don't want to go too high either.' He would not like to be top of the class because 'the teacher always thinks you should do more'.

Perhaps a most significant fact was that Martin had been under medical supervision for 9 months prior to his assessment. According to his parents he was suffering from anaemia which gave rise to symptoms of fatigue and lethargy and made him feel anxious about his performance in school work.

Martin must stand as an example of a boy with very high general ability which, not functioning obviously in classroom work, was not recognised. The intensive interest and substantial knowledge of country life at his age had not been valued as indicating a high intelligence with academic potential as much as it might have been. His parents wished to protect him from educational pressure and he had learned to be protective about himself in this area too. Should anyone intervene in the judgment of a son who was hypersensitive and delicate, and in his element out of doors where his mind and body thrived?

2. ROY was selected as gifted because of his exceptionally high Draw-a-man score (group 1). He was adopted by professional people in social class I. He attended a church school and was to go on to a fee-paying grant-aided school. His IQ was 146. He was very keen on mathematics and science, somewhat less keen on English and music. At interview he was described as 'tall, thin and athletic, enthusiastic and outgoing, positive in attitude towards tests, full of interests, especially in sport and natural science; socially well adjusted and probably very popular with other children'. He wanted to be an ornithologist and described himself as 'always happy; it's happy to be me'.

His family found him 'very emotional and very thoughtful. He doesn't like the dark, he's a bit timid. It's difficult to get to the bottom of him, you can't imagine his secret thoughts. He dislikes family friction and is very sensitive to it. He's very clean and well-groomed. Science is about his keenest subject, it's something he's got to think about and sort things out for himself, and do little researches on his own. He's captain of the school football team.'

Roy was rated only average in general knowledge, use of books and oral ability, but above average in mathematics (top 6–30 per cent). The teachers did not fill in the answers to the personality questions, but they predicted that he would get five O levels and probably do work involving the welfare of animals.

The tests indicated above average ability. Roy came in the top 20 per cent for reading and mathematics. He worked in a class of children mostly older than himself; his mother said, 'He's always top of the class.' He had been accepted for the grant-aided secondary school on his head teacher's recommendation. It was difficult to reconcile the teachers' average ratings with the rest of the picture of Roy. He might have been underestimated because insufficient weight was given to his youthful age in the group, or perhaps his less keen attitude towards English met with some disfavour. Whatever it was, Roy was not obviously suffering from the teacher's lack of perception in those areas of under achievement. He was happy, keenly interested in a wide range of activities, going to a secondary school of his parents' choice and well adjusted and popular with his friends.

3. WILLIAM had an IQ of 140, his father, a miner, died when he was 5 years old. His mother wrote to us saying: 'He is exceptionally good at

maths. At 4 years old, instead of singing when out on car jaunts it was always mental arithmetic, he is very good indeed at it' (Group 7).

His teachers put him in the top 5 per cent for mathematics and the top 6–30 per cent for general knowledge, but only average (middle 40 per cent) in use of books and oral work. He was described as 'polite and co-operative' and it was thought he might become an industrial chemist or computer expert.

William's mother said of him: 'He's happy and he's a good boy really. He charms the birds off the trees. He's always with a group, he has loads of friends; he's a lovable child, very good company, he can talk like an adult. If he's doing a job he likes to do it perfect, he can't botch it.'

The tests showed him in the top 11 per cent in mathematics, 25 per cent in reading. He was a pleasant and easy boy to interview as he answered quickly and competently throughout. He had few interests, most of his attention went on football and playing outside with his friends. The family had no academic interests, he was not encouraged to read and he did not voluntarily take to books.

It was perhaps the lack of interest in books that accounted for William's average rating on that item and on oral ability. There was no dissatisfaction on the part of school, home or William himself; he did well where his interest lay, in mathematics and football. Would increased pressure from school have brought development along other lines to above average standard? It might have put him off school altogether. He was not ambitious; his mother reported him as saying, 'What do I need GCEs for as long as I can add money up?' and she added herself, 'I don't think he's the type who could sit in an office. Teaching means staying in a class, he'd be no good where he has to stay in the same place. Something sporting—industry too—as long as he's doing something, making something, dealing with something.' Anyone who wanted to extend William's academic knowledge would have had to work hard to change his present attitudes and choice of direction.

4. PETER, IQ 145, social class II, rated average in use of books and oral ability, was a similar case to William in some respects. He was very keen indeed on mathematics and was considered outstanding in this respect by his teachers and his parents who recommended him for inclusion in the 'gifted' survey (group 7). He came in the top 3 per cent of the cohort on the mathematics test and top 17 per cent in reading. His main interest outside school was sport and he was keen on clubs, playing out of doors and chess. Reading did not appear in his chosen activities at all. His teachers expected him to do something with mathematics attached to it, such as accountancy, but Peter saw himself as a pilot. He had lots of friends and presented no difficulties in the family situation. It could not be said in this case that Peter was not encouraged in academic interests; his parents were educationally ambitious for him and

sent him to a private school to get the benefit of teaching in small classes. However, his specific ability and interests lay in other directions at that moment.

5. NIGEL, IQ 154, selected on a high Draw-a-man score (group 1), social class III manual, was rated average in mathematics and oral ability, above average (top 6–30 per cent) in use of books and general knowledge.

Nigel's case was one that called for concern, for despite his exceptionally high all-round ability he was not selected for a grammar school place. The system for selection in his area rested largely on recommendation by the school, and in the last year of primary education Nigel came up against a teacher he could not understand. 'My greatest worry', he wrote, 'is my teacher.'

The interviewer reported Nigel as one of the most outstanding boys in the gifted group, he was fluent and expressive, full of verbal quips and merriment, exceptionally well informed in science and skilled in technical-style drawing. He was despondent about his failure in the 11-plus and just could not understand how it happened, except that he thought his teacher hated children. He did not think the animosity was directed only to himself, but to the boys in the class in general.

There was nothing in his case study to account for his exclusion from a grammar school place. His results in the mathematics test put him in the top 1 per cent, and for reading the top 18 per cent. There was no indication of any adjustment difficulty on the Stott Guide. He had a wide range and variety of interests and every support at home. His parents were philosophical though disappointed at his secondary school placing and did not think of taking it up with the authorities.

6. SIMON, IQ 140, selected on attainment (group 5), social class III manual, came below average (bottom 6–30 per cent) in mathematics, average in use of books and oral work, above average (top 6–30 per cent) in general knowledge.

Simon's teacher was reported as upset because he was selected for the gifted study. His parents felt justified at last in their opinion of his ability. The mathematics test showed him to be in the top 11 per cent of his age group and he was in the top 17 per cent for reading. His written work was described as 'unintelligible'; his prospects 'to become a farmworker'.

The interviewer reported Simon as exceptionally tall and overweight, he had a large baby face and awkward gait. He was very nervous on stairs walking up and down more like a 3- than an 11-year-old. He was attractive in his general vulnerability and eagerness to please, but proved a challenge in the test situation because he needed so much coaxing into confidence. He loved science and making things and collecting, and was an avid reader mostly of non-fiction. He had great difficulty with writing and spelling and was terribly sensitive to his failure. He wrote: 'My teacher thinks I am good at tests but bad at work.' He had a high Stott social adjustment score (23) indicating 'maladjustment', which was revealed in his shyness, nervousness and isolation from village children because he was clumsy in sports.

An examination of his birth history data revealed a number of abnormalities which an obstetrician, who worked on the birth survey, said amounted to an indication of some minimal brain damage which could account for his physical ineptness and lack of oral fluency.

School, home and Simon himself were all puzzled and troubled about the unevenness of his academic performance, and they had all had to cope with the problem throughout the primary years. He may have fared better at the secondary school where he should receive more varied science and mathematics teaching and should meet a larger group of children older than himself with similar interests.

7. There was one other boy of IQ 143 who was rated only average on general knowledge, mathematics, use of books and oral ability. His case study is being presented in fuller form in chapter 13 (see JOHN).

IQ 130–140 'UNDERACHIEVING'

8. MALCOLM, IQ 133, social class I, rated average on general knowledge, mathematics, use of books and number but was selected on attainment (group 4). His teachers found him 'helpful and likeable, a good organiser, popular and mannerly'. They predicted that he would get some O levels, and thought he might become a draughtsman.

Malcolm himself wanted to be a chef. He had few interests, the main one was being outside with his friends cycling or climbing. His parents wanted him to go to a comprehensive school saying, 'He's a child who likes to choose his subject, he's not a delver, he likes more variety, and he won't get pushed at a comprehensive school. He lacks concentration and is easily persuaded by other children.'

The tests showed him to be in the top 25 per cent in mathematics and reading, so he had above average skills to use when he wanted to.

9. TOM, IQ 134, social class II, was selected on attainment (group 5). He rated average in general knowledge, mathematics, use of books and oral ability.

Tom wanted to be a chef. He had no strong interests, quite enjoyed sport and reading. He thought a lot about his achievement and behaviour. He wrote 'My teacher thinks I am stupid', but he said about himself 'I'm *not* average!' The tests supported him as he was placed in the top 10 per cent for mathematics and top 17 per cent for reading. He attended a private school because it was in the family tradition to do so. His parents thought it would make him independent and tough being in boys' company. His mother said 'He takes life too seriously, he's conscientious and persevering in what he does. He's a child who apparently suffers a good deal, but I get the sneaking feeling now that he enjoys it. I don't give as much credence to it as I used to. He has great black moments of despair, on other days he tends to be effervescent. He is certainly the odd one out in the family. His suicide threats were very genuine at the time, we had a great spate of them which stemmed from school not home, I think. He sulks, he tends to bear a grudge. He hates; he can hate a child for quite a long period of time. It's over in a flash with his sister; we tend to try and reason with him, we talk and talk. He finds it difficult to see other people's point of view, he really does. He's single minded, too, whatever he's doing seems to have his full concentration. I don't know whether he loves as passionately as he hates. He's got to an age where he's building up barriers and has more tempers and emotions. He's harder to see through. My other child you read like an open comic; this one's a book you never get the cover off.'

Tom must have had to bear a good deal of frustration if he felt he was being underestimated. He obviously had personality difficulties arising from swings of mood. He wrote, 'Sometimes I wish I could run away to sea', and 'Grown-ups are bossy'. So perhaps he felt himself subject to pressures on all sides. The fact that he was in a class of less than ten children must have made it difficult to judge his achievement in comparison with all 11-year-olds.

10. GORDON, IQ 131, social class III manual, was selected by parents' letter (group 7). He was recognised as above average in mathematics (top 5 per cent) but rated only average in general knowledge, use of books and oral ability. The teachers described him as 'stable and reliable, he has a questioning and lively mind'. They predicted that he would reach O level and probably be suitable for an office job.

Gordon, however, wanted to be a doctor. Although he was in the top 11 per cent of his age group for mathematics, he was only average on the reading test. His interests were practical and sporting, and he showed no spontaneous turning to books. His mother described him as 'a real good boy. He never grumbles if I ask him to do anything. He'll do anything for anybody. He knows he's adopted—he never says anything.'

Gordon wrote: 'My greatest worry is English for I hate the subject and it is boring', and 'My teacher thinks I am very good at everything, but I think I'm not and I know it.'

There seemed cause for concern here, for there was some lack of self-confidence intellectually which needed investigation if he was to be helped to realise his ambition. His high ability in mathematics at that moment ensured that he was not completely overlooked.

11. BERNARD, IQ 133, was selected on high Draw-a-man score and as an extra member of social class IV. He rated as average in use of books and mathematics, but above average (top 6–30 per cent) in general

knowledge and oral ability. The test results showed average ability in reading but above average in mathematics (top 28 per cent). His teachers described him as 'good natured and friendly', but added 'tends to act silly'. They thought he would reach O level but did not predict what job he might take up.

Bernard wanted to be an architect. His essay imagining himself at the age of 25 years was brief, and revealed his difficulties with writing and spelling.

There were some features from his interview that suggested some tendency to depression. When asked what he thought of life he replied, 'Not much'. He wrote 'I often feel . . . left out of things' and 'sometimes I wish I were dead' (a response given by only three other children). He said he worried a lot in case he did not get a good job when he left school.

He was interested in making models, painting, drawing and sport, but not in reading.

His parents found him 'very likeable, people think he's a nice boy, he's nice mannered, doesn't show you up. He's helpful at home and school, his reports say so.' They were not specially ambitious for him; they wanted comprehensive education because they saw it as offering variety on the non-academic side.

There was cause for concern, for this boy could be educationally handicapped by some of the factors associated with low non-manual social class status. He did not happily accept his condition as some of the children did who directed their energies more positively elsewhere. He had some 'immortal longings' in him and had as yet found no proper outlet for them.

12. STEPHEN, IQ 133, social class III non-manual, was selected on attainment (group 4). He rated above average in general knowledge and use of books, but average in mathematics and below average in oral ability.

He had a high Stott score (20) indicating 'maladjustment'. He scored on his excessive nervousness and shyness, lack of energy and timidity. However, he was gentle and kind and well liked by other children. At home he preferred to play quiet indoor games and draw. His teachers thought he would eventually reach A level and perhaps choose technical drawing or engineering as a career, if not hindered by lack of self-confidence.

His test scores were top 10 per cent for reading, top 25 per cent for mathematics, so he had ability. It was his withdrawn personality which inhibited him. His parents wanted him to go to a secondary modern school and leave early to get a job. His father in particular was unsympathetic to academic learning and found it difficult to understand a timid and quiet son.

His teachers had been sympathetic and understanding and had given him much help particularly in developing his keen interest in history.

They considered psychological help would have been beneficial had his parents been willing to co-operate. He might well be a late developer who could find his talents in the comprehensive school.

SUMMARY OF 'UNDERACHIEVERS'

Only one group of children defined as 'underachieving' in a specific way was examined. Other criteria could have been chosen and some different children might have been selected. For example, only one child, a boy, out of all those with IQs of 130 and over, achieved scores as low as average (middle 40 per cent) in both reading and mathematics tests, but his teachers rated him as above average. Seven more boys were average only in reading scores, two of them were discussed in the previous section—Bernard and Gordon—because their teachers rated them as average. One boy and one girl were only average in the mathematics test, but were above average on their teachers' ratings.

The examples showed the complexity of the task with which parents and teachers are faced. The children described do not form a homogeneous group. The overweighting of boys showed again the real need for further investigations into sex differences in educational performance. Some of the children when looked at all round were well-balanced, well-adjusted and quite competent enough in literacy and numeracy to achieve anything to which they set their minds. Their special abilities and interests showed that they selected one area for attention rather than another; these personal tastes are a feature of everyone's life, children's rights to them need to be respected as well as those of adults.

As a group, the children did not reveal the characteristics sometimes claimed to be associated with underachieving. There was no general tendency to undervalue themselves or other children, nor were they over-aggressive and self-assured, or generally more poorly adjusted. Only two cases had high Stott social adjustment scores.

Maladjustment

The teachers' ratings of the cohort children on the Stott Social Adjustment Guide showed the gifted children to be very favourably placed in this respect in comparison with their contemporaries (p. 23). Nevertheless it is important to examine more closely those individual gifted children who, in their teachers' estimation, gave rise to concern about their adjustment.

TWO CHILDREN 'MALADJUSTED' AT BOTH 7 AND 11 YEARS OF AGE

The one boy who came into this category had an IQ of 119. He was described as exceptionally quiet and withdrawn during his individual interview and seemed to lack energy and ability to concentrate. His teachers rated his work as average except in mathematics where he came into the top 5 per cent of his age group. The test results showed him as in the top 11 per cent for mathematics and top 30 per cent for reading. His teachers noted his lack of energy and concentration and reported poor general health and said, 'requires a great deal of sympathy and understanding; he lacks ability to communicate'.

His parents were separated and since that event he had lived in an all-female household with a mother, grandmother, aunts and five older sisters. His mother perceived no difficulty in him; it was she who put him forward by letter as gifted. She wrote: 'He is very intelligent, likes to play chess and do crossword puzzles and is interested in the scientific side of what makes things work.' She reported during her interview that he had suffered from constant ill-health since starting school and had had a number of spells in hospital. In spite of all this he mixed well with other children.

The boy was well observed and sensitively supported by his teachers. The physical factor seemed predominant in his symptoms. His mother perhaps overestimated him and overprotected him, though she tried not to. There was no direct evidence from the boy himself of emotional difficulties; the interviewing psychologist stressed his poor physical condition which seemed to require medical attention but did not rule out the possibility of psychological difficulties.

The girl who fell into the maladjusted category at both 7 and 11 years old had the lowest IQ in the group; her score of 90 represented a tentative estimate of her ability. She was exceptionally shy, and when she was interviewed had only spoken to her teacher once in two terms. She was rated as below average in all school work, and described as 'kind and keen to please. No personality or initiative. Shy.' Her parents and teachers showed concern about her, but specialist help which seemed indicated had not been sought. She was selected for the study as a result of her high Draw-a-man score at 7 years of age and the fact that her father's occupation rated in class IV manual. The child herself wanted to be an athlete. She was a very keen runner and surprised everyone by standing out from other children in this respect at the school sports meeting.

'MALADJUSTED' AT 11 YEARS ONLY—GIRLS

Two girls had Stott scores over 20 at the 11-year-old survey. They were considered shy, apathetic, trying to avoid adults and other children.

The first girl had an IQ of 127. She came from social class IV. Her mother put her forward as gifted because 'she tries hard at anything'. Her teacher rated her average in use of books and oral ability, but below average in number and general knowledge. The tests put her below average in reading (bottom 30 per cent) and above average in mathematics (top 30 per cent). At school she was shy, apathetic and tried to avoid adults and children. Her teacher wrote, 'an uninteresting child with few attractive characteristics, almost completely withdrawn and unresponsive'. The interviewer reported 'quietly co-operative, answered readily but without enthusiasm and at times sounded depressed. She has an unsatisfactory relationship with her father. Owing to lack of incentive and intellectual stimulation in the home the IQ may be an underestimate. In many ways a deprived child, socially, emotionally and intellectually.'

The picture the child revealed of herself was equally depressing. She said she had no interests and no friends. She had 'bad moods and tempers when Dad clouts me. He doesn't care what I'm going to be.' She wrote in the sentence completion test: 'My happiest time of the day is when . . . my Dad goes out', 'My greatest fear . . . when my Dad's in'. Did she think about serious things? 'Yes, death, that's all I think about—I wish I was dead plenty of times.' And what about life? 'I think it's just a waste of time, you're dead when you're first born, then you come to life and so many years later you just die again. I think it's just a waste of time, a way of wasting time.'

No one could doubt the seriousness of the child's state of mind. She had little acknowledgement or support. It was unlikely that her teachers knew that she was ill-treated by her father as her parents did not visit school and she was reticent. Her mother did what she could to encourage her children, but with an openly acknowledged violent and selfish husband she was limited in what she could achieve. Here was a child with potential but no outlet through which to express it. If the common criterion of high intelligence had been used for this study she would have been overlooked and her plight perhaps never exposed. Will her secondary teachers identify the spark that is there before she sinks into a hopeless adolescence?

The other girl in the 'maladjusted' category was selected for study on her high Draw-a-man score (group 1). She had an IQ of 112. Her father was an unemployed labourer and both parents were ailing in health and she was frequently kept away from school to nurse them or look after younger children. They belonged to a strict religious sect which kept them excluded from social life. The girl was unhappy when interviewed because the family had just moved from a district where she had some friends and liked her school. Her new teachers rated her average in use of books and oral ability but below average in mathematics and general knowledge. The tests placed her as average in reading and mathematics. Her difficulties over the move of house were appreciated by the school and efforts were made to help her feel more settled.

'MALADJUSTED' AT 11 YEARS OF AGE—BOYS

Two of the boys have already been discussed as underachievers, namely Simon and Stephen; they were both shy, quiet and lacking in self-confidence.

There were four boys whose maladjustment rating seemed due to inconsistent and erratic behaviour. They were said to get on well with children and adults, but they were moody and somewhat unreliable. Their IQs were 147, 125, 117 and 114. Three were rated above average in school work, one average. None of their parents reported having difficulty with them. They were all active and practical in their interests and saw their future careers as builder, footballer, farmer and chef.

There were three aggressive, 'delinquent' boys, at odds with teachers and children and engaging in antisocial behaviour. Their IQs were 127, 117 and 113; teachers rated the first two above average in school work, the last just average. Their parents were aware of their difficulties for they were often in trouble.

Finally, there was one boy with a high Stott score at 11 who was difficult to classify. He was a bit of an outsider but not shy; he was erratic in social behaviour, sometimes coming forward, sometimes hanging back. He was overtalkative and overfriendly with teachers, and a nuisance in the classroom generally. He was considered a powerful personality but too full of his own importance. He had an IQ of 154, a birth history which could account for his physical clumsiness, poor eyesight and slight deafness. He was rated in the top 5 per cent for general knowledge, number, use of books and oral ability. A full case history will be found on page 183.

Four of the fourteen children above were recommended to a special agency because of their difficulties. The whole range of IQ within the sample was represented and also all levels of attainment and all social classes.

The evidence from the Stott Social Adjustment Guide did not highlight any special group of children, certainly not especially the highly intelligent.

Summary

1. Ninety per cent of the 'gifted' group had at least one rating by their teachers (general knowledge, mathematics, use of books and oral ability) which indicated that they were in the top 30 per cent of their age group.

2. The teachers' ratings showed highly significant trends with IQ and other test scores, as expected.

3. Girls tended to be rated more highly than boys as a whole, but the boys varied more within the range of rating categories while the girls were steadier in level.

4. The changes in ratings between the ages of 7 and 11 revealed no bias for sex, level of IQ or social class.

5. Fifty per cent of the boys and 60 per cent of the girls were considered 'outstanding' in at least one dimension. The teachers did not concentrate on academic subjects only, or on children with exceptional IQs.

6. Children with IQs over 130 were significantly more often described in 'extrovert' terms by their teachers, but the 'introverts' were not overlooked in terms of their special abilities.

7. There was no evidence to support the idea that the most able were more often in conflict with authority than their peers.

8. A specially defined group of 'underachievers' revealed again the tendency for boys to be rated lower than girls. It also showed the need to take an overview of each child in many aspects of his life before making judgments about his functioning or underfunctioning in one.

9. The children who had high scores on the Stott Social Adjustment scale were not confined to any one IQ or social class group. Three girls and eleven boys came into the 'maladjusted' category at 11 years of age. The common suggestion that able children reveal social and behavioural difficulties is not supported by the opinions of teachers reflected in these results.

10. The teachers of this group of children appeared to have kept distinct the factors on which they judged their pupils; criteria of abilities and personality behavioural characteristics were not being confused. There were individual cases where there was some lack of perception, and these were regrettable, but they stood out to emphasize that rules of thumb are unlikely to benefit the lot of any gifted child; each one must be evaluated in his or her own context by the adults responsible.

6. The parents and their views

Education

CONCERN AND INTEREST IN EDUCATION

The fact that 85 per cent of the parents from the selected 'gifted' sample attended for the interview [appendix IIc] is an indication of their involvement and concern in their children and education. Even those who did not consider their children highly intelligent or gifted came along because of their interest in the survey in which they have taken part since the children were born.

This demonstration of co-operation from parents was not unusual: the Plowden Report quoted 95 per cent interviews from 3,237 parents in their primary school survey and the National Child Development survey also achieved 95 per cent (14,746) response from parents in the 7-year-old survey.

In the present study, the parent interviewers rated the parents on their expressed interest and concern in their child's education at the time of the interview, and they considered 47 per cent very interested, 42 per cent interested and 11 per cent less interested, but none could be rated as having little interest. The reports from the children's teachers claim 40 per cent very interested, 46 per cent interested, 2 per cent overconcerned and 2 per cent showing little interest. If the total '7-year-old' survey results are taken as a tentative guide, the 'gifted' children's parents showed greater concern and interest in their children's education because in the large sample the proportion of 'very interested' parents was 36 per cent and those showing 'little or no interest' 15 per cent.

Another way of assessing parental interest is by asking whether they have visited the school to speak to a class teacher or head teacher during the current school year (Table 6.1). Ninety-two per cent of the study parents had done so, 20 per cent being specially concerned about secondary school selection and the rest mainly because of interest in the general school progress of their child. The Plowden survey reported an average 18 per cent of parents having no talks at all with class teachers

Table 6.1. No class or head teacher seen

Social class	Plowden Report (%)	Gifted Study (%)
I and II	9	4
III non-manual	15	3
III manual	18	8
IV and V	25	18

or head teachers, but the time span was unspecified as the children had been different lengths of time at their particular schools. However, attention was drawn to the fact that amount of contact with school staff increased with social class and in a small way this was true for this study's children.

Only 6 per cent of the parents of the gifted said that it was not easy to see a teacher at the school, for the rest, 75 per cent said they could see someone almost at any time they called and 25 per cent said they could make an appointment on request. There were no social class discrepancies on this item.

SATISFACTION WITH SCHOOLS

In this study 87 per cent (as against 67 per cent in the Plowden study) were very pleased and satisfied with the school their child attended, 10 per cent had mixed feelings and only 3 per cent were not satisfied. Their satisfaction was mostly directed towards the teachers; 35 per cent of the favourable comments were to do with the friendly atmosphere created by the teachers for both children and parents, 44 per cent were pleased with high standards of work and modern methods (e.g. varied curriculum, individual project work and extra-mural visits), 11 per cent mentioned good facilities such as buildings, equipment and small classes. The non-manual and manual parents contributed equally to favourable comments about the schools, but when asked if they had any criticisms to make 46 per cent in the non-manual groups had none, while 66 per cent in the manual groups had none, showing significantly that perhaps the manual parents were more accepting of what was provided educationally for their children or were less articulate about it.

Most of the parents thought that if they were dissatisfied with their child's education they would or might intervene in the matter (60 per cent), but those who said they would not are represented more often in the children's under 130 IQ group and the manual occupation groups.

CHOICE OF SECONDARY SCHOOL

The parents were asked to which type of secondary school they would like their child to go. The answers were compared with the actual

allocation which teachers reported, and with similar results from the
Plowden enquiry on top juniors.

Table 6.2. Type of secondary school desired (percentages)

| | Plowden survey on top juniors | | Gifted study | |
	Parents' hopes	Actual allocation	Parents' hopes	Actual allocation
Grammar	51	23	50	53
Secondary modern	24	61	5	1
Comprehensive	5	7	13	22
Technical	5	2	2	1
Independent	2	1	24	11
Not known	13	6	6	12

Table 6.2 shows that the parents of the gifted were in a fortunate
position as their hopes for their children educationally were substantially
being fulfilled. Some parents were disappointed at their children being
allocated to comprehensive schools; these parents were largely from
non-manual occupations and their fears were of possible lower academic
standards and lack of competition for their children. Parents from
manual occupations chose comprehensive, technical and secondary
modern schooling more frequently and parents from non-manual
occupations chose independent and private schooling more frequently.
The other significant difference connected with this point occurred in
answer to the question asked if husband and wife took equal interest in
the choice of secondary school. Fathers of manual occupations were
said to take less interest in the problem, a fact which coincides with the
findings of the Plowden enquiry.

FURTHER EDUCATION AND OCCUPATION

The parents were asked how long they would like their child to stay in
full time education. Twenty per cent had no clear idea to express on this
item but 35 per cent said 'university' unprompted, and a further 32 per
cent agreed to university when asked directly. The parents of children
with IQs over 130 answered unprompted 'university' more often than
the rest and even when prompted were more often in favour. There was
also a social grouping split here; more parents with non-manual occupations spontaneously stated that they wanted university education.

Fraser (1959) stressed that as well as parents' attitudes to education
those concerning future occupation of the child were important in
affecting children's attainments. Ninety per cent of the gifted study
parents considered one or both of themselves ambitious for their children
as regards future work, 60 per cent had a definite idea of what they

wanted their children to become, the rest required that their children should have a 'satisfying' job. Half of the parents had no strong views on whether their child should or should not take up occupations they themselves had followed; 30 per cent said they considered the idea favourably; 20 per cent were strongly against it. There was a more positive wish that father's occupation should be followed in the non-manual social groups.

IDEAS ON PRESCHOOL EDUCATION

At the other end of the age scale the parents showed their positive attitude to early education. Twenty per cent of the gifted sample had had nursery schooling of one kind or another, which compared favourably with the total provision in the country which from the 1965 census was 13 per cent (approximate figures taken from the Plowden Report, Vol. 1). Fifty-seven per cent of the gifted sample started school before the age of 5, whereas in the whole National Child Development Study 49 per cent began before the statutory age.

The early provision of education may account for the fact that nearly half the gifted group had at one time or another in their primary schools been accelerated, i.e. had worked with children at least 1 year ahead of their own age group. Thirty-one per cent of the 130+ IQ group and 16 per cent of the rest had been accelerated.

PARENTS' EDUCATIONAL BACKGROUND [Table A9.11, A9.12]

When the parents' educational background was examined what was expected as a result of previous studies was confirmed. Even in this small, above average intelligence group of children, those with the highest intelligence, IQ 130+, had parents who had more prolonged education; 39 per cent of mothers and 37 per cent of fathers in the study group had grammar school type education, about twice as many as in the population at large. This meant longer full-time school education and a greater likelihood of further education, and all these items showed the 130+ IQ group favoured.

There was, of course, a close association between the level of parents' education and the father's occupation, but a comparison with Plowden figures showed that the parents in this study in semiskilled and unskilled occupations had the advantage of longer schooling and further education [Table A6.1]. Twenty-one fathers in the gifted study went to university, fourteen of them had children in the 130+ IQ group; eight mothers went to university, seven had children in the 130+ IQ group.

Whether the parents considered they had enjoyed school or not, or had done well or not revealed no significant intelligence or social class group differences.

Forty-three per cent of mothers in the non-manual occupation group had worked with children (28 out of the 55 were teachers), 19 per cent of the manual mothers had worked with children (4 out of 21 were teachers).

From the parents' interview schedule it will be seen that a number of questions were asked with a view to obtaining some estimate of the degree of control exercised by the parents over their children.

The parents of the over 130 IQ group, especially those from non-manual occupations, considered that they were more strict than other parents. They also considered a greater proportion of their children 'difficult to manage', 20 per cent as compared with 10 per cent of the lower IQ and manual occupation group.

The parents in non-manual occupations of the higher IQ children were more inclined to state that if they asked their child who was busy to do something they would insist that he obeyed. However, there were no IQ or social class differences in the items asking if parents controlled what their children read and watched on television. So the control of parents differed according to whether social behaviour or intellectual behaviour was considered.

There were no differences between groups on the item relating to which was the stricter parent.

While the non-manual parents see themselves as stricter than manual parents, the manual parents saw themselves as more affectionate, for 63 per cent claimed to show quite a lot of affection in the family to 20 per cent fairly reserved, against the non-manual parents who claimed 46 per cent affectionate and 30 per cent rather reserved. There were no differences when they were asked whether their children showed affection or were reserved. It seemed as if the non-manual parents expected demonstrative affection from their children while being rather reluctant to admit that they showed it themselves.

Definition of 'intelligent' and 'gifted'

DO YOU CONSIDER YOUR CHILD HIGHLY INTELLIGENT OR GIFTED?

This question was put to the parents to see if they recognised the superior abilities of their children and to find out what criteria they were using in making their judgments.

'Intelligence' was on the whole used to cover general ability, whereas 'gifted' was definitely made more specific, either relating to subjects, special skills or mental processes. Not all parents elaborated their answers but those who did can be grouped into three main categories:

1. superiority taken as self-evident from the child's behaviour;
2. superiority acknowledged because of comparison with other children in the family or neighbourhood;
3. superiority indicated by school performance.

Some verbatim examples illustrate these points and reveal the confidence or otherwise with which they were stated.

INTELLIGENCE

● Girl: IQ 145, social class III, non-manual
MOTHER: Highly intelligent. Oh yes, definitely!
FATHER: She's able to cancel out what is not beneficial distinguishing taking what you *want*, from taking what you *need*. Education is no problem at all—first prizes all the way—with her you don't think about being second or first, it's a taken for granted thing. Her attitude is, 'Let's not discuss it further—it bores me to tears!'
MOTHER: In some fields she's definitely gifted—she has an absolutely fantastic memory.

● Boy: IQ 150, social class I
MOTHER: He's highly intelligent—not on a pedestal, but very special.

● Boy: IQ 146, social class III, manual
FATHER: I look on him as highly intelligent because of the subjects he can discuss.

● Girl: IQ 132, social class II
FATHER: I don't really know what the criterion is. As far as I can see, she is highly intelligent, but she hasn't any passion for anything except reading. Her vocabulary is excellent—she spells unusual words—she's gifted linguistically. She writes stories and poems—they're not particularly outstanding. She sits down and writes a poem—it's not marvellous but it's really quite interesting. You tend to forget she's only ten and talk to her as though she was much older.

● Girl: IQ 144, social class II
MOTHER: She is unusual surely—highly intelligent *and* gifted in art, swimming and poetry.

ECCENTRICITY AND GIFTEDNESS

Another child was described as both highly intelligent and gifted, and one statement showed that the idea of the eccentricity of gifted children is still lingering in current thought.

● Boy: IQ 140, social class I
FATHER: He's a very lucky boy, he has the best of both worlds. The head teacher said his class teacher could not think otherwise. She thinks a lot of him—says often she has had children who are highly intelligent who are a bit peculiar in other ways—he's a normal child—not eccentric.

Two parents made direct reference to eccentricity and only one child was in the IQ range that is usually called 'exceptional' (IQ 140).

It was a-typical of this group of children to show unevenness to such a degree that it could be classed as eccentric.

● Boy A: IQ 140, social class III, manual
MOTHER: Highly intelligent academically, practically he's useless—for practical reasons the child is no good. He couldn't learn to do up his shoelaces, he goes out with his clothes unbuttoned. Nothing will drag him away from a book; we call him the absent-minded professor. If his cup was on the edge of the table he'd not think it wasn't safe.

It seemed worth noting that in this case the boy had a verbal IQ score off the scale, 155+, but a performance IQ in the average range, 114. So that the unevenness in his abilities made him appear 'odd' to a certain extent. This oddness was attributed to his general or academic superiority whereas it probably stemmed from the average level of his visual-manual skills.

● Boy B: IQ 132, social class III, non-manual
There was an unevenness in this boy which the parents did not quite understand. On the test he had a verbal IQ of 120, but a performance IQ of 140. His 'weakness' was not manual like the previous boy, but rather a narrowness of interest in book learning.
FATHER: I have a parent's attitude—he has too much intelligence but no common sense. I think there's less need for academic qualifications now. I've known people with qualifications who were not happy as people, and people without them who were—I know this is against the trend. Of our three children he seems to be the one who finds it easy to learn—but he can do nothing else—even post a letter—he'll forget it completely. There's nothing but that gift (to learn); he just can't do anything else. I have a brother who's gifted in—expert in—history, but he can't mend a fuse. To me I'd rather have someone like my other son who's an all-rounder.

RELUCTANCE TO BOAST

Some parents voiced an unwillingness to express their judgments because they feared it would be taken as boasting by other adults, or they were afraid that their children would get too great an idea of their own importance.

One mother illustrated well some of the features of her highly intelligent son's behaviour, but had to moderate her enthusiasm in case he (or she herself) became 'big-headed'.

● Boy: IQ 155+, social class I
MOTHER: Highly intelligent. He has enormous powers of concentration which have brought him to the top. In the past I've never thought of him as being out of the ordinary. Though the impression other people give—they say he's 'so clever'—I don't think he has got that extra flair

but he has powers of concentration and memory. He's consistently at the top of the class—that doesn't mean anything out of the ordinary. Other people are good in ways he isn't. I wouldn't want him to get big-headed. I don't think he's any brighter than a lot of the children at school are. I think he'll make the eleven-plus. Where he's gained enormously—he's widely read. You just don't know what is ability and what is acquired, do you? For instance, when he started stamp collecting he learned quite a lot about geography. He has a tremendous interest and I do think it's got him a long way. It's given him a good general knowledge. Again, when he's asked things I've felt he could find out for himself—it helps them to try to find out. What's ability and what's knowledge? I don't know.

Further examples of this inhibition were:

● Girl: IQ 128, social class II

FATHER: It's recognised that she's good at most things—we're very careful not to sound big-headed.

MOTHER: We're divided—we do think she's gifted and intelligent but we're too afraid it sounds big-headed. We may find her more so than other children when we make comparisons. We're so anxious not to create an impression that we're big-headed, but some of her new ideas do surprise us. Some of her handwork and drawings—the teachers don't believe she's done them on her own. Her pictures—people say: 'Did you trace it?'—it's such a shame—no one ever believes her that she's not copying or tracing.

● Girl: IQ 136, social class III, manual

MOTHER: I don't know what they class today as highly intelligent. She seems to take everything in. I suppose I'd say *highly* intelligent, she is most of the time. If she sees something on TV she gets her atlas out and finds out where it is—she's interested in almost anything. If she's reading and watching TV she can tell you what's happening on both. I used to worry that it might make her big-headed because she was doing well at school, but I was told not to. They say it doesn't affect her at all with the other children. Everything has just got to be the way she wants it. If there is a slight error, it has to be scrapped and started again.

● Girl: IQ 134, social class II

MOTHER: Very bright—intelligent certainly—probably very. I try not to think of them this way, because if you say this to people they think you're all cocky because she's got better marks than the other children. But it surprises you when you find she knows things you didn't think she would. She's a good speller—she knows the meaning of a word—her doll's clothes and her sewing leave a lot to be desired but I'm surprised she gets the shape she wants. This again is her patience—she will fiddle around till she gets a shape she wants.

Several parents voiced their doubts about the meaning of the terms 'intelligent' and 'gifted'.

● Boy: IQ 146, social class I
MOTHER: It depends how you measure intelligence. If it's school work he's top of the class and he always has been.
FATHER: He's a conservative boy—he's not *very* but reasonably intelligent—he's not behind the door at all!

● Boy: IQ 152, social class IV
FATHER: Gifted with his drawing and I should think a little bit above average intelligence. I wouldn't know how to define intelligence—it's not for a parent to say.
MOTHER: Especially if he's the only one! You're always apt to think your own child is best. How much he's above average, I don't know. We used to do a lot of travelling. He read from a very early age.

● Girl: IQ 125, social class II
MOTHER: I feel unsure on this—I don't know—we seem to get different reports—we're waiting for some proof.
FATHER: A sign! Perhaps we now have it! (i.e. being selected for the gifted group).
MOTHER: We didn't know—the school has always completely played it down—we would have had a yardstick if she'd passed the eleven-plus. I would have thought intelligent but not *very* from our experience—not gifted either. I can think of children at the school where I teach who were equally intelligent. Her school reports are not outstanding. I would say above average.
FATHER: I don't know. How can you judge your own child's intelligence? You judge by your own intelligence. The school has tested it. We don't know the result. *She* has a good opinion of her intelligence!

COMPARISON WITH OTHER CHILDREN
Some parents tried to find a foothold on the problem by comparing their child with other children.

● Boy: IQ 115, social class III, manual
MOTHER: He's above average. I'm going on children who are average. He's so superior to them, they seem like children while he's grown-up as far as I reckon—but I'm his mother!

In some families it was a disadvantage to be compared with siblings. The next child was exceptional verbally, but her full scale intelligence quotient was lowered because of her difficulty with visual—spatial tests in the performance scale. She was being judged on extremely high standards.

● Girl: IQ, Verbal 152, Performance 101, Full scale 131, social class II
MOTHER: I think she's a good 'A' stream grammar school pupil—not
anything outstanding—definitely not in the same class as her brother
who has an IQ of 170. She'll be about 135. I don't think she is *very*
intelligent.

RELIANCE ON TEACHERS' ASSESSMENTS

Parents of only children found judging their child a particularly difficult
task.

● Boy: IQ 152, social class III, non-manual
FATHER: We think he's highly intelligent but we haven't anyone to
compare with.

In this and other cases parents relied heavily on reports from school;
in fact, the majority of replies referred to school performance.

● Boy: IQ 132, social class I
FATHER: It was always easy to teach him anything—soon after he
started school the head teacher said, 'He's got something special.' He's
able to encompass a lot and reach a good standard. We've no idea of his
intelligence quotient.

● Boy: IQ 136, social class III, non-manual
MOTHER: He's highly intelligent. The teacher said the most scientific
child she's ever come across; if she doesn't know something she asks him.

● Boy: IQ 133, social class I
MOTHER: I personally think he's average, but people tell me he's
exceptionally good. The school teacher in the junior school says he's an
absolute gift to teach but we can't see it. At the age of two he could tell
me the names of every car on the road—whether that's a gift or not I
don't know.

● Girl: IQ 131, social class II
MOTHER: She's very intelligent, going by her record. I can't think much
else when her reports come from school.

● Boy: IQ 141, social class III, manual
MOTHER: I think he's highly intelligent, until a few months ago I always
thought of him as average but the last school and this school told me he is
quite bright. I asked the headmaster's advice—he rather changed my
opinion.

● Girl: IQ 145, social class III, non-manual
FATHER: I'd certainly say highly intelligent.
MOTHER: I didn't know till I saw the work of other children. Still the
teachers tell us we can't compare. She's a great character. I wouldn't
put it past her to be top of the school.

• Girl: IQ 146, social class II

MOTHER: I certainly think intelligent. It's difficult with your own children. I've never taught her in a class. I wouldn't place her as high as a child I did teach once, but by her results in school I know she does well.

• Boy: IQ 140, social class III, non-manual

MOTHER: Yes, I think he's highly intelligent.

FATHER: I'd say from the reports I've seen and his general attitude that he's highly intelligent. He does a lot of tests and takes them in his stride. The head teacher and other people have said how high his IQ is.

SPECIFIC GIFTS

The gifted category did not seem to present so much difficulty; it seemed to be a more clear-cut decision to make and reference to school was rarer.

IMAGE OF THE PRODIGY

Here two parents were wavering because of a specific image of 'giftedness' referring to a musical prodigy.

• Boy A: IQ 131, social class II

FATHER: We think he is highly intelligent.

MOTHER: And creative.

FATHER: We don't know how to determine giftedness!

MOTHER: I always think of 'gifted' as playing the cello at 5 years of age.

• Boy B: IQ 145, social class II

FATHER: I would say he's very intelligent. If you define gifted as a childhood prodigy who plays the violin at 14 years, no, he's not a genius!

Another misleading idea was that high ability functions without effort. There are a number of examples of it; one mother saw her clever child having to work and thought this immediately put her out of the 'gifted' category.

• Girl: IQ 145, social class I

MOTHER: She's probably intelligent. Very? Who am I to say? I can only compare with other children I have and she's more intelligent than they are. A 'gifted' child to me is one who does things with real ease, not having to work for things.

PERSONAL QUALITIES

Some of the gifts described were not in terms of a subject but rather as qualities of skill or mental processes which a child appeared to possess and use to his own advantage.

● Boy: IQ 134, social class I
FATHER: He's very intelligent and gifted, but not creative. He's got a gift in that he doesn't give in. You can talk to him and have TV on and nudge him, and he'll go on with his mental arithmetic. He has a great deal of perseverance. We don't show we think he's anything special, I think that would be very bad. I don't think he thinks his parents think he's gifted.

● Girl: IQ 136, social class III, manual
MOTHER: She's gifted—from a baby she's always been able to help herself.

● Boy: IQ 138, social class III, non-manual
FATHER: He's gifted: he surprises us sometimes with his ability to work to improve himself, e.g. football and elocution, he's really worked at them. He'd like to do a diploma to prove it to himself; you never have to force him to do it.

● Girl: IQ 128, social class II
MOTHER: She's gifted in that she can teach herself things—like music— she has a phenomenal memory.

It was unexpected that the word imagination was used so little in these definitions; when it was, it seemed to signal something more than just being good at something. The parents and teachers were noting the children's inner control over what they did.

● Boy: IQ 125, social class III, non-manual
FATHER: He's not highly intelligent—average—but gifted in drawing and he has a flair for things. He won first prize at a local flower show for flower arranging and a certificate for painting. His drawings, little scribbled men, really look as if they are doing something—he has imagination.

Another parent conveyed this extra dimension by reporting a subtle distinction observed by a teacher.

● Boy: IQ 124, social class III, manual
MOTHER: He's very intelligent and gifted. His teachers say he's gifted in sport; they say, 'He doesn't just play at it, he *thinks* it.'

GOOD WITH THEIR HANDS

Then there were the children who were manually dextrous. Sometimes the idea of being good with the hands was offered as a proof of worth where academic ability was weak. This does not apply to the following children who although they were not of exceptional general ability were by no means poor academically. They mostly came from the manual occupation group where work with the hands might be considered to have particular value.

● Boy: IQ 124, social class IV
MOTHER: Gifted, yes I think he is, he amazes me the things he makes with his hands.

● Girl: IQ 117, social class I
MOTHER: She has good average intelligence.
FATHER: She's gifted in as much as she has dexterity in her hands.

MUSIC—ART—SPORT

● Girl, IQ 134, social class III
MOTHER: No, not highly intelligent, not *very* intelligent—no, intelligent and gifted with her voice. I'd like her to go on with singing, but I'd like her to have a good education as well. I think they need both. If she's keen I'd love her voice trained later.

● Boy: IQ 131, social class II
FATHER: He's very intelligent and gifted in that he has an ear for music and words.

● Girl: IQ 124, social class III, non-manual
MOTHER: Well compared with us she's gifted musically and artistically.

● Girl: IQ 110, social class II
MOTHER: Oh no, not highly intelligent—gifted in drawing and diving, but it's more her determination.

● Boy: IQ 125, social class III, manual
FATHER: I think he may be gifted—he's got a good aptitude for drawing and he's keen on the sports side of life. I think with some encouragement he will be able to do further art and sport—these are his dominating features.

Summary

The parents thought 35 per cent of the children highly intelligent, 18 per cent intelligent, 14 per cent gifted, 11 per cent both highly intelligent and gifted and 22 per cent neither. There were no significant sex, social class or IQ group differences.

The parents reflected the difficulty of finding appropriate criteria on which to judge children of this age. They did not use the 'gifted' category very much, perhaps because of the lack of agreement as to what constituted a 'gift', or perhaps because the children of eleven were not yet showing a clear line of specialised knowledge or ability. It seemed as if in having to deny the highly intelligent category which was assumed to be high general ability, the parents fell back on to 'gifted' to take into account some special feature in which the child was doing well. The proportion in the 'neither' and 'intelligent' categories showed that not all the parents considered their children exceptional even when invited to do so.

Teachers have the advantage of being able to compare a child with many others of his age group either in the teaching situation or by standardised tests. It would seem that, when parents and teachers confer, parents need to be given information to help them make reasonable assessments of their child's standing in relation to his peers, and teachers need information about the child's special interests and abilities as observed by his parents.

Personality of the children

SOURCES OF INFORMATION

It was decided at the outset of the study to include both parents as far as possible. As it was known that some fathers would not be able to attend the interview, a rating sheet of personality items was prepared for them so that it could be taken home and returned by post if necessary. The ratings were taken from Terman's study with some slight modifications and a seven-point scale was used instead of thirteen [Table A6.2]. One hundred and eighty-seven sheets were completed.

Direct questions were asked during the interview on health items (illness, absence from school, sleep); social items (liking for company and leadership); emotional items (independence and resilience). There are popular stereotypes of the impractical but intellectually gifted child, the social isolate too clever to mix and the physical weakling too timid to play games. It was in order to examine some of these ideas in relation to our group of gifted children that assessments of general personality attributes were sought.

Much research has been directed towards children in difficulty so it was not easy to frame questions to describe the normal and above average child. The Newsons' books (1963, 1968) have demonstrated recently that parents are willing to co-operate and mostly enjoy talking about their children once they get going, so an open question on the child himself was posed to allow freedom to the parents to say what they liked in the way they liked. 'Could you tell me something about X him/herself, what is he like, what sort of person is he?'

Other questions that were included in the parents' interviews will be found on sheet C of their schedule [appendix IIc].

FATHERS' RATING OF PERSONALITY

The mean rating of each item was obtained and a rank order of items produced for IQs above and below 130.

The over 130 IQ group had a difference of six or more places higher on intelligence, originality and perseverance, while the under 130 IQs have a similar difference on sympathy only.

The intelligence test results for boys and girls combined were matched against the personality ratings by trend tests [Table A6.2].

The most significant personality traits in relation to the intelligence test scores were intelligence, desire to excel, desire to know, humour, originality, self-confidence, leadership and practical skills. It was encouraging to see the strongest association between the parents' ratings of intelligence and the IQ scores because it adds confidence to the interpretation that the other items when rated highly are likely to select the most intelligent children.

Shields (1968) using teachers' ratings replicated Terman's scale and found a high degree of correspondence between the rank orders of items. This present study of fathers' ratings had fewer items and used a seven-point scale rather than a thirteen-point scale, so cannot be compared as a whole with the two previous results, but it is worth noting that the same items appear at the top of the list when the over 130 IQ children are abstracted:

Terman (1925)	Shields (1968)	'Gifted' study (IQ 130+)
Intelligence	Intelligence	Desire to excel
Desire to know	Desire to know	Desire to know
Desire to excel	Originality	Intelligence
Common sense	Desire to excel	Humour
Perseverance	Common sense	Originality
	Perseverance	Perseverance

On the open-ended questions directed to parents, the children seemed to present few problems.

HEALTH AND SOCIAL BEHAVIOUR

In the over 130 IQ group 72 per cent were rated as having 'very good' health (Tanner, 1961) with 59 per cent in the under 130 IQ group. Only 15 children (6 per cent) were in poor health. The children were socially confident, only 27 (11 per cent) were thought to show some awkwardness in the company of adults. Half the children were considered grown-up for their age, only 22 (9 per cent) being young and immature. Only 12 (5 per cent) were seen to panic in new situations, the rest coped well. Physical timidity revealed more unease than other items; 60 children (25 per cent) were said to be physically timid, but 107 (45 per cent) were fearless in this respect. There were no differences of significance in sex or IQ.

SLEEP

Sleeping difficulties are often said to be a problem with gifted children, but no evidence was found to support this. Seventy-four per cent were said never to have any difficulty at all; those who did were evenly distributed throughout the IQ range. Time spent sleeping revealed no particular oddities, the average time was about ten hours and this was the same for children above or below IQ 130.

FIND LIFE EASY OR DIFFICULT

In answer to the question, 'Does he find life easy or does he tend to find it difficult?', 70 per cent of the children were said to find it easy. There were more children in the under 130 IQ group who found it easy, perhaps not surprising since the 130+ IQ represents greater complexity of thought, and such children perhaps were aware of a wider range of problems in their lives. This item matched that from the 7-year-old survey where it was shown that the brighter children showed more tendency to worry.

SEX ROLES

Sex roles have been investigated (Littlejohn, 1967) in relation to 'gifted' children and it was claimed that they had greater flexibility than others being able to allow themselves to show both feminine and masculine characteristics. This was confirmed in this study as far as boys were concerned; the 130+ IQ group boys were considered to have feminine aspects to their personalities more often than the under 130 IQ group. The trend for girls was the reverse, the under 130 IQ girls were more tomboyish than the rest.

OBSTINACY

Another concept that has been explored in regard to the gifted is their obstinacy. They are said to resist outside pressures more successfully than others. Again, the answers to the question on obstinacy provided no support for the idea that this was a special feature of the children with exceptional IQs (over 130). However, this could just be due to the age of the children, 66 per cent were said to show obstinacy in some respect and many parents were aware that their children were entering adolescence and a new period of independence which showed itself in greater resistance to external pressures.

GROWN-UP OPINIONS

The over 130 IQ group were thought to like talking about grown-up things and also to hold strong opinions about them more than the rest, showing another facet of the greater maturity of highly intelligent children.

PARENTS' SUMMING UP OF THEIR CHILD AS A PERSON

Perhaps the most important evidence on the children's personalities was that given by the parents in answer to the open question about what they considered their child to be like as a person.

The parents selected those things they thought most important. There was such variety in the answers that they were categorised in several ways. First of all they were assessed for warmth of response (W) if they seemed to pick out things on which they could appreciate and value their child. The opposite was a critical (C) rather than cold response. Some parents seemed only to mention the faults of their children.

Secondly, the answers were assessed on the parents' objectivity, i.e. were they describing their child as a separate person (O), or in relation to themselves (S)? When these two judgments are combined there are four groups:

1. Parents speak warmly of their child, appreciate and value him as a person, WO because of qualities in his own personality which are seen to be valuable (objective), WS because of the closeness of identification with parents (subjective).
2. Parents speak critically of their child, focus on faults more than virtues, CO because the qualities they see in him they judge rather harshly (objective), CS because their child does not come up to subjective demands. (Three assessors were used and a combined rating made the final grouping.)

Table 6.3. Parents' descriptions of their child

	WO	WS	CO	CS	Total
IQ 130+	54	26	14	20	114
IQ 129–	44	51	7	22	124
Total	98	77	21	42	238
Total %	41	32	9	18	100
Social Class					
Non-manual	64	26	16	22	128
Manual	34	51	5	20	110
Total	98	77	21	42	238
Total %	41	32	9	18	100

It can be seen that 73 per cent of the parents described their children in appreciative terms. Half were able to describe their children as separate and distinct from themselves, the other half still identified closely with the child and some of them found fault because the child did not fit their mould. It can be noted that the ability to be objective did not necessarily involve being overcritical.

There was a social class difference here in that the manual groups were less objective than the non-manual. Whereas the manual parents tended to express their ideas on their children warmly and subjectively, the non-manual tended to express their views warmly but objectively.

The following are some examples of the kind of comments the parents made:

● Girl A: IQ 107, social class II (WS)

MOTHER: I've found her most fascinating to bring up, never a dull moment, she always has something to talk about; she's very lovable and warmhearted in her ways, full of gaiety and very kind, she'd do anything for you. She just fascinates me, she's always something to talk about and do. She's quite a good conversationalist, always talking about something, politics, racialism, or whatever. She also has quite good perception, she knows what you're going to say before you say it. In planning things she's an enormous help to me, she reminds me about what I'm preparing. If she gets angry she goes up to her bedroom and generally erases herself, and comes down when there's the first signs of food. I never harbour any grievance, she doesn't get angry much.

[*Can you say what you most enjoy about her?*]

She's just my daughter, in every way she is fascinating to me. I just enjoy her company immensely. She's a treat to take out anywhere.

● Boy A: IQ 133, social class III, manual (WO)

MOTHER: He's polite.

FATHER: He's well-liked by adults, he holds very intelligent conversations about a number of things that he knows.

MOTHER: If somebody talks to him, he'll speak to them, he won't just stand there and say nothing.

FATHER: At the same time, away from grown-ups he is a boy, rough, tough, what have you—not aggressive—he doesn't like being pushed around—he won't stand it, but he wouldn't put himself out to push others.

MOTHER: He's very good with children—younger children accept him readily, he's accepted by everyone for what he is.

[*What do you enjoy about him most?*]

FATHER: I like him as an equal.

MOTHER: Well, he's a mate, isn't he?

FATHER: He's never one to be spoken to baby style, he's always spoken to as a grown-up, he's mixed more with grown-ups that's the reason he can hold a conversation.

MOTHER: You can take him out quite comfortably as a friend, that's unusual. He has a mind of his own, he knows how he wants to dress, he will tell me how to dress.

FATHER: You can talk to him more and more on the whole content of life, he'll sit there and understand; I enjoy having him around me.

● Boy B: IQ 134, social class II (CS)

PARENT: He has a very strong, quick temper which he's just beginning to learn to control, at one time he couldn't. He has a very strong inferiority complex yet he has to be top. He's found it difficult to compete with his sister. If he can't win he gives up. He doesn't like the youngest one at all. If I yell, he yells back, if I order him about he resents it. You're up against a brick wall if you try to get him to do something he doesn't want to do. He's very good looking and becoming more lovable; at one time I could not like him, I was fighting him all the time. I tend to give orders, the girls are more pliable, they will do it without smacking, with him it becomes a battle of wits that he is beginning to win.

● Girl B: IQ 148, social class II (CO)

MOTHER: She's pretty equable and cheerful mostly; she's not very suggestible, in fact downright obstinate over the last 2 years. She's not worried by school work, she tackles things reasonably well, sometimes tries to use one as a short cut to get out of dull work. She's quite a strong character with other children now, when she first went to school she was at the mercy of stronger characters than herself. She's not used to being in a group but she can look after herself pretty well. She's not a popular or unpopular child, but seems to fit in. Sometimes she's downright clever in the way she copes with other children's outbursts. I like to have an intelligent conversation with her. Perhaps it's when she reverts to being childish I'm most out of touch with her; because she's an only child we've always tended to talk to her as an adult, we don't keep anything from her, we discuss things, anything she wants to discuss. When my husband is there we talk as three adults not two adults and one child.

EXTROVERT–INTROVERT

The parents' responses were coded in a similar way to the teachers' comments. The positive, outgoing extrovert qualities and the withdrawn, shy, quiet introvert qualities were separated, a third category was made of those who said their child was 'good' or 'never gives me any trouble' as such remarks indicated a centring on the behaviour of the child in relation to his parents' expectations rather than on the child himself. The results showed that the under 130 IQ children were described significantly more often as behaviourally 'good' than the over 130 IQ children. When social occupation groupings were examined there were significantly more children from the 'manual' category described as 'good' and significantly more 'non-manual' children described in 'extrovert' terms.

There was 43 per cent agreement between teachers and parents. There was a tendency for the over 130 IQ children who were 'good' according to their parents to be 'extrovert' at school and those 'reliable' at school to be 'extrovert' at home. Where there was the greatest dis-agreement between parents and teachers the bias was for the under 130 IQs to be 'introvert' at school.

INTELLECTUAL VERSUS NON-INTELLECTUAL ATTRIBUTES

A third way in which the parents' responses were examined was by recording the number of areas they covered in describing their children, i.e. in referring to physical, social, emotional and intellectual attributes. The parents of the more intelligent children covered more areas in their descriptions than other parents and they mentioned intellectual attri-butes significantly more times. The parents in non-manual social occupations covered more areas than the rest in their descriptions and more often included intellectual attributes. The parents who presented a varied and complex picture of their children to outsiders were the ones who were likely to help their children construct varied and com-plex expectations of themselves.

Summary

1. The parents of the gifted sample showed greater concern and interest in their children's education than parents in general. The amount of contact with school staff was related to social class.

2. Eighty-seven per cent of the parents of the gifted were very pleased with the schools their children attended, only 3 per cent expressed dissatisfaction. Working-class parents were more reluctant to intervene if they were dissatisfied than middle-class parents.

3. There were class differences in the type of secondary education wanted for the children. Middle-class parents tended to choose grammar and independent schools, working-class parents were prepared to accept comprehensive, technical and secondary modern as alternatives to grammar schools. The working-class parents confirmed the general tendency to leave decisions concerning education to mothers.

4. The parents of the gifted acknowledged themselves as ambitious for their children's future occupation; 60 per cent had already thought what they wanted their child to become.

5. The gifted had more nursery education and an earlier start at in-fants' school than the population at large. Half of them were 'accelera-ted' at some time in the primary school.

6. Parents of children with IQs over 130 had longer education than the rest. This applied to working-class as well as middle-class parents. Forty-three per cent of middle-class and 19 per cent of working-class mothers had worked with children.

7. The middle-class parents of highly intelligent children considered themselves strict in their control. Working-class parents saw themselves as more openly affectionate.

8. The parents reflected the difficulty of finding appropriate criteria on which to judge children of this age as 'highly intelligent' or 'gifted'. There was need for more consultation with teachers on the matter.

9. The most significant personality traits in relation to the intelligence test scores of the 'gifted' group were originality, desire to excel, desire to know, self-confidence, leadership and practical skills.

10. Almost all the children had very good health, were socially confident and able to cope with new situations. There were no special sleeping problems connected with exceptional intelligence, but there was an indication that they (IQ over 130) found life 'more difficult' than the others.

11. The over 130 IQ boys were considered to have feminine aspects to their personalities more often than the under 130 group.

12. Obstinacy was a general characteristic of this group of pre-adolescents.

13. Working-class parents tended to express their ideas on their children warmly and subjectively, while middle-class parents tended to be warm but objective in their descriptions. Working-class parents were biased in favour of behaviourally 'good' children; middle-class parents more easily identified the 'extroverts'.

14. The parents of the more intelligent children (IQ over 130) mentioned a wider range of personality attributes when describing their children and were more likely to include intellectual aspects.

7. The children and their views

School

On the whole, this group of gifted children expressed at their interviews positive liking for school. Seventy per cent of them really enjoyed it and their keenness was supported by their parents' comments. A further 17 per cent found it satisfying in most respects, 9 per cent had some doubts about it, and only 4 per cent said they really disliked school.

It has already been demonstrated that they were successful in their work as compared with their peers. They were conscious of their abilities, at least two-thirds of them considered themselves to be 'exceptionally good at something'. Over half found no difficulty with school work at all: of the rest, the only subject that stood out was mathematics with which 21 per cent of the girls and 11 per cent of the boys had some difficulty.

When it came to things the children specially enjoyed about school, the parents reported that in 60 per cent of cases it was sports and the company of other children. This reinforced the picture that these children were normal, sociable and active 11-year-olds, for the most part especially happy when engaging in joint activities with their peers.

The things the parents reported that their children did not like about school were divided into personal and specific items. The only item of any frequency was a dislike of school meals which was mentioned by 15 per cent with some spontaneity and humour. More than half the parents could not think of anything their child disliked.

FAVOURITE AND MOST BORING SUBJECTS

The children were asked to put in order of preference the subjects they studied at school. The mentions received by each subject were then summed to produce the table overleaf.

It can be seen that there were differences in position for boys and girls, and for those above and below IQ 130. The most able boys revealed their

69

Table 7.1. Favourite subjects

	Proportion of children mentioning subject as most liked (up to 3 named)		
IQ 130+ Girls (41)		**Boys (73)**	
	(%)		(%)
Art	54	Maths	58
English	44	Art	34
Maths	44	Science	33
History	27	PE	32
PE	22	Craft	27
Craft	22	English	25
Science	20	Projects	21
Geography	17	History	21
Projects	12	Geography	19
Foreign language	7	Music	11
Music	7	Foreign language	3
RI	5	RI	1
IQ 129− Girls (72)		**Boys (52)**	
	(%)		(%)
English	56	PE	62
Art	46	Art	46
Maths	36	Science	33
Music	28	Craft	27
History	25	Maths	25
PE	25	History	25
Craft	18	English	23
Geography	17	Projects	19
Science	14	Geography	10
Projects	13	Foreign language	4
Foreign language	7	RI	1
RI	1	Music	0

maths-science bias and the others chose PE and games strongly, with mathematics and science lower down the list but still above English. The girls showed their preference for English and a relatively low placing for science.

The children were also asked to name the subjects they found most boring in school. They were not limited in the number of choices but were encouraged to name up to three. Despite these efforts, twelve children said there was *nothing* they could say was boring at school, a third of the rest could mention only one subject, a third mentioned two and a third mentioned three. The number of mentions given to each subject produce the table opposite.

The tables reflected the interest in practical subjects of all children. Forty-two per cent of the children regarded themselves as above average

Table 7.2. Boring subjects

Percentages of children mentioning subjects as boring (up to 3 named)

IQ 130+ Girls (36)		Boys (71)	
History	30	Music	58
English	23	History	43
Geography	22	English	42
Art	19	Geography	41
Maths	18	Foreign language	39
Foreign language	16	Religion	39
Religion	16	Maths	36
PE	12	Art	20
Music	12	Craft	9
Craft	11	PE	6
Science	9	Science	2
Projects	3	Projects	0
IQ 129– Girls (69)		Boys (50)	
Maths	52	English	41
History	52	Music	38
Foreign language	45	Religion	27
Geography	35	Foreign language	25
Science	34	Maths	24
Religion	27	Geography	23
Music	20	History	22
English	18	Art	12
PE	13	PE	11
Art	12	Science	8
Craft	11	Projects	6
Projects	5	Craft	2

in skill with their hands and only 5 per cent put themselves below average. No child of IQ 140 and over considered himself or herself lacking in manual skill. Though 'Projects' did not come high in the list of favourite subjects they appeared to be some of the least boring activities the children engaged in, and this was regardless of whether the projects concerned were self-chosen or set by a teacher.

The under 130 IQ girls showed their poor evaluation of mathematics and science again. The over 130 IQ girls did not rate science highly as a favourite but did not find it as boring as their less able peers.

The boys showed clearly again their low estimation of English. A third of the children really enjoyed writing, i.e. getting ideas on to paper, a fifth of them really disliked it and these children were evenly distributed throughout the IQ distribution, though slightly more boys (25 per cent) than girls (17 per cent) admitted to distaste for writing. The biggest difference was in music which was disliked by a third of the boys but only a tenth of the girls.

WERE THEY 'STRETCHED' SUFFICIENTLY IN THEIR WORK?

The question asked about doing 'more' work than the teacher expects was rather unsatisfactory, a better phrasing would have been 'harder' work. This was how some children interpreted the question, but others took it to mean a greater number of sums or pages of work. But bearing this in mind, it is still worth noting that 47 per cent of those with IQ 140 and over thought they could do more, while only 28 per cent of those with IQ 119 and under thought so.

In summary, it seemed that these children were well-balanced in their choices of subjects, except for the under 130 IQ boys who opted strongly for PE and games. There was no special bias because of high ability towards only academic subjects. The differences between the boys and girls on mathematics and science versus English only confirmed what common observation and other studies make clear. The low placing of religion, foreign languages and music also reflected general trends in the population[1] and are not confined to this small group.

REASONS FOR PREFERENCE OF FAVOURITE SUBJECT

The reasons the children gave for a subject being a favourite or the most boring showed where their interests lay.

Table 7.3. Reasons for favourite subjects (percentages)

	Boys (125)	Girls (113)
1. The subject is enjoyed both at home and at school	38	40
2. Ability to gain high marks or standard in the subject	28	25
3. The subject is different from others, e.g. PE and sports are out of doors and do not involve reading or writing	20	15
4. The subject is challenging and makes the children think	10	8
5. The teacher is interesting on the subject	4	12

The outstanding subjects in which the children linked their home and school interests were art, science and games for the boys and art and English for the girls. The subject liked most because it yielded success in terms of marks was mathematics for all children. There were no special trends for social occupation groups or higher and lower IQ groups.

REASONS FOR BOREDOM

The boys lay stress on repetition as boring, the girls on difficulty in understanding. The number in the case of individual school subjects

[1] (Enquiry 1 H.M.S.O. 1968)

was too small to reveal any general trend, and there were no clear IQ or social class group differences.

Table 7.4. Reasons for a subject being the most boring (percentages)

	Boys	Girls
1. Repetition—'it's the same thing over and over again'	40	30
2. Lack of understanding of the subject	29	50
3. The teacher is not interesting on the subject	18	16
4. The subject is not useful	9	2
5. The subject is liked at home but not at school	4	2

THE CHILDREN'S IDEA OF A 'GOOD' TEACHER

The children had no difficulty in expressing themselves on the question that asked for their ideas of a 'good' teacher, even the least verbal children were able to answer satisfactorily. There were no significant differences between the IQ groups. It was thought that the brighter children might give more responses in several categories, but this did not prove to be the case. It was also thought that perhaps the more able children would opt more for the 'skill' of a teacher and the others for personal qualities or discipline, but this was not confirmed. There seemed general agreement that teaching ability is uppermost in their minds and this result is in line with other research on children's perceptions of their teachers (P. H. Taylor, 1962).

'Skill' as a teacher in most of the answers meant skill as an explainer or interpreter. It stood out clearly that the teacher who could build an effective bridge of understanding between the material to be learned and the children was highly valued. The other definitions of 'skill' were divided between the teachers' organising ability which allowed for freedom of work in the classroom and their sympathetic understanding of children.

Table 7.5. The children's idea of a 'good' teacher (percentages)

1. Skill as a teacher	38
2. Discipline	26
3. Content of work	13
4. Personal qualities	13
5. Relationship with children	10

Examples

SKILL AS AN INTERPRETER

● Boy: IQ 140

'The teacher's got to be patient, because lots of kids can't get it first time like other kids; they're paying attention but they just don't see it

first time and lots of teachers just say, 'Oh, you should have listened.'
I've got a good teacher now—if she sees you're trying and you can't do
something she has you out to her table and she explains to you about it.'

● Girl: IQ 140

'Somebody who, instead of getting in a temper or telling you off or
anything like that, can help you with your work that you've done wrong,
show you how to do it so that you can do it better next time.'

DISCIPLINE

The most important item categorised in 'discipline' was that of balance;
these children demanded control in the classroom but were aware that
the extremes of too great strictness or easiness were unhelpful. The
rejection of shouting as a mode of control was the second item mentioned
frequently by these children.

● Boy: IQ 125

'I like a teacher to be firm, but—what's the word for it—nice, firm but
nice. I'm not so keen on teachers too old or too young—ones that have
just come from college. I think all teachers should really get used to their
class, and they should find out what these children like and what they
don't like. I don't like teachers who shout. If you do the slightest thing
wrong they pick on you. Some have a favourite and a least one, and
you could be the least one and it's terrible then. I like teachers who are
helpful, not a person who says they help you by shouting.'

CONTENT OF WORK

'Content' covered three items equally: the facts that teachers have
knowledge to offer, that they can make subject matter interesting and
that they can make school more enjoyable by a varied curriculum.

● Boy: IQ 154

'Someone who is good at all the subjects really top, like model-making,
art, gymnastics, as well as all the other subjects like maths and English.
Not someone who sets out everybody in rows. I'm not interested in that
because you come in and it's just always four rows and you're in one of
them. I like how you have it in the infants, you can have group activities,
it's a lot more interesting and it gets you more interested in your work.'

● Girl: IQ 154

'I think one that takes different subjects—various things, not the same
thing every time you have a lesson; one that takes a lot of interest in you
and is strict but not too strict. Some people give you a book and say,
"Do this" and leave you to it. I like teachers that come round and look
at your work and help you on with it—in case you're stuck on anything.'

PERSONAL QUALITIES

The personal qualities mentioned were most often kindness and patience.

● Girl: IQ 120

'Not a teacher who is impatient. Impatient teachers sometimes want to be more ambitious than the children can understand.'

● Girl: IQ 128

'A person who is considerate, who understands you and isn't angry if you cannot do things right . . . does not expect more than you yourself can do. A person who is willing to help and has time to see you and talk to you and help you along with things. I know there isn't always time because of the large classes, you can't see every child for quite a while.'

● Boy: IQ 134

'Teachers on the whole should be interesting and kind and they should be tolerant. My favourite teacher is a kind man. He goes off the subject sometimes and gets caught up in the things he's telling us about but he does get back to the subject eventually.'

PROFESSIONAL ATTITUDE

Closely related to personal qualities were those remarks indicating a special relationship with children, a professional enjoyment of the job.

● Boy: IQ 130

'Well, a good teacher would be quite strict, but he would think about us, the children, more than he does himself.'

● Girl: IQ 107

'She must enjoy her work otherwise there's no use teaching, and she must enjoy the children too, because they can't do anything very enjoyable without her liking children.'

The children were also asked to define a teacher who might not help children to get on well. They made only half as many comments as on the idea of a 'good teacher', but these reflected again the importance of skill as an explainer or interpreter and ability to keep balanced discipline.

The examples showed that some children were able to answer the abstract question with an abstract answer, but others slipped into describing a specific teacher or even needed encouragement to think about a favourite teacher to make answering easier.

Perhaps the last word can be left with a girl of very high ability who ranged cleverly between abstract and specific statements and gave a great deal of information about herself and her problems in relation to two different teachers.

● Girl: IQ 148

'I have been in different classes where the teachers are totally different
to the same children so it's hard to answer. I think that you should have
a reasonably strict teacher or else they'll get nothing done and they'll be
doing all sorts of things they shouldn't. I like a kind teacher and a
teacher that explains things well to you and doesn't give you the answers
but explains how to do it well. I think a teacher should not have a main
subject. Whenever there's a choice between two they say we've got to do
arithmetic instead of something else. I think the teacher should have an
assortment of things to do. Our teacher doesn't teach art or anything.
His main subject is music, sometimes we have about a quarter of an
hour of religion and the rest of the time music when we're supposed to
have half and half. He stretches out a bit on the music and he thinks it
doesn't matter about PE.

'The last teacher always joked with us and we used to go to her and
tell her anything that happened at home, but if we go up to the teacher
now, he just says we've got better things to talk about. He is more all
school and we don't talk about other things.

'When they know a child is doing their best to do what they really
can, I do not think a teacher should try drumming into them that they
can do better when the child is already all out to do what he can. Last
year I really went all out to get everything right, but this year I can't
get much further than I was last year, but the teacher expects me to
double my intelligence. Really, I was trying too hard last year.'

THE CHILDREN'S IDEA OF A 'PERFECT' PUPIL

The children were asked for their definitions of 'a teacher's idea of a
perfect pupil'. Again, this was a question they found easy to answer.
The answers were categorised in different ways, firstly to separate those
children who put the emphasis on success in work (e.g. 'somebody who
knows everything and can do everything well') from those children who
put the emphasis on behaviour (e.g. 'a pupil who obeys and doesn't
bother the teacher'). The second categorisation separated those whose
emphasis was on the teacher, either in connection with work or with
behaviour (e.g. 'a pupil who gets everything right, a pupil who likes the
teacher's subjects, and a pupil that does what he's told') from those who
saw the effort lying in the child himself (e.g. 'teacher likes a person who
can get on by themselves without having to be told what to do every few
minutes', and 'a child who doesn't mess about, doesn't talk too much').
Differences between the sexes, between higher (130+) and lower
(130−) IQ groups, and between social occupation groups, manual and
non-manual, were sought, but none proved significant.

The interest in the answer lies in the relation it bears to the child who
gives it. The brighter children gave longer answers and included more
items. The following boy was thought by his parents to take life too

seriously, he is too conscientious and persevering and suffers a good deal (See Tom, p. 40). His sensitivity extends to his teachers:

● Boy: IQ 134
'I think a perfect pupil is not a snob for a start, not a sneak or a tale teller. I think a perfect pupil sticks hard to his work. He must be kind to the teacher. Some teachers—you may not realise it—but they are weak and I know one at our school and poor chap, some of the bigger boys in our form really make life hard for him. I'm really sorry for him sometimes. They should be kind to the teacher and they shouldn't be rude. There's no need—and I mean this—they don't have to be clever at work, as long as they stick at their work, I think teachers like them, unless you've got a nasty teacher.'

As in the case of this boy, most children answered the question with their own idea of what an ideal pupil might be like, few acknowledged the slant that had been given to the question, 'a teacher's idea of a perfect pupil', in order to see how far the children were capable of taking another's point of view rather than answering from their own. Only a few children acknowledged the particular phrasing, mostly these were the very bright children.

● Girl: IQ 140
'I think, from what teachers have said, that they don't mind if you get things wrong so long as you try hard to do it right and so long as you don't just give up.'

● Girl: IQ 140+
'I don't think they expect us to be really perfect, because no one is, but they think we ought to come to lessons with everything ready and our books ought to be neat—which is more than you could say for mine!'

● Girl: IQ 109
'A perfect pupil can be someone who is always quiet and gets on with their work and does their best all the time, and is always willing to help and likes the things that they have chosen—but I don't really think a teacher likes a person who is *very* good, I think teachers like a bit of fun in their work, too.'

CHILDREN WHO DO NOT LIKE SCHOOL

Of the thirty children who admitted to some dissatisfaction with school, eighteen were boys, twelve were girls, a not untypical pattern. Twelve of the boys had IQs over 130, but only one girl with an IQ of over 150, so it was the brighter boys and the less bright girls who rejected school. It was difficult to sum up the reasons for their doubts about liking school because each child was reacting to his own particular set of circumstances. However, there did seem to be two categories that most of the boys could be divided into, those who were not scholastic in their interests and turned away from academic work and those who wanted more academic work because they were rather bored at school. All the boys (6) with IQs under 130 came into the first category. They were boys who liked games, PE, art and playing outside with other children. Six of the boys with IQs over 130 also came into that category.

● Boy: IQ 132
'I don't like maths and I don't like English. I like football, cricket, books, acting. I'm no good at drawing and making things.' He does not like writing things down, in fact he says he likes football because 'It's running around and you don't have to write.'

● Boy: IQ 130
MOTHER: He will not admit he likes school. I can't understand it. I could if he was a lazy child. His school reports say 'A's all the way, excellent, well done, very good progress'. The boy himself gave the impression at interview of being nervous and unhappy, he said he felt 'no good and hopeless at things'. He dislikes reading and writing.

● Boy: IQ 112
PARENTS: He likes the outdoor life, he can't sit still to concentrate on lessons.' His favourite occupation out of school is helping a coal merchant. He is at the bottom of an 'A' class, and dislikes writing things down.

● Boy: IQ 102
A boy who likes art and games, but dislikes reading and writing. His main interest is helping on a farm in his spare time.

It will be remembered that earlier on in the chapter it was shown that the children who were really keen on school had favourite subjects which they followed through as interests at home. There seemed to be a sharper division between home and school for the above boys who did not carry on the same interests in both areas of their lives.

The four 130+ IQ boys who wanted more academic work at school all complained of boredom in one way or another.

● Boy: IQ 154
He changed schools in his last year in the primary stage. He says about the first school, 'We did a lot more work and we didn't get bored and I had lots of friends there. And the teachers, well, if you had any troubles or anything, you just told them and they did their best to help.'
His parents said, 'To be honest, at this school he's rather bored. The one he came from was more advanced than this. The work he's doing now he did 2 years ago. His previous school was marvellous, very go-ahead.'

● Boy: IQ 136

This boy was above average at school but he just did not enjoy many lessons so that he developed a general attitude of dislike.

MOTHER: I think there's too much PE and too much art and other things are left out like history and geography. They fall down on that. At the moment they're not all to the same standard in the class. He's capable of a bit more of a higher standard—I'm told he's bright. I don't like non-streaming. In his class there are four groups. They're all different levels—that's not fair to the children—it's certainly not fair to the teacher. Some children in his class can't read. The teacher spends so much time with them she leaves the clever ones to themselves. They're told to do this and that lesson out of the book. He resents it. How can a teacher cope with three types of lesson? It's quite recent, the past two years, in the second year he was streamed, he was in the A stream. I went to see his teacher and she was there with the group that couldn't read. She's very conscientious, young and ambitious, but she can't cope with four different types.

Perhaps the mother voiced the difficulty of the boy, a lack of realistic standards for his ability.

Two boys were shy and sensitive and did not like the hurlyburly of school life. In this, they resembled the girls, for one common feature that could be found in six of the twelve girls was shyness and nervousness.

● Girl: IQ 126

'She has never settled down since the day she started school. She can't take exams, she gets so sick and nervous, she couldn't do the eleven-plus exam.'

● Girl: IQ 98

'The work is too hard for her. She gets upset when she can't do it.'

Like one of the boys, one girl had changed schools. She moved from a lively and interesting school to a more traditional one and she found the slower pace more trying, and her loss of companions distressing.

Three of the girls had no interests at home; they were committed to household tasks and looking after younger children, so again there was no carry over of any aspect of school work into the home. One of the brightest girls was bored and wanted more to do. One less able girl whose main interest was swimming found 'a lot quite boring', by which she meant the subjects she did not care for. None of the girls mentioned dislike of reading and only one did not like getting things down on paper.

It appeared that girls and boys needed to be considered separately in this context of dislike of school, although there was some overlap of the aspects found distasteful. The boys were more concerned with what they did there, the girls perhaps with how they felt about it. Although boredom was mentioned in several cases there was little evidence to support the contention that the most able children were understimulated and insufficiently stretched. Most of the children in the group found school very satisfying indeed and it was a small minority who complained of lack of work at the standard they felt they could manage.

It is perhaps worth while to finish with two rather longer examples of children's records, just to show the complexities that there are in each individual case with dislike of school constituting one common factor. The cases are that of a boy with an IQ of 140 and a girl of IQ 150.

- Boy: IQ 140

This boy was the youngest of a large family. He was born in this country though his parents are Indian. His brothers and sisters all went to university and he was expected to follow in the family tradition. His teachers thought well of him, rating him 'above average' all round except in number work where he was considered of average ability. They said he was a favourite among his companions but rather withdrawn when speaking to adults. He was thought to have a happy nature and to be kindly towards others in trouble.

The interviewer found him to be a good-looking, alert and responsive boy.

INTERVIEWER: How much do you like school?
BOY: Not very much. I don't like the lessons much. I like history, only we don't do much of it. I'm not very good at art but I do like it. I like English composition; I don't really like the English grammar questions, just the compositions. I like writing stories and things. I try at home but I never finish them, there is always something else to do. But at school it is okay because we've got to finish them. I'm not very good at making poetry, but I don't mind reading it and drawing about it.
INTERVIEWER: What about drama?
BOY: Well, I like that but we never do that at school, not in our class, just like we don't have much art, we don't have physical education. We have games; I like that. We don't do crafts, we don't do any woodwork or anything. We do music; we have no instruments, just singing. I like it, it's okay. It's not something I'm very attached to, though.
INTERVIEWER: Which is your favourite subject?
BOY: Well, I think I'd like craft best if we did it. I like English composition best of the ones we do at school.
INTERVIEWER: Do you like science?
BOY: Well, we have it on the radio at school. We don't do any experiments. It would be okay if we could hear the words properly. The man hasn't got a boring voice but he sounds boring. I don't do much geography. We don't do the geography of the land, we do the people, like farming and industries and coals and things like that. I don't like it. I don't like religious instruction because I've heard it all before. We have been told the same stories all over and over again.

When the interviewer looked into the interests of this boy, she found that he liked active physical things; he did not like reading: 'I don't really read very much. I've read *Journey to the Centre of the Earth*, and, well, I don't read books really. I hardly ever read them. I look up the *Encyclopaedia Britannica* only to find out things, like something for projects at school.' He did not appear to derive much satisfaction from the work that was provided for him, and the things he was interested in he saw sparsely represented in his curriculum.

His mother said: 'He keeps telling me he doesn't like school but he has never yet made a fuss about going. For some years now he says he doesn't like it. I like the school very much, I don't know any other. All my other children went there. The teachers are very friendly. The head teacher seems to be very interested in our family as a whole. The boy is a great chatterbox. May be the teachers don't see eye to eye with him in chattering. He doesn't seem to have any trouble with his work. He is not terribly above average; a little. Concentration is a little difficult; his mind is on other things. There is nothing else he finds particularly difficult. He has a lot of trouble because of his colour. He comes home and says, "So and so, he called me names." He doesn't like it very much, but we don't make much of it. He's got to live with it all his life. Children are hurtful. He has a great interest and keenness in sports and games. He thinks he's a great runner but he isn't. They're not encouraged as much as they could be in the juniors. He likes to be noticed by everyone else. He thinks he should be noticed by everyone else. He thinks he's good. He's joined a gym club. He's as keen as anything. He found out about it from the boys at school. I'm very glad. He said, "That's Monday evening and Tuesday evening. Now I've got to find something else for the other evenings." He's not all that keen on his own company. He likes swimming, football, going out with friends.'

It was clear that at that moment the boy's interests were not academic. He was finding ways for himself of dealing with his physical energy and need for activity which staved off the frequent boredom which was noted in him at home. He had the problem of his colour to deal with and was getting little sympathy over it at home and his school saw him only as popular with others, so may not have been aware of his predicament.

His essay was somewhat surprising as it dealt with the more sordid aspects of adult life which other children did not deal with:

Now, at the age of 25, I have a job at the cake factory. In my spare time, I sometimes take the neighbours' children out to the cinema. Sometimes, I might go to the pub down the road, have a couple of pints, and then stagger home to the flat.

A couple of weeks ago, I went fishing with some of my friends. We didn't get far though, the first pub we got to we got drunk and forgot to take our fishing rods from there. We had a small accident just as we started to get back after finding—or should I say—'not finding', our rods. You see, we stopped at another pub, and we were so drunk that time that I've got into the wrong car, and crashed into the side of the supermarket. We paid a fine of £30, by pooling our money together, and when we found that it was £30 each, we again went to the pub to think it over with a couple of pints.

Last Thursday I went to a soccer match, and, as my home team lost, I got into a fight with one of the other team's supporters at the 'King's Head' pub. A copper had to go and break it up though. Saturday night, I planned to rob a big store with a couple of other men, but the police were tipped off by one of their rotten spies. They were ready for us, and now, in jail at Slogmoor prison, I find myself without a pub, barred windows, and hopeless food. Still I suppose it's better than having to buy food, new clothes, and not having to pay rent.

Still, though, come to think of it, I wish I never got mixed up in all these things.

This could be seen as a production out of character for a boy from a middle-class intellectual home. He liked writing compositions so this could just be a particular flight of fancy of the moment, or it could be an expression of some antisocial ideas he felt strongly and wanted to express in some way.

It remained to be seen whether a secondary school could cultivate intellectual interest in this boy so that he could make fuller use of his high intelligence and get some satisfaction from it.

● Girl: IQ 150+

At 7 years of age teachers rated this girl in the top 5 per cent in oral ability and reading, the next 25 per cent in awareness of the world and creativity, and average in number work. Drawing and painting were said to be her favourite activities. She was not considered a good mixer, she associated with one other child and mostly ignored the rest.

At 11 years of age her teachers said she was of outstanding ability in reading, story-writing, and oral work, and very good on general knowledge and mathematics. It was predicted that she should do very well at secondary school, being encouraged by her family. Her future career was seen to lie in something creative, story-writing or dress-designing. Her teachers said: 'She is very neat and tidy in all her work, which is very creative. She is capable of great attention to detail.' In connection with weaknesses or drawbacks of personality or character, 'She is tall for her age and somewhat plumpish. In a class where her classmates are smaller and more active she's inclined to be retiring as if self-conscious and outgrown in her strength. With her height and ability she could assert herself far more than she does.'

The interviewer considered her a very pretty child with an attractive smile and expression. She was co-operative in the interview but reserved and slow in response. She said she had one or two close friends but seemed to be rather lonely and worried about bullying from other children. She said very little during the interview. She answered in a word or a phrase and did not elaborate despite encouragement.

INTERVIEWER: How much do you like school?

GIRL: Not all that much really. I don't like getting up in the morning.

INTERVIEWER: Which subjects do you find most interesting?

GIRLS: Mathematics, history and art and music.

INTERVIEWER: Any others?

GIRL: No.

INTERVIEWER: Which do you find boring?

GIRL: English and games. I don't like going out much.

INTERVIEWER: Are you exceptionally good at anything?

GIRL: I think I'm better at art.

INTERVIEWER: How do you know?

GIRL: Because all my friends say I am.

INTERVIEWER: How much do you like getting things down on paper?

GIRL: Oh, a lot, a lot.

INTERVIEWER: What is your idea of a good teacher?

GIRL: One that doesn't interrupt all the time telling you things, and don't disturb you when you're hard at work.

INTERVIEWER: Is there anything you would like to change about school if you could?

GIRL: I can't really think of anything.

INTERVIEWER: Some children have mentioned equipment, lessons, teachers, children.

GIRL: I'd like the children to stop bullying. Last year there was this boy always bullying me and there was this girl last year as well.

INTERVIEWER: Has it stopped this year?

GIRL: Yes.

INTERVIEWER: Tell me about your friends.

GIRL: I've only one really good friend.

INTERVIEWER: Tell me about your interests.

GIRL: Drawing, playing the piano, knitting and sewing.

INTERVIEWER: Do you write stories?

GIRL: No.

INTERVIEWER: Or plays?

GIRL: I did once but the teacher says it wasn't any good.

INTERVIEWER: Poems?

GIRL: Yes. At home and at school.

INTERVIEWER: Do you enjoy doing it?

GIRL: Yes.

INTERVIEWER: How much do you use books?

GIRL: A lot.

INTERVIEWER: Do you belong to a public library?

GIRL: Yes.

INTERVIEWER: How many books do you own?

GIRL: I don't know. I don't count them. I've got quite a few, about sixty or seventy.

INTERVIEWER: As a reader how do you compare with other children?

GIRL: I think I'm better than most of them.

INTERVIEWER: What are the other members of your family interested in?

GIRL: My dad likes mending things; he reads the newspaper.

INTERVIEWER: Mother?

GIRL: I don't really know.

INTERVIEWER: Tell me about yourself. What kind of a person are you?

GIRL: Shy.

INTERVIEWER: What would you like to be when you grow up?

GIRL: A teacher.

INTERVIEWER: Do you know what you have to do to become a teacher?

GIRL: I've got to go to college and learn about children.

INTERVIEWER: Tell me about your friend.

GIRL: She's the girl who lives across the road from me.

INTERVIEWER: What is it you like most about a friend?

GIRL: She can think of something to do when I'm bored (*laughs*).

The child gave little away in her interview. It was her parents who gave a clearer picture of her.

INTERVIEWER: Does she enjoy school or not?

MOTHER: Sometimes she does, sometimes she doesn't. When she's bored in school, she doesn't want to go. She says; 'I know all that.' She's quite bright. When she was 8 years old she had the knowledge and ability of an 11-year-old. She won a first prize in a National Essay competition about 2 years ago. It was really marvellous. She's very good at drawing; she was runner-up in a Blue Peter competition. Her interests are that big that she easily gets bored. She wants to start new things. She really acts as an older person—sometimes the child comes through but she's usually older. In every way I'm really astonished at her. She wants to get contact with older children because her interests, speech and conversation are not satisfied with the ones in her age-group. I only wish she would stay that bright and not one day . . . I find that with children all of a sudden it goes.

INTERVIEWER: What type of secondary school would you like her to go to?

MOTHER: Grammar school. I don't feel very happy about comprehensives. If at a comprehensive school a child wants to get on, the others bully and tease all the while. That's what I've got against comprehensives. In the grammar school they're interested in lessons. If someone's interested they've got more go or push. If they are with other intelligent children, it's like a race. All the teachers in the comprehensive schools are more for general knowledge but the teachers in grammar schools have each got their own subjects. Discipline. If you achieve discipline in children you get more attention—when there's more attention, they listen to what you say.

INTERVIEWER: What does she choose to do in her spare time?

MOTHER: She's very musical. She plays the piano at home and the organ at school. She even tries to compose a little bit. She knits and draws, and writes poetry and plays. She's not so much for outdoor life. I have to say, 'Now it's time to go out.' When she goes out she likes to go where she can see things, old ruins, graveyards.

She likes to read a lot. She goes to the public library. She's allowed four books every fortnight. She likes dress-making. She has a pen-friend in Canada she writes to. She used to have piano lessons. I stopped them because I didn't like the teacher. He said it was a big mistake to stop it—that she was a very brilliant child musically and could take it up as a career, but she started to play the violin at school—I stopped it. The teacher was very disappointed. I said, 'I don't want any fiddle in the house.' She began playing the piano at 3 years of age on her own. I didn't know about it; she said, 'I can play the piano.' I said, 'Who taught you?' She said, 'Nobody.'

INTERVIEWER: Could you tell me more about her—what sort of a person is she?

MOTHER: She's very sensitive; if some children say or do something to her she really takes it to heart. It's a job to get it out of her. She's ever so untidy, leaves things lying about. I threaten her 'If you don't put them away, I'll throw them away.' It's no good—books, clothes, toys— that's something I really can't understand with her being so intelligent. May be this is an outlet—she's got to let go somewhere. She's a very obedient child, very well-mannered, very clean. If there's a spot on her dress she won't wear it. She takes a pride in herself. She's everything I wish for apart from being untidy.

INTERVIEWER: Would you say she's a sociable child who likes company?

MOTHER: She likes company but she's very reserved. This was one of the problems at school. She wanted to go to school but at playtime she wanted to stay in. I talked to the teacher; she said she was timid—that she should go out and mix with the others. She's not a great mixer, she's not so bad now but she used to be quite a problem.

INTERVIEWER: Have you thought what kind of work you would like her to do?

MOTHER: If everything goes all right she'd like to be a school teacher. I have nothing against it. I hope she comes through it. If she couldn't be a teacher the next thing is a hairdresser or dress-designer; those are the three things we have in mind. I'm quite happy, I always said to her, 'You aim for the highest first.' I don't think office or industry is her type at all. I think the jobs would be too tedious for her.

This child had problems of height and weight in relation to other children. She was withdrawn and unsociable and did not like the active pastimes of most children of her age. That she was exceptional in many ways was recognised by her parents and teachers. The school had ob- viously cultivated her creative talents as far as they could but the mother had curtailed this line of endeavour, perhaps searching for academic prowess in her daughter, the rare musical talent was perhaps not fully appreciated.

The child could have been lonely for the companionship of others more like herself, a small village school was perhaps restricting for her as indicated by the fact that she 'wants to get contact with older children'.

Interests out of school

The children were written to personally before their interviews and it was suggested that they might like to bring along some evidence of their interests [appendix Id]. At the interview these exhibits were discussed and further questions about interests asked. The word 'interest' had to be explored with the children and it was found that most of them equated it with hobbies and things they liked doing in their leisure time.

It may seem frivolous, but one could say that one could almost judge a child's ability by the weight of material he brought to the interview. Some children brought several bags and cases full of things and other members of the family joined in and helped in carrying these. There was never any difficulty with such children, they were eager to get into the room to start unpacking and talking about their things. The children who brought nothing were different in that it took longer to ease them into the situation and find some common ground to start them talking. Some, of course, had their reasons ready to offer—their models were too big or collections of rocks too heavy or their interest in a sport had not lent itself to producing anything that could be shown. The larger amounts of material certainly seemed to come with the most verbal children, many of whom could have spent the whole three hours just talking about their hobbies.

The idea was to get the children to talk spontaneously about their interests on the assumption that what they felt most involved in they would talk about most fluently. After that, if there were one or two areas of interest they had not mentioned, these were suggested to see if they were included in the child's range. Parents were interviewed in the same way, spontaneous comments were followed with questions on other interests they did not mention. When it came to putting the evidence together, the parents' and children's answers were combined and a decision taken on whether a particular activity was a 'keen' interest or 'occasional' interest or 'not done'. The activity a child chose as the activity he liked most and did most often was accepted as his 'main' interest. The combining of parents' and children's answers was done to try to avoid the difficulty that other workers have pointed out, that some less able children tend to say they do everything.

PREFERRED INTERESTS

The parents were asked if they considered their child busy or bored. The answers showed 80 per cent busy, as one would expect for children of this age, which is one of activity and involvement in peer group play. There were no significant differences between the number of boys and girls who were bored, or between the IQ groups over and under 130.

As in the case of previous studies on children's interests at 11 years of age, it was found that the order of preference for certain activities was different for boys and girls.

Table 7.6. List of interests in order of preference (percentages)

GIRLS considered main or keen interest (N = 113)		BOYS considered main or keen interest (N = 125)	
1. Reading	62	Sports	75
2. Sports	49	Playing outside	50
3. Making (crafts)	47	Reading	45
4. Drawing	34	Making (crafts)	41
5. Music	29	Drawing	39
6. Playing outside	26	Collecting	33
7. Writing	20	Science	31
8. Painting ⎫	19	Clubs	25
9. Clubs ⎬	19	Television	21
10. Television ⎭	19	Painting	17
11. Collecting	15	Music ⎫	16
12. Keeping pets ⎫	11	Pets ⎭	16
13. Helping parents ⎭	11	Chess	14
14. Science	7	Helping parents ⎫	9
15. Inventing games	5	Inventing games ⎭	9
16. Chess	2	Writing	7

READING—WRITING—MUSIC

In a comparison between the sexes the girls tended to favour reading, music and writing, the boys tended to prefer sports, playing outside, collecting, science and chess. Both boys and girls in the over 130 IQ group showed more interest in reading than the others.

A quarter of the children played a musical instrument (not including the recorder[1]). It was anticipated that the more able children would reveal greater preference for classical than light music, but there were no IQ or sex differences on this item. Music was one of the interests most strongly rejected by some children yet it was fifth on the girls' list. The boys with IQs over 130 knew more definitely that they were not interested, and the under 130 IQ girls showed a similar strength of rejection. It should be remembered that music was one of the least favoured of school subjects. This might reflect the quality and content of the teaching.

A further 15 per cent of the children had some form of instruction out of school; speech training, sports training and dancing were represented.

---

[1] Recorder playing is commonly learned in school. It was excluded in order to focus on home interests.

A third of the children expressed strong interest in these activities, the others seemed less involved, perhaps only attending at the wish of their parents.

SPORT

Football was the sport that boys like best. It received 75 per cent of the mentions of sport. Only six girls managed to enter this male preoccupation, usually to join their brothers on the field in order to make up a neighbourhood team. There was nothing to attract the attention of girls in the same degree as football for the boys. Swimming was the next most favoured sport, 65 per cent of the girls and 63 per cent of the boys enjoyed this sport. Girls took the lead in dancing and horse-riding but even then only 10 per cent of them had tried one of these activities. In fishing, 8 per cent of the boys were keen in contrast to 2 per cent of the girls.

DRAWING AND PAINTING

A point worth noting was the greater interest in drawing than painting. Fifty-eight per cent of the children did not paint outside school, while only 29 per cent did not draw. It was the children who insisted on separating painting and drawing to consider them as two distinct activities. Those who could express their dissatisfaction with painting commented on the difficulty of the medium itself; they felt that it easily got out of control and could end in a confusion in which they lost their intention.

As a corollary to this it was noted that of the hundreds of pictures brought by the children, hardly any had been drawn freehand. These intelligent children seemed to put hours of effort into copying and tracing realistically, and seemed to gain pleasure and satisfaction in doing so.[1] Only four children, two girls and two boys, brought paintings which could be said to show appreciation of colour and some knowledge of the use of paint that would suggest they were 'exceptional' compared with others of the same age.

GENERAL PLAY OUTSIDE WITH OTHER CHILDREN

As for playing outside the home with other children, only 14 per cent of these children did not do this at all. There was a connection with intelligence here in that boys and girls in the IQ 130+ group showed less keenness on this than the rest, but this was probably only a matter of having the time, for the more intelligent children did more reading, science, collecting and other things which kept them indoors.

[1] This, too, may reflect the quality of the teaching of art in school!

CHESS AND SCIENCE

Forty-four per cent of the children played chess—28 per cent boys, 16 per cent girls, but only boys showed *keen* interest in the game, only two girls could match that degree of interest.

Interest in science was another divider of the sexes. The boys had science as a main or keen interest significantly more often than girls. And for both boys and girls the higher IQ groups were keener than the lower IQ groups. Science, of course, covers a wide range of activities. For the girls it was mostly restricted to nature study, particularly plants and animals, for boys it was either astronomical or physical, chemical or biological. Some boys seemed to have a vast verbal knowledge of astronomy, others had already reached the stage of the first chemistry and electronic kits and therefore turned to a more practical way of developing their interest.

The boys in the 140+ IQ group were outstanding in respect of their interest in science, thirteen had it as a 'main', ten as a 'keen' interest out of thirty-five. Burt (1962a) also drew attention to the fact that highly intelligent children tended to be interested in science.

COLLECTING

In collecting things these children were typical of their age, two-thirds of them had collections of one kind or another. Stamps were favoured by the 130+ IQ boys more than by the over 130 IQ girls, but there were no significant sex or IQ differences in collecting coins or natural phenomena. There were many collections mentioned which were too personal to classify, special toys, comics, books, souvenirs, cards, etc.

Time did not allow for a fuller analysis of these collections during the interview. It was the way in which the children ordered and classified their collections that was important. Some children obviously enjoyed amassing numbers of things of one general kind, but others were already more selective, narrowing their choice to one kind of stamp, e.g. British Commonwealth, or one range of coins, e.g. Victorian. Only the very intelligent and highly verbal children could discuss why they narrowed their choice and ordered their things in a particular way. The others showed how they stuck in their stamps and used the titled pages in their albums correctly, or arranged their coins in order of age, but probing questions about further orders or categories were not successful.

This is an area for future research, because children's ordering of their personal possessions gives information about their style and level of thought. Conscious knowledge of different ways of ordering and classifying these very meaningful objects could help towards better understanding of other types of categorization that are constantly being put to children in their daily work at school.

CLUBS

Half of the children attended clubs (other than those arranged by school), Boy Scouts, Girl Guides and other church affiliated clubs account for the majority of these; a further 25 per cent went to sports clubs and 10 per cent managed at eleven years of age to get themselves into youth clubs. There are a number of correspondence clubs for children connected with their comics or animal welfare or books, and about 12 per cent of the group showed sustained interest in these. There were no significant sex or IQ differences on this item.

TELEVISION

Television did not emerge as a positive interest for many children. Only two boys named it as their main interest and one of these was keen on drama, with an ambition to be an entertainer; the other was a reserved boy who lived outside a town and, not being academically inclined, probably relied on this form of entertainment. For the rest, six children had no television in the home and two expressed no interest at all; 19 per cent expressed a keen interest and 76 an occasional interest. This proportion cannot be translated into how often the children watched television, it only represented how far they considered it a definite interest rather than something to fall back on when there was nothing else to choose. When asked what their favourite programmes were, two-thirds of the children mentioned programmes that had some informational content (as well as others). *Blue Peter*—a programme specially designed for children—received half the mentions; it appeared to lead to much active involvement in making things, observing things and entering competitions, all of which the bright children enjoyed. The remaining children mentioned only light entertainment, cartoons and sport. (No significant sex, social class, or IQ differences.)

PETS

It was difficult to sort out from the replies on pets whether there was a genuine active interest or just a general interest in the family pet. As a number of parents pointed out, children of this age can be keen on animals but they are not yet able to sustain continuing responsibility for them. However, thirty-three children seemed to express a keen interest on this item; sixty-seven had no interest at all.

INVENTING GAMES

The item about inventing games was included because previous work had suggested that very able children liked to play with rules, varying them for their own purposes, creating something different from traditional forms of games. Only one girl made this her main interest and she had an IQ of 150+; sixteen children made it a keen interest. There was an indication that the more intelligent children engaged in this activity, but as over half the children did not choose it at all, the numbers were not statistically significant on sex or IQ.

HELPING PARENTS AT HOME

When it came to assessing how much interest the children showed in helping in the home, parents' statements were considered to be more accurate than the children's. Only one child gave it as a main interest, a girl who came from a strictly religious background where all activities were focused on family participation. Ten per cent of the children were said to show a keen interest in helping and 75 per cent helped occasionally.

TOYS

The children were asked to name their favourite toys. This was done to see if the more intelligent children would show maturity by rejecting the idea of toys more often than the rest, but this was not found to be so. A quarter did say they were no longer interested in toys but they were equally distributed between the sexes and throughout the IQ range.

SOCIAL CLASS DIFFERENCES

The analysis of social class presented only little additional information to what had already been said. The major difference was on the item about helping at home. It was clear that the girls in the manual occupation group had to use more of their leisure time on family chores than others. Non-manual group boys were more interested in collecting than non-manual girls; non-manual group girls were more interested in writing than non-manual boys. Non-manual girls showed more interest in reading than manual group girls, they also owned a significantly greater number of books. Boys and girls together in the non-manual groups more often owned forty or more books than the others. Only three children, all from social classes IV and V possessed no books of their own. Ninety-five per cent of the children owned more than five books and a third of them over forty. This reflected the difference in opportunity offered by the home environments of this special group of children, the Schools Council's enquiry in 1968 on *Young School Leavers* showed that just over a third of the *parents* of 15-year-old school leavers owned less than six books. The Plowden enquiry on a group of 10-year-olds found that 18 per cent had no books other than children's books in the home.

SOCIAL—AESTHETIC—ACTIVE—PRACTICAL

The responses on interest were further summarised into main areas: (*a*) social, including sports, playing outside, clubs, etc. (*b*) aesthetic, including art and music, etc. (*c*) academic, including reading, writing, science, history, etc. (*d*) practical, including all model-making, inventing, needlework and other crafts, and (*e*) collecting, which did not seem to fit into the other four areas, was kept separate [Table A7.1].

The results showed the tendency for the 130+ IQ boys and girls to have more interests in the academic area than the rest; they also had more practical hobbies and collected things with keener interest. The partiality of the under 130 IQ boys for interests involving social activities was also shown. There was the same trend for girls, but it was not significant.

The higher the intelligence of the children the wider was their range of interests; there was a significantly larger number with interests in four and five of the areas in the 130+ IQ group.

No clear pattern emerged as to the source of the main interests of the children. One child saw a television programme and was stimulated to make things, another read a book and found a passionate interest in travel developed, another was given a microscope and learned rapidly about science, another was jealous of a sibling writing a poem and decided to try, for another a friendly adult started a bird-watching club in the district and it became an absorbing pastime.

The variation in sources of interests and the chance nature of the starting points indicate that it is important for all children to be exposed to stimuli of many kinds presented in many ways. For underprivileged children, schools will have to take the chief responsibility for this.

The children in the 130+ IQ range were the most enthusiastic and verbal about their interests. They were able to convey something of their delight and the hard work that went into activities of their own choice.

Examples

● Boy: IQ 146

Interviewer's comments: 'Adrian is a boy who is immediately likeable. He is tall, dark haired and good looking with bright piercing eyes. He started off with zest from the first sentence, 'I'm interested in history!' He brought old history books, two written projects, a collection of old coins and several drawings of battles which showed a lively appreciation of the movement of crowds. He showed these things with pride and care. He tackled everything with energy and enjoyment giving the impression of a strong personality, yet was never arrogant or boastful. He had a wide general knowledge. He was, to put it in his own words, 'furious' that in having to do errands for the teacher as head boy he missed a weekly TV lesson which was the only work he had in history at school.

He was thought of very highly at school and was much appreciated by his parents for his vitality, optimism and cleverness.

ADRIAN: Well, I've always been interested in history ever since I was young. Every time I go to a jumble sale I always look up old history books and buy them, so I've got piles of history books . . . and, well, I just write . . . I do projects and poems in history and I've done thousands of them. I did one on war and I did one about kings, and I remember the first project I ever did was about the Crusades you see, because I love history, it's my favourite hobby. When our teacher said that you could choose what your thing was, I naturally chose history and I just got on and away with it. I brought all my ancient books to school, dusted the dust off them and just looked things up, and, well, put them in my own words and did poems about them and did drawings. They're a bit complicated but I like complicated drawings—and don't like them when they've got just one thing in them. I like thousands of things in them.

INTERVIEWER: Which books have you got?

ADRIAN: Well, I've got one . . . I think it was 1928. It's got about a thousand pages and it's ever so heavy, and that's one of my favourites. I like old history books specially because they give a more vivid account of the time, and I've got one that was in the nineteenth century. I can't remember what it was called. Another one, that was 1900. I prefer ones that don't have pictures in them . . . I prefer them with maps of the battle and lots of small print so I have to use a magnifying glass.

INTERVIEWER: What is your favourite period in history?

ADRIAN: Oh, the fifteenth century definitely. I don't know why really, I've always liked it best because of the kings for one thing and the army they had, well mainly, specially fifteenth century, but most of the Middle Ages from about 1200 to 1500. I like that period very much.

INTERVIEWER: Do you get any help with this interest?

ADRIAN: Well, when mummy and daddy go out and they do see a history book, they'll buy it for me, and sometimes mummy asks me a few questions about it, every now and then, you know, and she helps— she looks up books with me sometimes.

INTERVIEWER: Have you any other hobbies?

ADRIAN: Well, I like football. I support the home team and I collect stamps and I like reading a lot. I like reading history books best, but story books I like and sometimes I like adventure books, exploring, true life ones; oh, and I like playing with soldiers as well—Middle Ages soldiers—that's another thing. I've got Meccano—I like Meccano a lot because it's a creative thing and I like making things with it.

INTERVIEWER: What about drawing and painting?

ADRIAN: Yes, I like drawing. I like painting but I find painting more difficult than drawing because I remember when I was painting this picture and it was getting on fine, when it came to painting flesh in I got a bright red and it ruined it, and so I've tried to avoid painting as much as I can.

INTERVIEWER: Do you collect anything?

ADRIAN: Oh, cards every now and then, I've got a few cards and, let me think, what else? Oh, fossils—fossils and stones, and things like that. I've got my own museum of them in my bedroom on my dressing-table. It gets awfully dusty, and I collect coins. I've got two Edward VIII ones but, yes, they're South African, so I don't think—it's a bit, it's a bit cheaty but nobody else has got them so it's quite good.

INTERVIEWER: Do you invent games?

ADRIAN: Yes, I did invent one—it went on fine and then I found that somebody else had it at school. I mean, it was asking to be invented. It's a football game. I was disappointed when I found that it had been invented by Waddingtons, and it was funny because my mother was going to send it in to Waddingtons. Good job she didn't.

INTERVIEWER: Do you like music?

ADRIAN: Well, I can't play an instrument actually, I'm not very good at music but I like listening to music. I prefer classical music to pop music because I think pop music's a bit of rubbish nowadays. It used to be quite good.

INTERVIEWER: Are you interested in sports?

ADRIAN: Oh well, I love football, you know, it's my favourite, but I'm playing hockey, but now I'm delighted, you see I got picked for the hockey tournament.

INTERVIEWER: Do you play outside with other children?

ADRIAN: Well, I'm an only child so I don't. I usually play at home. But every now and again I have my best friend over to tea, which is about once every two weeks, and we go over to the field—the other side of our house—and it's a super place to play in with hills and things.

INTERVIEWER: Are there any hobbies you would like to have had?

ADRIAN: Well, not really, I mean I'm quite happy with what I've got, but I wouldn't have minded, well, being an author, a proper one who published some books. When I grow up I can be that.

INTERVIEWER: What are your parents interested in?

ADRIAN: Oh, touring old houses. Oh, perhaps that's how I got interested in history because I'm always touring old houses!

Adrian wrote the following essay at school for the second follow-up study. He used his interest to comply with the set task of imagining himself to be twenty-five years of age. He obviously accepted history as a permanent part of his life. He dealt cleverly with the concept of change on a number of items which few of the children were able to do.

I am just getting up, the time is 9.35. I switch on the automatic tea maker and I have a nice 'cuppa'. After that I get dressed. I read the newspaper, then I get in my hovercraft and go to work. I am a teacher. I work at one of the few 'old fashioned' schools where the teacher teaches. Today's lesson is History. We are writing about the world, fifteen years ago. I tell the class that the countries prime minister was Mr Wilson, how he was displaced by Mr Heath in 1970 and how in 1973 the rival parties joined together to make a united government. Britain's entry into the common market was an interesting subject. So was the prison system. Now the prisoners work their way out. What I mean, a prisoner is sentenced to a certain amount of work. In 1969 a prisoner was sent to prison for an amount of time. Football was the same then as it is now. In 1969 a team was awarded two points for a win, one for a draw and nil for a lose. Now you get a point for every goal.

My hobbies are meteorite collecting, (these fall very frequently in England), and coin collecting. Our home has the new inflatable beds and the 'home computer'. Also we have the 'A.S.S.T. Burglar Alarm MK11. This alarm rings a bell and drops a net on the criminal.'

● Boy: IQ 140
Interviewer's comments: 'Jonathan is tall and plump with slow and deliberate movement. He is full of good humour and can give and take a lot of teasing. At times he looks very mature and shows considerable mastery of thought and expression for his age. His language is fast and fluent ranging from slang to literary metaphor with ease. Everything goes well for him at school as he is good all round and an undoubted leader.'

His parents realised he was exceptionally bright and he had every encouragement in his pursuits.

Jonathan spent 2 years inventing a town:

'We invented buildings, my three friends and I, we call the town Brumley . . . Brumley Amusements Centre . . we've got our own government, our own transport service, our own money, pounds, shillings and pence. I don't think we'll use the shillings any more though. We have made coins out of cardboard. It all started 4 years ago when we started up a stamp business. It's grown up from that. We made the money and then we invented numerous banks which had to be taken over by other banks when they got a bit useless, something like notes going up to a thousand million dollars and that type of thing. It wasn't much good so we decided to start another one. We didn't have a mint so we returned to another note that we'd already made, the notes which I'd kept in stock so that if you lost a note or threw it away by accident you had another to replace it. We soon got bored with having the highest note at £500. Then we've got all sorts of things like trains, monorails, underground, buses, aircraft. We don't make all of it, we just pretend.

INTERVIEWER: Who helped you?
JONATHAN: We did it on our own, just the four of us.
INTERVIEWER: Whose idea was it?
JONATHAN: Mine . . . to start up a company and then Tom started up a stamp company after me and we branched out from there making companies and doing the paper-work, the leaflets, the pamphlets. The main one was a bus company, it had all sorts of things, like all about

season tickets and route maps, folders, and for the underground we made maps and for the aircraft we made time tables. Then we came to think that we'd just remembered something . . . we'd made a timetable for the bus to come every 45 minutes and we'd got 500 buses and there's only one bus on each route, so we decided to amend the timetables slightly and now we've got buses which come every five minutes.

INTERVIEWER: Do you make up people?

JONATHAN: Not really. We like being ourselves most of all. I don't really pretend to be other people, just myself doing some other job.

Jonathan also used his main interest to write his essay at school. He had not the time sense of the previous boy: he used the theme in the service of his current thoughts with little attempt to deal with the future. However, he saw himself in a leading role with responsibility.

It is 7.30 and the morning paper has arrived. I go out and collect it from the front door. I read it, get washed dressed and have my breakfast. Time to go to work I walk across the road into the forecourt of the Wood Garage of Brumely Transport Group. Up the stairs and into my office. B.T.G. the largest transport group in the Brumley Area. They own both British Leyland and Daimler and to finish it off, Atlantean. Work on my desk. Extension of Trolleybus lines to Croft Avenue, scrapping of the 32 to Ington War Memorial and the 182 to Nottingham Lane. Start of the 109 to Upham. Oh dear, more and more. Then I am called out. '1 Driver short on 23,' says Jock head inspector. At the same time my secretary calls and says 'Bill is here.' Bill is head of Maintenance and supplies. 'Do we need more Bus Stop stickers. We're running out.' Bill is always concerned with supplies. Anyway, the 23 to Five Ways is one driver short so I think I'll have a run or two until lunch break. Pete, Assistant Head, can take over while I'm out. The 23 BCB (Brumley Corporation Buses) Wood Garage, Rye Jersey Drive, Upton Corner Main Gate Old Rd Terminus Main Gate Army Offices Five Ways The Junction The Square and back the same way excluding the Extension to Old Road Terminus. On I go until Five Ways. Might as well stop for a drink. Finished the drink and back to the Bus. Round the route three more times and then Lunch break. After lunch, back to desk work. Should we have a pipeline supply of fuel from McNab fuel Ltd. Should we or not. I don't know? Its all up to fuelling and tanks department. More Work. It piles up. However, its now 5.30 and time for home. Across the fore court. Past the Brumley Air Bay. Past the Brumley Mono rail sheds. Past the Brumley Underground Station. Over the carpark and home. Time for dinner and relaxing in front of the TV. Whats on 'This is BBTVC2 and now Spy Pie'. The music and then another day is nearly over!

● Boy: IQ 136

Interviewer's comments: 'Angus is small for his age but he is neat and compact. Everything he does has an air of competence about it, he is very much in charge of himself. He is doing very well at school and his parents are surprised by his sustained interest and enthusiasm for science.'

INTERVIEWER: How did your interest in astronomy start?

ANGUS: Well, it's a long time ago really. When I was in the infants, well I'm in the last year of my top school now, going into the secondary school after that. Well, in the infants this boy brought something to school, a little model he'd made about a spaceship, and I decided to find out a bit about it. Well, now I'm doing quite a bit on it. I just get books on astronomy from the library and read them. Now I'm really doing about the stars. I've got a telescope to look at them with.

INTERVIEWER: What kind of telescope is it?

ANGUS: Well, it's about 2½ foot long or 3 foot, and it's got—it isn't a reflecting telescope, it's just an ordinary one, and it's got the ten to sixty power but it's only got a small stand. It'd be about so high . . . which isn't very good, 'cos I've got to take a stool out every time I want to look up.

INTERVIEWER: What's your favourite planet?

ANGUS: Saturn. Well, it's got these dust rings round it, it looks quite nice when you look at it through a telescope. You can see all the colours and everything.

INTERVIEWER: Who shares this interest with you?

ANGUS: Well, usually I do all the projects on my own. There's not many people in our class that like it. Most people like about dinosaurs and things like that.

INTERVIEWER: Have you any other interests?

ANGUS: Yes. Biology and zoology. And I like making things that I think might happen in the future, like cars in the future and things like that, or rocket ships. Oh, another interest is micro-science, you know. Looking through the microscope. I've got a good one.

INTERVIEWER: What kind of person are you?

ANGUS: (*he laughs*): I'm all right. It depends on what your friends think!

● Girl: IQ 135

Interviewer's comments: 'Susan is a tall, attractive girl, very graceful in movement and hypersensitive to the feelings of others. She has friends, but feels herself sometimes estranged from them because of her intense interest in reading and writing stories and poems. She does well, but it not exceptional at school, though her literary bent is acknowledged. Her family considers her mature in outlook for her age and gives her every support in her interests.'

INTERVIEWER: What is your main interest?

SUSAN: It's too hard to choose really. Suppose writing is and music.

INTERVIEWER: When did your interest in writing start?

SUSAN: As soon as I was able to hold a pen (*laughs*). No, it was when my brother wrote a poem and I think I was a bit jealous, so I started writing poetry . . . then I wrote a little story and then I wrote another which took 2 years because I kept on having spasms of writing a bit, and I wrote as much as I could in the time, and then I did other things. And then I went on with it until I was about 10. I thought it would be a good size for a children's story so I thought if I just kept it in this book it would be a good size for them.

INTERVIEWER: Do you get any help with this interest?

SUSAN: I do it mostly myself but mother writes poetry and father writes books, but they're grown-up books.

INTERVIEWER: How much do you use books?

SUSAN: Well, I read a terrific lot. They complain at school that every book the teacher reads for us, I've read—it's actually true. I have read all the books they pick out to read to the class. We play a dictionary game at school: the teacher gives us a word from the dictionary and asks us to explain what it means, and I have read so many books I know most of the words and they complain I've read the dictionary!

Susan took seriously her intentions to become a writer. This emerged again in her essay written at school for the 11-year-old survey. She did not deal with material changes in the world 15 years hence, but gave herself a job, a husband and children like the majority of girls in the group. However, she was unusual in that she acknowledged the reciprocal nature of future relationships which few children of her age can.

The alarm-clock goes off with a horrible noise at about 7 o'clock and then it's 2 hours to get up and about, have breakfast, pack the children off to their school down the road, and then catch the bus for my school, where I teach. I sit down with 10 minutes to become calm and composed in. Then in come the children.

'Lo, miss!' 'Nice day, miss.' 'What are we having today, miss?' It's English, so out come the books and twenty childish brains bury themselves in the problem of the past tense.

What has Fate done to allow us to be cooped up in one room, twenty children and one grown-up all longing for escape to the brighter world outside.

('Please miss, shall I shut the window, 'cause its raining?' 'Yes it is raining, you better shut it!' Who said outside was a brighter world? Now we can't even go out at break.) Some people might laugh at that.

Eight hours in school and then, all out. Now it's back home to welcome John and Mary and make my husband a cup of tea. Wash the dishes, the floors (who invented dust?) and then make the supper, eat the supper, wash up the supper, and then evening. Blessed evening!

Evening, when you can rest, talk to Peter, and even think. When you're rested it's out with the pad and pencil, making those little marks on the fresh white sheet of paper. Little marks that mean so much to me. And then (where does the evening go?) its time for bed.

Time to relax the mind from all. Till tomorrow, tomorrow's school, work, and then another evening with talking and thinking and writing, yes, even writing.

● Girl: 144 IQ

Interviewer's comments: 'June is a well-developed athletic looking girl. She has unbounded energy, she can't get things done fast enough, even her words compete for speed of utterance. She brought more evidence of interests than any other child, it took five members of the family to help her carry her cups and medals for swimming, her novels and poems, paintings, drawings, craftwork and collections of various kinds. She does well at school, but it is in swimming at the moment that she excels. Her parents give up a great deal of time to helping her pursue her talent.'

Her essay included reference to swimming, but at that moment she saw herself as a journalist at 25.

> At 18 I decided to try for Bristol University. The main subject I wanted to study was English Literature—I am interested in languages too. Now I am 25 I am staying at home at the moment on holiday. I still keep swimming hard. I swum for Bristol in the student games and that made me keener than ever . . .

INTERVIEWER: What is your main interest?

JUNE: I told you I was interested very much in swimming. Well, these are some of the things I've got for it (*she shows some certificates obtained in County Championships*).

INTERVIEWER: How often do you train?

JUNE: Well I train on Monday, Tuesday, Wednesday and Friday. And I went on a weekend course. On Monday it's from nine to ten at night, but you know, I have a sort of nap before I go, but some people—they don't really understand that I really enjoy it very much and it's important to go swimming, and they say, 'Oh dear, that's why you get ill', but I don't get ill very often.

INTERVIEWER: Does school encourage your interest in swimming?

JUNE: Well, we don't do any swimming because they've stopped it. I don't think the head master or anybody minds me doing it as long as I don't fall asleep half-way in the lessons. I don't really think that our head master is very interested. I mean, we didn't go in for any of the galas . . . I was disappointed in that because we've got some quite good swimmers at our school.

DISCUSSION

(*a*) Barker-Lunn (1970) pointed out that the greatest single factor affecting interests at the top primary age was the sex of the child, and this would hold also for this gifted group. The highly intelligent were distinguished for the extensive range, type and complexity of their interests, and also for their ability to discuss with confidence what they do.

(*b*) Whatever the source of an interest, the more intelligent a child is the more likely he is to carry it out with enthusiasm and concentration. The bright children have to do a good deal of hoarding to retain the results of all their pursuits, and parental tolerance must sometimes be strained in the accommodation of the paraphernalia. Perhaps the children of middle-class parents have the advantage because their interests tend to include the academic which are encouraged for their educational value. It will be remembered that these children more often had a link between school subjects liked and those pursued for interest at home.

(c) Primary school teachers know that conversation about a child's hobbies or interests is often a starting point for the acquisition of further knowledge. The variety of interests the level of complexity of thought about them and the ability to express pleasure in their pursuit gives clues to the width of apprehension a child has of his culture. No standardised tests reveal the quality of enjoyment in the mastery of skills and knowledge and their functional use in the child's life.

Personality

THE CHILDREN'S VIEW OF THEMSELVES

'What kind of person are you?' is a difficult and unusual question to ask directly. An adult might immediately want to know in what sense the word 'kind' was being used, to get his bearings in what was expected of him before he answered. It was considered that a child of 10 to 11 years of age would not be so sophisticated in thought as to ask what was in the mind of the questioner, but would answer according to what the question meant in his own terms. It was expected that perhaps some of the children would have begun the kind of self-reflectiveness that starts in adolescence, i.e. the point at which a person becomes consciously self-aware to a sufficient degree to be able to take himself as an object of thought.

The children's reactions to this question were some of the most illuminating in the interview. There was no doubt that the question touched on something in the children quite different from any other question asked. The immediate response in nearly all cases was an involuntary gasp, sometimes followed by laughter, embarrassment or stillness which indicated withdrawal from the situation. One bright boy expressed his ruffled feelings quite clearly by saying rather sharply, 'That's a personal question!' and indeed it was, and for this reason no child was asked it a second time or pressed to give an answer. A third of the children did not answer, half saying 'I don't know', the rest remaining silent. There were no sex, social class or IQ differences associated with willingness to answer. The more intelligent children were not content with a straightforward 'don't know'; they were inclined to give some explanation:

'I haven't thought about it yet.'

'I can't really mirror my own thoughts.'

'I don't really know, I think you ought, sort of, on that aspect, to ask somebody else about that.'

'I can't boast about myself, so I don't know what to say.'

Those who did answer gave varied replies, the more intelligent, more verbal children giving longer descriptions than others, and therefore mentioning more varied aspects of themselves.

The replies have been categorised to show the main themes that emerged:

1. *Self-assertiveness.* In this group were twenty-six children who seemed to want to convey their independence either by saying so directly, or by indicating their strength of reaction towards others in certain situations, e.g. 'I can be bossy', 'I get angry if I'm teased', 'I'm not slow to retaliate if someone calls me names'. These children seem openly prepared to reveal their aggressive side.

To summarize:

		Social class	
IQ over 130	20	Non-manual	17
		Manual	3
IQ 129 and less	6	Non-manual	1
		Manual	5

Seventeen children in the group had IQs over 140 (three in manual social class). It therefore seemed that it was the highly intelligent, non-manual children who could respond in this way spontaneously.

2. *Intellectual qualities.* Children referred to themselves as 'intelligent', 'clever', 'creative', 'inventive', 'imaginative' as follows:

		Social class	
IQ over 130	19	Non-manual	14
		Manual	5
IQ 129 and less	15	Non-manual	11
		Manual	4

Eleven children had IQs over 140 (one manual social class). More than twice as many non-manual children referred to intellectual aspects of themselves.

3. *Physical activity.* Eighteen children described themselves as active children, wanting to be 'on the go' rather than sitting still as follows:

		Social class	
IQ over 130	8	Non-manual	7
		Manual	1
IQ 129 and less	10	Non-manual	5
		Manual	5

Two children with IQs over 140 (both non-manual social class). The IQ groups were similar but there was still an advantage for the non-manual children on this item.

4. *Neutral responses.* This category was made for those children who replied 'I'm ordinary', 'I'm average'. (It also had to include the response of a boy of IQ 150 who answered 'Homo sapiens'. He accepted the question as one of categorisation and the speed of his answer and the level of abstraction used signalled to the interviewer a probable exceptional intelligence.)

To summarize:

		Social class	
IQ over 130	11	Non-manual	4
		Manual	7
IQ 129 and less	13	Non-manual	6
		Manual	7

(Two children had IQs over 140 both non-manual social class.)

5. *Social qualities.* Thirty-six children related themselves to other people, claiming to be 'friendly', 'generous', 'helpful' and generally co-operative in some way:

		Social class	
IQ over 130	16	Non-manual	10
		Manual	6
IQ 129 and less	20	Non-manual	6
		Manual	14

(Six children had IQs over 140, 3 in the manual social class.)

6. *Emotional qualities of shyness and quietness.* Seventeen children mentioned only their shyness or quietness, thirteen girls and only four boys. This was the only group that showed an obvious sex difference:

		Social class	
IQ over 130	4	Non-manual	1
		Manual	3
IQ 129 or less	13	Non-manual	7
		Manual	6

(One girl with an IQ over 140, manual social class.)

The numbers are small, but they showed that the trend was for the lower IQ group to mention subdued characteristics.

7. *Unhappy responses.* Four children only came into this category, their IQs were 143, 129, 117, 114 (two manual social class) (see ch. 5).

The results on the question must be looked at in the context in which it was given. They showed the degree of willingness of these children to answer an unexpected and personal question asked directly by someone unknown to them. The willingness did not depend on IQ level or social class, but these affected the quality of the answer.

THE CHILDREN'S IDEAS ON 'LIFE'

Another question of similar kind was asked at the end of the interview, 'You're eleven years old now, what do you think about life?' It was inserted to see what the most intelligent children could do with it on the spur of the moment; whether they could generalize in any meaningful way. The answers were categorised as follows:

1. *Spontaneous enthusiasm,* e.g. 'It's marvellous', 'I love it', 'It's fun'. Such responses were given immediately and with liveliness (N. 35).

2. *Positive-active,* e.g. responses that indicated the subject felt it was up to him or her to make the most of it, a suggested active intervention in affairs (N. 50). 'There's lots of chances but you have to take the chances when you get them!'

3. *Accepting-positive,* e.g. 'It's all right', followed by a positive remark like, 'it's usually good' (N.32).

4. *Accepting-neutral,* e.g. 'It's all right' (N.50).

5. *Accepting-negative,* e.g. 'It's all right', followed by a negative remark, 'terrible things can happen' (N.26).

6. *Negative-an expressed rejection,* e.g. 'I think it's just a waste of time' (N.6).

7. No answer and 'don't know' (N.39).

It was not only what the children said that was interesting, but also the style in which they chose to express it, and it was the 'enthusiasts' and 'positives' that revealed some probable differences of sex, IQ and social class:

Enthusiasts		*Social class*	
IQ over 130	11	Non-manual	11
		Manual	0
IQ 129 and less	24	Non-manual	12
		Manual	12
Boys 13 Girls 22			

(Two children with IQs over 140, non-manual social class.)

Positives		*Social class*	
IQ over 130	35	Non-manual	20
		Manual	15
IQ 129 and less	15	Non-manual	8
		Manual	7
Boys 32 Girls 18			

(Seventeen children with IQs over 140, 10 non-manual social class.)

This question showed the 140 IQ children to advantage as 67 per cent of those who answered were in one of the first three categories mentioned as compared with 46 per cent of the rest of the children.

IDEAS ON 'SELF' AND 'LIFE' COMBINED

The children whose replies were placed in the first three categories on 'self' and 'life' were considered together. There were 29 boys and 22 girls, 35 in the non-manual, 16 in the manual social class groups. Two-thirds were in the over 130 IQ group to one-third in the rest.

The results perhaps only revealed better verbal ability on the part of the more intelligent children, but in comparison with the results of the teachers' and parents' descriptions of the children they provided further evidence of the confidence and positiveness with which the most able children were able to present themselves.

DO YOU EVER THINK ABOUT SERIOUS (GROWN-UP) THINGS?

This question was asked because Burt (1962a) suggested that highly intelligent children of this age think about some of the life themes that usually emerge in adolescence, and that they can be troubled by philosophical ideas which perhaps they do not express to others.

The question was asked openly to begin with, but if no answers were forthcoming, the items raised by children in the pilot study were suggested, i.e. space, being grown-up, religion and politics. The majority of children who mentioned thinking about being grown-up looked forward to it, but some did not for they were already seeing that it involved greater responsibility; politics were largely ignored, only four children had any comment to make; ten children were troubled by religious doubts, beginning to be aware of the problems involved in reconciling religious belief and scientific proof; ten were troubled by death, asking the question 'What happens next?' In the foregoing there were no signs that degree of intelligence in this group of children was having any influence, but in the answers on 'space' it did, for, of eighteen children who referred to the idea of infinity in connection with space, sixteen had IQs over 130 and nine of these were over 140. The children were genuinely disturbed by the idea of 'infinity'; 'They say it *must* go on and on but it *can't*!' was the type of answer given and some children admitted that they were frightened to think of it. The children were asked if they had discussed the problem with someone, but they all said they had not.

The primary school stage of development is one that is often referred to as one of 'concrete operations', to use Piaget's term; for the most part children of this stage are more concerned with the here and now and need provision educationally for work which deals with empirical experience, but for those who are beginning to assimilate more abstract ideas there is a need for adult help in learning the ways in which to handle these intellectually.

FRIENDS

The gifted children on the whole were very sociable with other children: only two said that they had no friends. One-third liked a friend who shared their interests and activities; one-third liked those who had acceptable personal qualities such as kindness, generosity and lack of boastfulness; the remaining third mentioned liking a degree of permanence and reciprocity in the relationship. It was thought that the most difficult concept in friendship was 'reciprocity', and that perhaps only the highly intelligent children of this age would be able to express ideas about this, but it was not so.

The children themselves felt most valued by others for co-operativeness, humour and being able to make a contribution to a relationship because they were good at something. They thought they were most disliked for bossiness, failure to conform and because of jealousy when they could excel.

These findings represent a picture of the age group in general and no IQ, sex or social class differences were apparent.

However, in leadership the most intelligent children came into their own. Fifty per cent of those with IQs over 130 stated that they were the leaders in their friendship activities; only 25 per cent of the under 130 IQs claimed that privilege. The results gave further evidence of the greater confidence and positiveness of the over 130 IQ group.

The parents confirmed the general friendship pattern; they described regular exchange of visits for 80 per cent of the children, most of them preferring to play with friends rather than on their own or with siblings. It was thought that more of the most intelligent children would prefer being alone or having one special friend with whom to share an interest rather than having a wide circle of friends, but there was no evidence to support the idea.

SUMMARY

(a) There were no sex, IQ or social class differences influencing whether children were willing to answer a direct question about their self-image. However, more children with an IQ above 130 saw themselves as 'self-assertive', and more whose IQ was below 130 saw themselves as 'shy and quiet'. Social class differences were present, the middle class children being more inclined to acknowledge self-assertiveness, intellectual qualities and physical activity in themselves.

(b) Of the children who had the most positive attitudes to life, the over 130 IQ children were more likely to express them in terms of making life yield what they want, while the under 130 IQ children tended to express a spontaneous and enthusiastic acceptance of what happens.

(c) There was one item in particular that suggested that the highly intelligent children had philosophic difficulty. They were troubled by the concept of infinity which was frightening because they could not control it intellectually.

(d) The 'gifted' children revealed no unusual social peer group patterns. They were more typical than atypical of their age group. However, the most intelligent among them emerged clearly as self-appointed leaders.

8. Discussion of previous literature

Introduction

'Gifted', 'genius', 'talent', 'creative', 'divergent thinker', 'inventive', 'exceptional intelligence'; these are some of the words in current usage by which we try to express our judgments and insights about human qualities and behaviour patterns that are considered outstanding. As far as the study of children is concerned, the words seem to appear in current educational thought for two reasons. Firstly, it is considered by some writers important to search for excellence and the promise of excellence in children so that they can be offered education which will lead to their personal satisfaction through the full and proper use of their talents, on the assumption that lack of opportunities for knowledge and development of special skills will lead to frustration and perhaps misdirected energies. Secondly, some writers emphasise the economic value of the 'gifted' to a society and point to the loss and wastage to the community if individuals are not chosen and trained to use their exceptional abilities. These reasons are separate but not distinct; the needs of individuals and society are interdependent, but focusing on either the individual or society could lead to very different procedures being adopted for the selection and the methods of education employed to fulfil the aim.

In the Plowden Report it is said that 'at the outset giftedness meets with an irrational obstacle', the latter being an 'egalitarian' suspicion of the whole concept of 'giftedness'. But the irrationality perhaps has a longer history than that, one which goes back to the notion that genius was a demon or god and a 'gift' bestowed by supernatural powers. These meanings linger on in the fear that some parents have of their child being called 'gifted' and that some teachers have of being faced with the task of teaching 'gifted' children. It is not surprising that genius and madness came to be equated for neither was understood in the times when these meanings evolved; even if neither is as yet fully explicable we have at least enough knowledge to be able to make some clearer distinctions.

106

Early studies

The most intensive and extensive attempt to study the 'gifted' is, of course, that of Professor Lewis Terman of Stanford University, USA. Anyone who wants to come to terms with the concept must take into account his lifetime's study of a group of 1,500 (approx.) subjects from their childhood to mid-life. There are to date five volumes (1925; 1926; 1930; 1947; 1959) and still more to come from Terman's successors. The range of measurements and the thoroughness with which the whole study has been carried out ensures his work the title of 'a classic'. However, it must not be forgotten that, as Burt reminds us by quoting Sir Robert Morant, 'Britain was the first nation to recognise the importance of making special provision for the education of her ablest children' (Burt 1970). In an introductory essay he traces the history of the search for the ablest from every social class in order to educate them to fulfil the ever-growing demand for 'clerks, lawyers, justices, court bureaucrats and local officers—to assist in the elaborate administrative system created by Anglo-Norman Kings'. He refers to the establishment of endowed grammar schools and university colleges from the thirteenth century and records the beginning of the British scholarship system which has continued and developed through the different eras to the present time.

Sir Francis Galton's book, *Hereditary Genius* (1892), was a landmark that presaged the measurement of 'mental capacities' and the identification of the most able from all classes of society. He took up the idea that genius is inherited and traced the lineage of 300 families to demonstrate his point. Further research on individual families and uniovular twins has been carried out since Galton's original work, but the controversy about genetic and environmental factors recurs again and again because no one yet has produced a satisfactory solution which would help in understanding something of the complexities of the relationship that obviously exists between them.

Sir Cyril Burt has consistently drawn attention to the evidence for heredity exerting the major influence in a child's development, but he acknowledges that environmental circumstances can facilitate or hinder development. His own words are: 'As regards individuals, the only generalisations that can be safely drawn are (i) that their genetic constitution endows them with a certain potentiality which may or may not be realised as they develop, and (ii) that it sets an upper limit to what they can, in favourable circumstances, be expected to achieve' (Burt 1962a). As the first educational psychologist in the country, appointed by the London County Council in 1913, Sir Cyril Burt searched for children who were suitably endowed to receive scholarships for secondary education. This was at the time of the development of mental testing, when psychologists like Burt, Binet and Spearman were trying to measure general ability or intelligence free from the interference of cultural-educational factors. These new tests were taken up and used to find the abler type of pupils regardless of the economic and social conditions of their homes.

TERMAN'S LONG-TERM STUDY

Terman also turned to 'intelligence' tests to find his able children: his first study was for his doctoral thesis, an experimental study on the intellectual processes of the seven brightest and the seven dullest boys in a large city school. He was inspired to do this because of prevailing attitudes of 'early ripe, early rot', and he wanted to investigate the precocious in more detail. This first study convinced him that the new mental tests were important and valuable for research, so he began helping in the Stanford revision of the Binet Scale. The contrast in the intellectual performance between the brightest and the dullest children intensified his interests in the former and determined him to start a special research programme. This he began in 1921. From his earlier researches, from teachers' estimates and group tests, he gathered nearly 1,500 children from kindergarten to high school levels whose average Binet IQ was approximately 150, and 80 quotients were 170 and over. He had two main aims, firstly to find what traits characterised children of high IQ, and secondly to follow them for as many years as possible to see what kind of adults they might become.

The subjects were given medical examinations, achievement tests, character and interest tests and information about their behaviour and personalities was obtained from parents and teachers. The results showed that children of IQ 140 or higher were in general superior to other children; appreciably superior in physique, health and social adjustment, markedly superior in moral attitudes and vastly superior in their mastery of school subjects (about two grades beyond their normal age grade).

The children were generally so able that they achieved high standards in all subjects and so Terman claimed to have refuted the traditional belief that gifted children are one-sided.

Follow-up studies on this group (98 per cent followed up) in 1927, 1939 and 1951 showed them to be still superior in many ways to the population at large, the incidence of mortality, ill-health, insanity, alcoholism being lower at each age of examination. They were socially well adjusted and the delinquency rate was 'fractional' compared with the population. On a specially constructed Concept Mastery Test they have been shown to be as far above the average as adults as they were as children. 90 per cent entered college; 70 per cent graduated; 30 per cent honours and two-thirds did post-graduate studies.

Eight hundred case histories of men at mid-life showed that they had published 67 books (41 science, arts and humanities, 21 fiction), 1400 scientific and technical articles, 200 short stories, novelettes and plays.

These numbers did not include TV, radio, journals and newspaper articles.

Seventy-eight men had obtained Ph.D.s or the equivalent, 48 medical, 85 law, 74 teaching, 51 research in physical science and engineering. All these numbers are twenty to thirty times greater than would be found if 800 were picked at random from the population at large.

Terman (1954) concludes that:

> Tests of general intelligence given at 6, 8 or 10 years tell us a great deal about the ability to achieve now and 30 years hence. Such tests do not predict what direction the achievement will take . . . granting that both interest patterns and special aptitudes play important roles in the making of a gifted scientist, mathematician, artist, poet or musical composer, I am convinced that to achieve greatly in almost any field, the special talents have to be backed up by a lot of Spearman's 'g', by which is meant the kind of general intelligence that requires ability to form many sharply defined concepts, to manipulate them and to perceive subtle relationships between them: in other words, the ability to engage in abstract thinking.

Another interesting study related to Terman's work was that carried out by Cox who wrote *The Early Mental Traits of 300 Geniuses* (1926). She examined the biographies of 1,000 eminent men in history and then assessed their probable IQs from the evidence written about them at three stages in their lives. Although this book study has been criticised as somewhat fanciful, Terman said that one aspect of special interest was that the facts clearly contradicted the legend that geniuses were often labelled as backward in childhood. The people he quoted did not excel in school subjects, but outside the classroom the evidence of natural talent in one direction such as writing verse or stories or carrying out scientific investigation was prolific. Out of 100 of the test documented cases, Terman said in more than half the cases there was a 'marked foreshadowing' of the direction their future excellence would take. He quoted Leibnitz who at fourteen was writing philosophy and logic, Pascal, who at eleven secretly constructed a geometry of his own and Macaulay, who at six started a 'Compendium of Universal History'.

Replication of Terman's study

A study which replicated Terman's to some extent was that of G. Parkyn of New Zealand (1948). He reported results similar to Terman's, but he was more concerned with the organisation of the New Zealand education system and its effect on highly intelligent children. He showed that children of parents with professional occupations were over-represented in the highly intelligent category (over IQ 134) and drew attention to the relationships between intelligence, schooling and parents' occupational status. He considered that, with New Zealand's social policy of non-selective education at that time, adequate differentiation was not being made in the curriculum for the benefit of brighter children.

It has to be remembered that New Zealand worked on a stringent grade system and set syllabuses. Other social factors may have accounted for the slight differences from Terman in personality trait ratings that Parkyn found. His children stood out strongly in moral and especially social qualities, perhaps not surprising in a social setting of which Parkyn said 'There is a tendency to undervalue the claims of scholarship.' He also found a greater interest in scientific and technical hobbies amongst his bright children than Terman reported which again could relate to prevailing attitudes in the community.

Many other studies have followed Terman's work but usually with smaller numbers of children. The latest carried out in England is that by Lovell and Shields (1967). They selected a group of fifty children (35 boys, 15 girls) between the ages of 8 years 5 months and 11 years 7 months, whose Verbal IQ score on the Wechsler Intelligence Scale for Children was 140 or more, and gave them tests of divergent thinking, logical thinking, mathematics and essay writing. The study was designed to obtain up-to-date information on the abilities and personality traits of highly intelligent children. The introduction of some Piaget-type tests was an innovation in the field and they yielded some interesting results. Lovell and Shields confirmed some ways in which children reveal high ability and referred to their fund of general knowledge, keen powers of observation, outstanding quantity and quality of vocabulary, stability of temperament, moral strength and social success and health. With reference to Terman's work on ratings of personality, they summarized: 'If we note that one study is a contemporary study of a relatively small number of children in two northern cities of England, and the other is a study of a much larger number of children in California more than forty years ago, the degree of agreement of findings is remarkable.' The degree of agreement on traits of intellectual, volitional, emotional, moral, social and physical was +·90 (Spearman Rank Difference). In the logical Piaget-type tests the children showed themselves well advanced in the concrete operational stage of thought, but only occasionally capable of formal thought where hypothetical deduction is required.

Is intelligence enough?

Another series of British studies has been carried out by Hudson. He took up the point that current intelligence tests pick out the bright children effectively but do not give enough information to distinguish the most able children in the bright group in different subject areas. In his book *Contrary Imaginations* (1966) he maintained that an important distinction to be noted amongst able children was the divergent or convergent thinkers, and these types he related to ability in the sciences or ability in the arts. He was critical of American concepts of 'creativity' which saw 'the diverger as potentially creative, and the converger as potentially uncreative'. He considered the relation between divergence and creativeness to be complex and quoted Roe and Mackinnon's works as compatible with his own evidence that both converger and diverger may be creative in his own field. In his second book, *Frames of Mind* (1968), Hudson moved even further in the direction of acknowledging the complexity and diversity of human performance.

> Although there is excellent evidence that people become set in their ways, I have never seen why someone should not drift slowly over a period of years from convergence to divergence and vice versa. Nor why someone should not be divergent in some moods and convergent in others. . . . I have become more interested in the experiential life of the individuals measured. Slowly I have grown aware, too, of the complexity of the relations between major psychological dimensions: that freedom is one area of a man's life may counterbalance constraint in another. Also that convergence and divergence do not exist in a social or historial vacuum.

His varied attempts to clarify his converger–diverger polarity make interesting, entertaining and instructive reading.

The concept of 'creativity'

The last two studies made reference to and use of the word 'creativity' and this introduces a whole new field of thinking and experiment that has grown rapidly in the last 20 years, although similar ideas can be traced in the literature to individuals who tentatively explored the topic earlier. Indeed, searching for references on 'giftedness' is a limited task until one comes to the era of 'creativity' when suddenly the number of books and articles appearing each year begins to multiply steadily. The information on 'creativity' has to be reckoned with in relation to the 'gifted' because one of the reasons for the sudden spurt on creativity research was dissatisfaction with the acceptance of high intelligence test results as an adequate definition of 'gifted'. Guilford, Torrance and Mackinnon, some of the leading American champions of 'creativity' claimed that it is different and distinct from intelligence as measured on current standardised tests. It is said that in selecting 'gifted' pupils by IQ only many who are exceptional in creative ability and/or divergent thinking are overlooked.

The word 'creativity' which has crept into our vocabulary is not in the dictionary yet. No doubt it soon will be because of its frequency of use in current speech. Psychological terms tend to be adopted by everyday speech; for example, intelligence was used in a specific psychological sense by Spearman but now is a common term in public use. But there were valid reasons for using the word intelligence, whereas the validity of 'creativity' as a comparable global value term is yet to be satisfactorily established.

The American psychologists started off the new vogue in 'creativity' in the 1950s when their society had a sudden preoccupation with the space race. It was considered necessary to examine their education system closely to see where it could be improved to produce more and better research scientists. The stereotype of the American undergraduate selected on intelligence and other standardised tests to receive the traditional academic college courses was criticised and the ideal of a dynamic, inventive, imaginative, original type was suggested in its place. The term 'creative' was no longer to be accepted as synonymous with 'artistic talents' to the exclusion of other types of achievement requiring inventiveness and originality.

The word 'creativity' is in considerable confusion, even a philosopher's article (White 1968) trying to make clearer the meanings takes the matter little further when his own prejudices seem apparent. He uses 'creative' when referring appreciatively to Dostoievsky, Einstein and other important historical creators, but when referring rather disparagingly to certain children's activities he speaks of 'creativity'. He is referring to the publicly acknowledged meaning in the former case, i.e. 'creative' appears in the dictionary as one sign of this acknowledgment and aesthetics deals with the creator in this sense, but he is using a specifically psychological term when using 'creativity', a concept which is under consideration by psychologists and educators, not yet formally defined, and to which he gives a pejorative overtone. The use of the word 'creative' with its long historical tradition is not necessarily synonymous with the comparatively modern term 'creativity'.

The creative act

A 'creative' person in the first sense of the term is one who makes some product (mental or physical, i.e. ideas or objects) in a specified field or fields of endeavour (i.e. art, science, music, literature, etc.). He or she has the intention to produce something which then is judged by himself and others in terms of the acknowledged standards of the particular discipline. The first exposition by Graham Wallas (1926) of the phases in creation have become generally accepted. They are incubation, when ideas are mulled over; preparation, when all relevant information and skills are surveyed; illumination, when the original idea is born; expression, when it is expressed in a given form; and lastly, verification, when it is judged to be true or satisfying in the meanings of these words that are acceptable to experts in given disciplines. The description takes into account the processes involved and judgment of the object produced.

Patrick (1935, 1937), in examining poets and artists at work in an experimental situation, confirmed the different aspects of the process of creation, but questioned that they came in always the same order. Her subjects showed much variation in their patterns of work.

Mackinnon also stressed processes and product in creative persons and said that it seemed more profitable to examine adults who had achieved success in their field of endeavour than to look for creative potential in children and adolescents. His best known work was a study of architects (1961). Roe (1951, 1953) made studies in detail of physicists, biologists and psychologists who made 'creative contributions to their sciences'. Barron and Welsh (1952) produced evidence on artists versus non-artists and created a special art scale to help in differentiating them. Cattell and Drevdahl (1955, 1958) studied research scientists, artists and writers. This type of evidence has shown that those who have made creative contributions to their subject can be distinguished from their equally successful but 'non-creative' peers on personality grounds. The results vary according to the methods of investigation used, but they all reveal that 'creative' persons in the different areas examined showed great independence of mind, felt freedom from social conformity and were prepared to acknowledge the unusual and unconventional. They attached high value to aesthetic and theoretic interests and pursued these with strong persistence.

The specific psychological processes or abilities that lead a person to produce innovations in his chosen discipline are sometimes referred to as his 'creativity'. It is assumed on the whole that everyone has a degree of 'creativity' in the same way that everyone has 'intelligence'; some people have it in quality or quantity sufficient to lead them to the heights of originality in their professional work; others perhaps reveal it in their performance of everyday tasks and engagement in social relationships.

Measurement of 'creativity'

There are many and varied abilities and traits subsumed under the term 'creativity'. Guilford considers that ability to see problems, fluency of thinking, flexibility of thinking, originality, redefinition and elaboration are the types of cognitive abilities important for 'creativity'. He designed a number of the divergent type tests to measure these and submitted his results to extensive factorial analysis. Some research workers support his results, e.g. Barron (1955) and Chorness and Nottleman (1956), others have shed doubt on their validity: Drevdahl (1964), MacKinnon (1961) and Gough (1961).

Torrance also created a battery of tests, both verbal and non-verbal, to measure 'creativity' in children. The scoring of the tests relates to Guilford's factors of fluency of thought, flexibility of thought and originality. He was primarily concerned with the creative potential of children, and carried out experiments to show that training in how to produce ideas can increase performance on divergent type tests (1961). He published suggestions and programmes for teachers to increase their ability to identify and promote 'creativity' in the children they teach (1965a, b). He believed that teachers themselves should be intellectually adventurous in their approach to teaching. This idea gets support from

British research by Haddon and Lytton (1968) who compared children
from schools with 'progressive' or 'traditional' methods of teaching and
demonstrated that, where emphasis was laid on self-initiated learning,
the children were superior on tests of divergent thinking. Barker-Lunn
(1970) also showed that children's scores on divergent thinking items
were related to certain methods of teaching and certain types of pupil–
teacher relationship; those teachers favouring non-streaming taught
children who were higher scorers on divergent type tests.

Intelligence versus creativity

A work that is frequently referred to in connection with intelligence
versus 'creativity' dispute is that of Getzels and Jackson (1962). They
studied two groups of children from sixth grade to high school level who
were selected on the basis of intelligence and 'creativity' tests:

1. Those in the top 20 per cent (average IQ 150) in an intelligence test
but not in the top 20 per cent of the 'creativity' tests (28).
2. Those who were in the top 20 per cent on the creativity tests but not
the top 20 per cent (average IQ 127) of an intelligence test (26). The
two groups were then compared to see 'what the pupils so selected are
like as students, individuals and as members of their family'.

The results showed the groups equal in school attainments, but the
'high IQ' group were considered 'more desirable' as pupils by their
teachers. The 'high creative' group tended to diverge from the expectations of their teachers and conventional standards of behaviour. There
were differences in home background in that the 'high IQ' group's
parents tended to be in professional occupations, exercised stricter
control over their children's lives and provided a more academic
background generally; the 'high creative' group's parents tended to
be in commercial occupations.

The Getzels and Jackson work has been criticised on many counts
(Burt, 1962b; Marsh, 1964) but it remains a widely quoted study and
one that has stimulated much further research. Hasan and Butcher
(1966) partially replicated the study on a group of Scottish children and
reported a much greater overlap between intelligence and 'creativity'
test scores. They formed four groups, adding to those of Getzels and
Jackson the child 'high' on both types of tests and 'low' on both types of
test, and were not able to support the previous findings. Edwards and
Tyler (1965) working with American junior high school pupils came
to the same conclusion.

Wallach and Kogan (1965) were disappointed that after so many
studies the intelligence–creativity question was not answered. They
decided that perhaps the test-like situation was not conducive to best
performance on the divergent tests. They argued that the nature of
creative work in adults demanded unlimited time and freedom to

operate in one's own style. So they carried out an experiment which was designed to make the children (10- to 11-year-olds) at ease and unaware that they were being tested. This was done by getting teachers to co-operate in allowing the experimenters to give the creativity tests more as games during normal school days after they had worked in the school for several weeks and were familiar to the children.

The creativity items used were similar to those of Guilford and Torrance and included both verbal and non-verbal material. Wallach and Kogan achieved a clearer distinction between 'creativity' and intelligence than other workers in this way, the average correlation between the tests of creativity was $+ \cdot 41$ and that between tests of intelligence and creativity $+ \cdot 09$. They formed four groups of children and compared them on a variety of points, summarised as follows (1965, p. 303):

> High creativity—high intelligence: these children can exercise within themselves both control and freedom, both adult-like and childlike kinds of behaviour.
> High creativity—low intelligence: these children are in angry conflict with themselves and with their school environment and are beset by feelings of unworthiness and inadequacy. In a stress-free context, however, they can blossom forth cognitively.
> Low creativity—high intelligence: these children can be described as 'addicted' to school achievement. Academic failure would be perceived by them as catastrophic, so that they must continually strive for academic excellence in order to avoid the possibility of pain.
> Low creativity—low intelligence: basically bewildered, these children engage in various defensive manoeuvres ranging from useful adaptations such as intensive social activity to regressions such as passivity or psychosomatic symptoms.

Wallach and Kogan claimed that flexibility in both types of thinking, open and closed, is necessary:

> It seems reasonable to expect that if one were to make an accurate assessment of children's creativity and intelligence status and if one were to apply environmental aids appropriate to the child's mode of thinking, many children could conceivably be moved toward higher levels of cognitive functioning.

However, they realised as all other workers in this field, that there were still questions of the validity of creativity tests to be solved, and that longitudinal studies are necessary.

> It is unlikely, however, that we shall soon find a psychologist or team of psychologists to do for creativity what Terman and his associates have done for intelligence.

A brief summary cannot do justice to the large amount of work that has been carried out on creativity. There are many fuller statements on the problem in recent literature (Butcher 1968; Freeman, Butcher and Christie 1968; Thouless 1969; Vernon 1970). All writers consider the concept an important one, especially for education, largely because it has raised issues concerning the relationships between the intellectual, social and emotional aspects of personality, which in turn lead to questions about current teaching methods.

Despite the unresolved difficulties in defining and measuring creativity, psychologists recommend the continued attempt to use tests of a divergent type as well as the more traditional intelligence type. In cases where this has been done there has always been a group of high IQ *and* high creativity scorers, and perhaps these are the children to be rightly named 'gifted' for they demonstrate a flexibility of thought that leads them to excel in a variety of tasks.

Burt states: 'Creativity without general intelligence produces nothing of interest or value' (1962a). What needs to be validated is that creativity *and* intelligence produce something of exceptional interest and value.

Part III
Subsidiary Studies

9. Intelligence versus 'creativity'

High intelligence and/or high creativity

Convergent and divergent type tests [Appendix IIa] were used in this survey. It was decided to see whether, at the top end of the scale, the most able children could be divided into groups, distinguished from each other in a number of ways based on intelligence and creativity criteria. The study could not replicate the work of Getzels and Jackson (1962), Haddon and Lytton (1968) or Wallach and Kogan (1965), but it was thought that it could be similar enough in aim to add some evidence to the controversy raised on the intelligence-'creativity' issue.

The relationships between the intelligence test and divergent thinking tests have been discussed in Chapters 4 and 8. It was shown that all the tests correlated and showed significant relationships. It would appear, therefore, at the outset that it might be difficult to separate groups on intelligence and 'creativity'. However, a number of writers have suggested that, above the level of IQ 120, intelligence becomes more distinct from 'creative' abilities (Barron, 1963; McClelland 1958; Mackinnon 1962; Yamamoto 1964), in which case it should be possible to make the required subdivisions in our sample.

On the basis of the full-scale intelligence test scores and the summed standard scores of divergent test measures, three main groups were formed; boys and girls were selected separately on their results since the boys' mean IQ was significantly higher than that of the girls which, if they had been considered together, would have led to overweighting the groups with boys.

I. The high intelligence-high 'creativity' group (HI-HC)
These were subjects in the top 23 per cent in intelligence and the top 23 per cent in 'creativity', giving a total of 28 subjects (15 boys and 13 girls).

II. The high intelligence group (HI-LC)
These were subjects in the top 23 per cent in intelligence but below the top 23 per cent in 'creativity', giving a total of 28 subjects (15 boys and 13 girls).

III. *The high 'creativity' group (HC-LI)*

These were subjects in the top 23 per cent in 'creativity' but below the top 23 per cent in intelligence, again giving a total of 28 subjects (15 boys and 13 girls).

The mean intelligence scores and the mean 'creativity' scores for the three groups and the significance of the differences between them are given in the appendix [Tables A9.1, A9.2].

The groups as defined were analysed within four broad contexts:

1. Attainment in school.
2. Other test results.
3. Interests outside school.
4. Personality.

1. *Attainment in school*

(*a*) *Reading* (scores taken from the reading test used in the second follow-up study). The results showed the high IQ—high 'creativity' groups to be significantly higher in reading attainment than the other two groups whose scores were not significantly different [Table A9.3].

(*b*) *Mathematics* (scores taken from the mathematics test used in the second follow-up study). The differences between the high IQ–high creativity groups and the high intelligence–low creativity groups were not significant, but they both had significantly higher scores than the high creativity–low intelligence groups [Table A9.4].

(*c*) *Teachers' assessments* (sum of ratings on general knowledge, number work, use of books and oral ability; second follow-up study). The boys' high-on-both group was rated significantly higher than the other two groups; the girls' high-on-both group was only significantly higher than the high creativity–low IQ group. When the boys and girls were taken together there were significant differences between all three groups, the high-on-both receiving the highest sum of ratings, the high IQ–low creativity next and the high creativity–low IQ last. The results revealed again the tendency for teachers to rate girls more highly than boys and the positive relationship between the teachers' estimates and IQ results [Table A9.5].

When the items rated were taken separately, the girls' high-on-both group differed significantly from the other two groups on number work and the boys' groups were similarly differentiated by the oral work ratings. The high-on-both boys also scored better than the high IQ– low creativity boys on use of books. There were no significant differences between the high IQ–low creativity and high creativity–low IQ groups for any of the ratings whether boys and girls were taken separately or together. It must be noted here that several factors had to be taken into account; the small numbers involved, the coarse grouping of the teachers' estimates and the high intelligence quotients of the children involved (only two boys + three girls with IQ just below 120).

This school data suggested that the high-on-both groups tended to do better than the other groups all round, the high intelligence–low creativity groups were more similar in achievement to the high-on-both groups where mathematics was concerned, but more similar to the high-creativity–low IQ groups where verbal material was concerned.

This was supported by the results of the test nearest in kind to mathematics, the logic test, if the boys and girls were taken together; the high-on-both and high intelligence–low creativity groups were not differentiated but the high-on-both and high creativity–low intelligence groups were significant [Table A9.6]. The high intelligence–low creativity group did not do as well as the high-on-both in the more verbal social reasoning test [Table A9.7].

There were no significant differences between the scores on the Barron-Welsh Art Scale of any groups. This test had the lowest correlation with the WISC intelligence test of any test in the battery (0·026). It was thought that it might have singled out the high-creativity–low intelligence groups.

No boy in the high IQ–low creativity group put art as his favourite subject whereas five in the high creativity–low IQ group did. Five girls in the high IQ–low creativity group put mathematics as a favourite subject but only one girl in the high creativity–low IQ group did. These slight trends of the arts-science preference as revealed at this age need following up as the children get older to see how far they are valid.

2. *Interests at home*

The high intelligence *and* high creativity groups showed their superiority in the range of interests they covered and their greater preoccupation with academic and executive or practical interests. The boys particularly stood out in this group because of their strong interest in science.

The high creativity–low IQ groups tended to have a narrower range of interest than the others, although this was not significantly different from the high IQ–low creativity groups. This finding was contrary to Getzels and Jackson who found their high creativity–low IQ children showing more specific and numerous interests.

Each interest was examined separately to see if the high IQ–low creativity and high creativity–low IQ groups could be differentiated, but none of the results was significant. A slightly higher proportion of children in the high creativity–low IQ group chose drawing, writing stories and poems, and music than the others (57 or 43 per cent) which may be another sign that this group was opting more positively for the arts.

3. *Personality*

The high-on-both group again showed more superiority according to the parental ratings: they were rated more highly in self-confidence, forethought and originality than the high creativity–low intelligence group. The high intelligence–low creativity group was superior in 'forethought' only to the high creativity–low intelligence group.

Another test of relevance to this discussion was the 'Outstanding Traits Test' which referred to the parents' attitudes towards the traits they would prefer to see in their children. [Appendix IIc]. It was given by Getzels and Jackson to the children in their sample, but in the present study it was given to the parents. The test contained a list of thirteen 'desirable traits' which the parents were asked to arrange in order of importance [Table A9.8]. The result worthy of note was that the parents of high-on-both groups ranked the intellectual quality of goal directedness (the one who knows best what he wants and works steadily towards getting it) higher than the other two groups for both boys and girls (cf. children's ideas of 'self' and 'life', Chapter 7).

There were no differences between the groups on the 'extrovert–introvert' dimensions formed from the comments of teachers on the positive qualities of their pupils. There were not significantly more comments made on the weaknesses of personality in the groups: the comments that were made, however, showed some noteworthy differences. The high-on-both groups contained the most comments about exhibitionism, 'showing off', bragging (I:25 per cent; II: 11 per cent; III: 4 per cent); the high intelligence–low creativity group contained the most shy and diffident children (I: 18 per cent; II: 36 per cent; III: 21 per cent) and the high creativity–low intelligence group contained the children most in need of supervision for aggressiveness or indolence and laziness (I: 4 per cent; II: 7 per cent; III: 39 per cent). So there was the suggestion that teachers as well as parents were faced with different types of adjustment problems to deal with in the different groups [Table A9.9].

The teachers were asked to predict, if they could, what kind of job they thought the child might undertake eventually. The results again showed the leaning of the high-on-both groups and the high intelligence–low creativity groups towards occupations requiring mathematical-scientific ability (I: 43 per cent; II: 43 per cent; III: 14 per cent).

Family and home environment

Getzels and Jackson suggested that perhaps not only were there different types of children, i.e. intelligent versus creative, but also that these children had different types of parents. They found that the high intelligence–low creativity group had more fathers in academic or educational occupations and that the mothers were less likely to go out to work. They also found these parents more critical towards their child's school in that they made a greater number of unfavourable comments about it.

In our gifted sample the number of children from parents of manual occupations was deliberately increased to make the ratio to parents of non-manual occupations approximately equal. There was a significantly larger number of non-manual occupations represented in the three small groups under discussion if taken together. There was a significantly larger number of boys in the high intelligence–low creativity non-manual group than the high creativity–low intelligence group, but the girls were equally distributed throughout the three groups [Table A9.10].

The fact of mothers working was not significant, nor the amount of further education they received. The high intelligence–low creativity groups tended if anything to have more parents with no further education than the other groups [Tables A9.11, A9.12].

The most comments about schools came from the parents of children in the high-on-both groups with the least from the high intelligence–low creativity group. More parents of the high-on-both boys' group made unfavourable comments than the others [Tables A9.13, A9.14].

Summary

The groups that were formed had IQ means of +1, +2 and +3 standard deviations above the mean of the WISC. It was not surprising that the groups high-on-both intelligence *and* creativity tests were the most outstanding in other ways. The evidence that seemed most worthwhile to follow up was that which suggested that the high intelligence–low creativity groups had a mathematics–science bias whereas the high creativity–low intelligence groups had a verbal–arts bias.

The intelligence test alone would have provided data from which to identify children with particular interests and abilities in certain areas of knowledge, i.e. arts and/or science. It is unfortunate if commonly accepted intelligence tests favour those with mathematico-deductive modes of thought more than those with attitudes and abilities orientated towards the arts, for the latter may appear 'inferior' because they obtain 'lower' scores. The exceptional children (IQs over 140) are not affected for they can show excellence in a wide range of activities, but for the next IQ band of children who tend to show preference for one mode of thinking rather than another we need tests that indicate these differences as matters of kind rather than simply of degree.

10. Social occupation groups

Compensatory weighting

Earlier studies on gifted children contain a higher proportion of children with fathers of non-manual than manual occupations (Bereday and Lauwerys, 1962). This could have been true of this study had it not been for the deliberate inclusion of additional children in social occupation groups IV and V from the Draw-a-man test and school performance results (selection groups 3 and 6, p. 8). This was done so that the performance of children in the skilled manual and unskilled manual categories could be examined more adequately against the non-manual groups.

It was considered that it would be fairer to the lower social groups if they were compared with those selected on the same criteria, so the children with the highest results on the Draw-a-man test (selection group 1) and educational performance results (selection group 4), and those selected from parents' letters (selection group 7) were dropped from this analysis. This left those who were selected on the slightly lower Draw-a-man results and educational performance results (selection groups 2 and 3, 5 and 6) (N = 104) [Table A2.3].

RESULTS

Verbal ability and the middle class

There were no significant differences between the three social occupation groups on the full scale or performance scale of the intelligence test. Other studies which have included a wider range of IQ have found differences. Floud, Halsey and Martin (1957) and Robbins (1963) and Musgrave (1965) have drawn attention to the fact that the lower the IQ the greater was the difference between the educational and vocational chances of the broad social class groups. For the present sub-study's children, who were from the above average IQ band, it was the verbal scale of the intelligence test that revealed significantly lower scores for the manual social occupation groups, a result that was anticipated from the work of Bernstein (1960).

Superiority in verbal ability was evidenced in other tests. On the reading test the non-manual children had significantly higher scores than the manual; also on the Social Reasoning test, the Definitions test, the Information test, and Words test. There were no such differences on the Mathematics test or the Divergent Mathematics test or the test of Logic.

Progress between seven and 11 years of age

The two main social occupation groups (non-manual and manual) were distinguishable in the teachers' estimates of children at 7 and 11 years of age. When the estimates at the two ages were examined, those for the social occupation groups IV and V were seen not to have altered significantly, but the skilled manual (IIIm) and the non-manual groups obtained significantly lower assessments at the later age. The figures were taken from a summation of teachers' estimates. However, if the results were broken down into specific subject areas, the social occupation groups IV and V improved on general knowledge; the skilled manual group (IIIm) was lower on general knowledge and oral ability; the non-manual groups taken together were not rated as highly at eleven as at seven on use of books or oral ability. As the trend was for non-manual groups to have higher teachers' estimates at both ages, their drop in scores at eleven was probably a statistical regression to the mean, lessening the gap between them and the manual groups. This result was not altogether expected as Wiseman (1964) and Lawton (1968) have pointed out that educational 'distance' between the social groups increased with age. However, this study's group of lower working-class children were of *above average* ability and seemed to be able to hold their position during the junior school period. Douglas (1964) showed that by the end of the primary school middle-class boys were catching up with girls, but not the working-class boys; again, this was not the case for this study's special children, the boys of manual and non-manual groups overtook the girls. This was probably due to the fact that the boys in this sample were of higher intelligence if judged on the WISC.

The teachers anticipated that a third of the whole sample would go to university, approximately half from the non-manual group and a quarter of the manual group; this, of course, was related to IQ score which, if taken into account, reduced the difference between the predictions for each group, i.e. 68 per cent manual group with intelligence quotients over 130 were expected to go to university as against 75 per cent of the non-manual group. How these results are judged depends on how far one believes the IQ score to be inherently affected by social occupation grouping in the first place.

School and interests

All the social occupation groups contained a large proportion of children who liked school very much, but the manual group contained more who did not have positive feelings about it. The manual groups children tended more often to choose non-academic subjects as their favourites and liked them because they did not involve reading and writing, e.g. sport and art. The non-manual group children, because they tended to enjoy academic subjects, said they were 'favourites' because they did well in them. From the parental answers it was obvious that significantly fewer children from non-manual groups found some subjects difficult at school, the subject presenting most difficulty was mathematics, particularly to lower manual groups and especially to the girls in them.

Interest in reading again brought out a sharp contrast between the groups. The non-manual groups, regardless of level of IQ, chose reading as a main or keen interest more often than the rest who, if they chose reading at all, tended only to have it as an occasional interest. Obtaining books from public libraries and owning books also differentiated the groups; 30 per cent of the non-manual group children and 5 per cent of the manual group children owned over fifty books. The lower manual parents said they exercised control over what their children read more often than the others.

The non-manual groups had much more instruction out of school than manual groups and expressed a keener interest in it. They also played more chess and claimed to be above average in manual skills significantly more than the others, but in all groups it was the higher (over 130) IQ children who claimed greater manipulative skill.

When asked about their ideas of a 'good' teacher, the non-manual groups mentioned skill as an interpreter (can explain things to children) as most important, whereas the manual groups rated skill as a disciplinarian most highly. There were no social group differences in what they liked most about their friends.

The unskilled manual group said more often than the rest that they would like a profession as a career, mostly as teachers. This result coincided with that of Jackson and Marsden (1962) who found that among working-class 'successes' a larger proportion than among the middle class chose teaching as a career. The non-manual children chose from a wider variety of careers all involving special skills, although sometimes non-professional in the academic sense.

Parents' views and background

The non-manual group parents reported more of their children as having very good health and having fewer difficulties of timidity and adaptability in new situations. At their individual interviews the non-manual children were rated more highly on self-confidence and perseverance than the others; the unskilled manual group were rated the lowest on perseverance and the skilled group lowest on self-confidence.

The non-manual parents, when asked for favourable or unfavourable comments on the school their child attended, made more comments than the others. They were particularly concerned with standards of work and teaching methods in contrast to the lower manual group who were more concerned that their children had teachers they liked. In line with other research (Musgrave, 1965; Plowden Report, 1967; Douglas, 1964; Davie, Butler and Goldstein, 1972) fathers of non-manual social occupation groups tended to take more active interest in their child's education in choice of school, talking about and helping with school work. These parents were also more confident that they would intervene in their child's education if they were dissatisfied, and teachers saw them as more concerned over their children's education than manual group parents, probably because they visited schools more often.

Mothers and fathers in the non-manual groups stayed at school longer and had selective education more often than in the two manual groups. The mothers in the non-manual and skilled manual groups left school earlier than the fathers, but fathers left earlier than mothers in the lower manual group. It was only in the non-manual groups that parents had gone to have late training some time after compulsory education was concluded. It seemed almost too obvious to state that the non-manual parents were the ones who expected the majority of their children to go on to university and professional work; 70 per cent in contrast to 20 per cent in the other groups.

Summary

The most important result from this section was perhaps the significantly lower verbal ability of the manual group children. This accounted for the main difference in test performance between the groups and was reflected in their parents' own shorter educational history and less confidence in educational matters. They had held their above average position in their teachers' estimates but were still lower than non-manual group children and the prognosis for their further education was considered less favourable by both their parents and teachers.

11. Social class and language

Language analysis

The effects of social and cultural environment on intelligence and attainment are well documented. It was no surprise to find in the present study that children from the manual social occupation groups did less well on the verbal intelligence scale and other tests involving verbally expressed answers than non-manual groups, although it seemed possible at the outset that the generally high level of intelligence of the total group could have produced atypical results.

When it had been established that there was a significant difference between the social occupation groups, the next step taken was an analysis of the language used by the children to see if some special differences could be isolated to distinguish the different social groups in more detail.

There are many ways of analysing language, both in its content and structural aspects. Most recent developments involve lengthy and complex procedures that could not be carried out in the context of this study. Therefore, a simple grammatical analysis of language structure was followed from the work of Lawton (1968) in his consideration of the theory of Bernstein. A brief account of the theory would do an injustice to the work of its author and is not attempted; the main concepts which have been used for this study are those of the 'elaborated' and 'restricted' codes, two types of speech patterns with characteristics enumerated (by De Cecco, 1967) as follows:

RESTRICTED CODE

1. Short, grammatically simple, often unfinished sentences with a poor syntactical form stressing the active voice.
2. Simple and repetitive use of conjunctions (so, then, because).
3. Little use of subordinate clauses to break down the initial categories of the dominant subject.
4. Inability to hold a formal subject through a speech sequence; thus a dislocated informational content is almost inevitable.
5. Rigid and limited use of adjectives and adverbs.
6. Infrequent use of impersonal pronouns as subjects of conditional clauses.

7. Frequent use of statements where the reason and conclusion are confounded to produce a categoric statement.

8. A large number of statements/phrases which signal a requirement for the previous speech sequence to be reinforced 'Wouldn't it? You see? You know?' etc. This process is termed 'sympathetic circularity'.

9. Individual selection from a group of idiomatic phrases or sequences will frequently occur.

10. The individual qualification is implicit in the sentence organisation: it is a language of implicit meaning.

ELABORATED CODE

1. Accurate grammatical order and syntax regulate what is said.

2. Logical modifications and stress are mediated through a grammatically complex sentence construction, especially through the use of a range of conjunctions and subordinate clauses.

3. Frequent use of prepositions which indicate logical relationships as well as prepositions which indicate temporal and spatial contiguity.

4. Frequent use of the personal pronoun 'I'.

5. A discriminative selection from a range of adjectives and adverbs.

6. Individual qualification is verbally mediated through the structure and relationships within and between sentences.

7. Expressive symbolism discriminates between meanings within speech sequences rather than reinforcing dominant words or phrases or accompanying the sequence in a diffuse generalised manner.

8. It is a language use which points to the possibilities inherent in a complex conceptual hierarchy for the organising of experience.

The codes were said to be 'functions of particular forms of social relationships, or more generally, qualities of social structure'. Bernstein suggested that middle-class children were likely to have the advantage of the use of both types of code, the elaborated one learned at home and a restricted one used with peers, while working-class children were more likely to have the use only of restricted codes.

Bernstein and Lawton carried out empirical studies on the language of small groups of children from manual and non-manual social groups, Bernstein on twenty-four boys of mean age 16 years, and Lawton on ten boys aged 12 and ten aged 15. They both found differences on social class in the predicted direction on some elements of grammatical structure and syntax. Lawton found that the differences were less marked at age 12 than age 15 and also less apparent in an individual interview situation than a group discussion.

SELECTION OF SUB-SAMPLE

The gifted study provided an opportunity to use the previous work, examining more children all above average in intelligence and including girls in the sample.[1] A grammatical analysis is a time-consuming activity,

[1] The language analysis was carried out by Mrs J. James, assistant research officer to the project.

so it was decided to limit the sub-sample to forty-eight children. The study group was divided into eight sub-groups on sex, non-manual v manual social occupational status, and degree of responsiveness during the interview (assessed on the number of sentences used in reply to questions, non-responsive children were those who used only one or two sentences throughout, the rest were considered responsive). Six children were selected from each sub-group matched on IQ as far as possible, and where there was a gap of one standard deviation between the verbal and performance scales on the intelligence test scores, these were matched also. This meant that there were sixteen small groups of three which could be made into larger groups for the purpose of examining the different variables. Thirty-eight scripts were analysed and the matching of the groups was maintained as far as possible.

There were no significant differences on the full scale and performance scale intelligence test scores between the non-manual and manual groups, but there was the expected lower mean for the manual group on the verbal scale scores [Table A10.1].

It was decided on the evidence of Lawton's study to examine two types of speech, that which was used in the interview, which gave opportunity for spontaneous and personal replies to be given to questions, contrasted with that which was used in answer to the questions 'What is science? (or history, geography, art, mathematics and poetry)' which asked deliberately for the highest level of abstraction in thought that each child could bring to such a question. All the answers on these definitions were analysed, but in the case of the interviews the ten longest uninterrupted replies were selected from each child's typed interview schedule. It had to be acknowledged that there were some interview questions which elicited abstract replies, but for the non-manual group a mean of 1·6, ranging from 6 to 0 replies, and for the manual group a mean of 1·3, ranging from 4 to 1 were of this type. These differences did not seem large enough to affect the decision to treat the two types of responses as distinct. The interview responses are referred to as 'descriptive' and the definitions as 'abstract' in the results.

Results

The type of analysis and findings are described together.

1. WORDS OMITTED FROM THE ANALYSIS [Table A10.2]

Table A10.2 shows the number of words omitted from analysis in Lawton's and the gifted study. Under this heading were counted repetitions, false starts, socio-centric sequences (e.g. you know, isn't it? etc.) and egocentric sequences (e.g. I think . . .).

The gifted study children had a greater percentage of words omitted by the non-manual children in both descriptive and abstract sections which was consistent with Lawton on the former but not the latter.

The words omitted in any sentence, if consisting of more than two words, were called 'a maze', a measure defined by Loban (1963) who predicted in a longitudinal study that children with high verbal ability would become more fluent each year and decrease the number and length of their mazes. Although the result was as predicted in general, there was an increase in mazes around the 10- to 11-year-old age, which seemed to indicate a renewed struggle in verbal planning to reach higher levels of verbal construction. The non-manual group children in the 'gifted' study had a higher percentage of mazes—58 per cent than the manual group children—37 per cent, which, although not statistically significant, is in line with the idea that children of higher verbal ability at this age are attempting more complex verbal strategies. This was supported by the fact that the non-manual children had a significantly higher percentage of mazes on the more difficult definitions task.

2. ADJECTIVES AND ADVERBS

These parts of speech were abstracted and examined in relation to the total number of words used.

Rare adjectives and adverbs were obtained by counting once only each different example used by a child, omitting those which appeared in McNally and Murray's list of the hundred most common English words.

Lawton showed no significant differences on these measures, but claimed there were trends showing the non-manual children superior on all four adjective counts and two (descriptive) adverb counts. The gifted study had even smaller differences; they were in the same direction on all counts [Table A10.3].

3. PERSONAL PRONOUNS TO TOTAL WORDS AND ALL 'I'S TO TOTAL WORDS

Girls and children with lower (under 140) IQs had significantly higher proportions. On the definitions test, boys, the less responsive children and those with higher verbal than performance IQs had significantly higher proportions of personal pronouns. This study yielded no social occupation group differences. Bernstein and Lawton reported that manual group children were inclined to use personal pronouns where a noun or noun phrase would convey more meaning. Their non-manual children used 'I' more often which suggested more emphatic insistence on ego differentiation.

4. PASSIVE VERBS AS A PROPORTION OF ALL ANALYSED VERBS

In both Bernstein and Lawton's studies the non-manual children consistently used more passive constructions than the manual children and the difference between them increased with age. In this study the proportions were weighted in the same direction but were not significant.

5. SUBORDINATE CLAUSES TO TOTAL FINITE VERBS ANALYSED

There were no significant differences between the different groups, though the proportions were weighted in favour of the manual group. Lawton noted a similar weighting in his more spontaneous situation, but it was reversed in the more abstract one. In his work he found non-manual children used more complex types of subordination and fewer clauses; the simple conjunction of clauses leads manual children to give more examples.

6. COMPLEX VERBAL STEMS TO TOTAL FINITE VERBS ANALYSED

In this study, girls and children with performance IQs higher than verbal IQs were significantly superior in the number used. Lawton's 12-year-old manual group children has a higher proportion than the others. The slight differences in this study favoured the manual children in the definitions only.

7. EGO-CENTRIC SEQUENCES EXPRESSED AS A RATIO TO SOCIO-CENTRIC SEQUENCES

The difference was most marked in Lawton's study in the more abstract situation, the non-manual group as expected using 'I think', 'I feel', 'I would say' in contrast to the manual group preference for 'you know'. However, the reverse was true in the gifted study, because the non-manual children tended to go one stage further in abstraction when defining by using the pronoun 'one' rather than 'I', e.g. 'What is history?' 'In history one studies the past.'

8. STRUCTURAL PATTERNS

As a final investigation, it was decided to observe how conversant the children were with the basic structural patterns of English. Loban (1963) listed nine such structures, but only seven were examined here because questions and commands were not elicited. The phrases were identified as present or absent in each child's schedule and groups compared to see which used less and which more [Table A10.4].

The seven basic structural patterns were:

1. Subject + verb as predicate
2. Subject + verb + object
3. Subject + linking verb + complement
4. Subject + verb + indirect object + direct object
5. Subject + verb + direct object + objective complement
6. Subject or representative subject + linking verb + subject
7. Passive verb

In the interview sample of speech nine non-manual group children used all the speech patterns to seven of the manual group, but this was reversed in the definitions when two manual group children used *all* and only one non-manual child. However, the differences were so slight that the conclusion was that there were no significant differences in the use of basic structural patterns between the two social class groups [Table A10.5].

9. CODE SWITCHING

The hypothesis of code switching, derived from Bernstein and utilised by Lawton, stated that 'elaborated code' speakers would tend to switch easily from one code to another according to the demands of the situation, whereas restricted code speakers would tend to be confined to one code or experience great difficulty in switching to another.

This was tested by examining the results on the definitions to see if the non-manual group children scored higher than the others on some aspects of speech structure which are attributed to the elaborated code. The definitions required a high level of generalisation, producing succinct and precise replies. It was therefore expected that a smaller proportion of adjectives and adverbs would be used and fewer personal pronouns than on the sample of interview speech since the more abstract task demanded more impersonal phrases or noun phrases. This left a possible six items on which differences could be expected. The majority of non-manual children used more passive verbs, complex verbal stems and mazes in the abstract task in contrast to a minority in the case of manual children [Table A10.6].

The median test was applied to all the proportions calculated from the children's speech: eight items were significant [Table A10.7]. However, as 120 tests were performed six could appear significant at the 5 per cent level by chance and therefore the results are negligible in terms of any generalisations that might be made.

An analysis of variance test confirmed the median test results in five cases and differed on another three. The descriptive and abstract samples of speech were examined for straight class distinctions and for interaction effect between social class and sex. No social class differences were revealed on the amalgam of scores or in the individual items of which that score was composed [Table A10.8]. It had to be accepted again that eight items out of 156 tests could be significant by chance.

Summary

In this selected sub-sample of children with high intelligence quotients, social occupation group differences in the use of some aspects of language, although observable, were not large enough to demonstrate the existence of two types of linguistic code.

These children appeared to be linguistically competent in the grammatical sense, regardless of sex, social class, degree of responsiveness and greater ability in verbal or performance test items on the intelligence test. The children from the manual social class groups were perhaps not typical of that group; their high intelligence quotients had been a better predictor of their grammatical usage than their social class.

Lawton drew attention to the fact that the level of language structure used by his subjects depended on the context in which he obtained his data. His structured interview was considered to have enforced expression in a more complex way than was reached in a group discussion with peers. In the gifted study the interview was considered an opportunity for spontaneous response in contrast to the 'definitions' which required thoughtful reflection. It was assumed that there would be a difference in the results of the two tasks, but it was acknowledged that the questions in the interview were selected to pick out exceptional children in the group and did demand a response in terms of the adult's context rather than the child's.

It is, perhaps, in the content of language that one has to look for the differences between children in terms of their intelligence levels and social occupation groupings. Most writers on gifted children refer to the vast store of general knowledge which they can retain and relate with apparent ease. This goes with their extensive use of books for knowledge and pleasure, which, as has been shown, relates to social occupational status in the extent to which these books are available.

12. The children's definitions of six areas of knowledge

Most studies examine children in English and mathematics but omit other subject areas. Time is always against the investigator; intelligence tests, English tests and mathematics tests assume more importance because they yield information quickly about children's general and basic abilities. Tests of this kind are also more numerous and well standardized.

The children's general knowledge

It was decided to try to get some measure of the sample children's reactions to other subjects to which they would have had some introduction in their primary schools, namely science, history, geography and the arts. This was done in two ways: first, four short information tests were given orally (p. 11). It was thought that particular biases in interest in specific subjects might be supported by high scores in the information tests. This was not the case, for most children maintained the same level across the four tests and the correlations with the intelligence test result and each other were highly significant [Table A4.7].

Secondly, the children were asked a very difficult question about each subject: 'What is science? (history, geography, mathematics, art, poetry)'. On the surface these would seem perhaps rather irrelevant questions to pose to 11-year-olds who have no knowledge of philosophy, when experts in each field argue, define and redefine the nature of their subjects. And yet one cannot help wondering what these children think they are about when they have lessons in subjects at school, especially the children of advanced mental age who are beginning to reflect in a self-conscious manner on their experiences. Of course the evidence is only on what they say and it cannot be inferred from their words alone what functional knowledge they have of the subjects. However, in learning at school it is often through words that new ideas are introduced. If these definitions represent at all their intellectual organisation of ideas about these subjects they should help to show which children are most ready for the more subject biased teaching they are likely to receive in secondary school.

It was not possible to establish how great a part school or home plays in the formation of knowledge and its values. There were many variables in the problem, not least the way in which subjects were taught. Some teachers might have aimed for straight information with their primary age pupils, some encouraged experimentation, using techniques and tools appropriate to the subject, others might have aimed to convey larger issues concerned with a subject as a form of knowledge or way of structuring experience. The range of categories that emerged in each subject from the children reflected all these approaches and teachers might find it of interest to look at the content of the statements by this national group of children.

Assessment of the definitions

The answers were rated on a five-point scale. The assumption was made that most of the children would be at the stage of concrete operational thinking (marked as Grade 3), i.e. able to form concepts in the various disciplines when these can be derived from situations within personal experience, and able to express these in language involving simple generalisation. Some children would be at an advanced concrete operational level using concepts of greater complexity in the subject and able to express these in more comprehensive generalisations (marked as Grades 1 or 2). It was expected that other children would find the task too difficult, and resort to word association answers referring to specific school situations without attempts to generalise (marked as Grades 4 and 5). A first sort was made and a description of the various categories in each subject was produced. Three raters were employed for each subject, always including one specialist (i.e. a graduate) in that subject area who also had experience of teaching children of this age, as had the other raters. The answers were typed out from taped recordings and the children identified only by a number, no sex, IQ or other data were supplied.

No satisfactory statistical technique was found for comparing ratings so if the ratings differed on more than 10 per cent of the cases, the categories were redescribed and the ratings repeated.

The table of percentages in the different categories and IQ groups showed the correspondence of ascending and descending grades [Table A10.9].

Each subject will be illustrated in turn to indicate the range of responses received from children of different IQ levels. [For the full range of vocabulary see Appendix IV.]

What is science?

CATEGORY 1

Although the answers may seem slight and fragmented in comparison with what an educated adult could say, these children were well ahead of their age group in their ability to acknowledge that a variety of studies are subsumed in the subject and that they involve problems of 'what' and 'how' and 'why' types. The children attempted to derive from their experience some all-inclusive generalisations which they formulated in objective statements.

(a) Girl: IQ 136, Verbal IQ 150+, social class II
She had a marked interest in science, and though a great reader on all subjects declared less interest in the arts. The attempt to differentiate the arts and scientific modes of thought suggested a high level of intellectual abstraction.

'Biology is the study of animals and plants—a study of living things; chemistry's the study of things that are not living and yet can move—well, they can't always move, but things like the study of atoms and elements and compounds and things like that, and it's the study of things that are not included in—I'm finding it hard to say—physics. Physics is about different forces like pressure, mass, weight and these are all mixed up, and they should go to physics. They're all in one group—the biology being living things, things that are definitely alive—chemistry being things that—solids, liquids and gases—but most of them can move, that is, gases can, water can—liquids can take the shape of the vessels, and things like the metals and nonmetals—there's a metal that can take the shape of the vessel—mercury, the bromine that is the only other liquid. . . . They are grouped together because it's something you really have to study to find out about—things like poetry, or English, you don't have to find out, you've already found out, but science, you do not yet know everything about—you can always find out something more. There's always still something to find out that you don't know. Other things, once you've got most of it you've got it—if you've drawn something, you've drawn it there—you've drawn a complete picture, I mean there isn't any more to put in, whereas if you think you've drawn a complete picture of what science is, then you probably haven't, because you can still find out more in various experiments. An experiment is finding out about something that you don't really know the answer to when you begin, or else you know the answer to, but you want to see whether it really does work like you said it will.'

(b) Boy: IQ 154, social class II
A boy with a wide range of interests covering all areas of the curriculum.

'Science is the study of reaction in chemistry, in living things and living things in relation to dead things. The reaction particularly of atoms and molecules and the things around us—the way they move and how life is formed and how it functions. For instance, the movement of air forming vacuums and that sort of thing: how things move because of vacuums and chemical reactions; fission, division, multiplication, that sort of thing; the movement of atoms and the way they live.'

(*c*) Girl: IQ 148, social class II
This girl had good ability all round but was particularly keen on literature.

'Science is increasing the human knowledge. You do experiments to prove theories. At school we do experiments that other people have done before us to prove they work. Science goes in lots of directions—going to the moon, science about animals, there's all kinds of science really, underwater science. It helps us cope with problems, helps us to find solutions to our problems. Tells us when volcanoes are going to erupt and when there'll be earthquakes. We devise new weapons and invent things to do jobs.'

(*d*) Boy: IQ 131, social class II
This answer was given a high rating partly because of the child's awareness of his own developing concept of the subject.

'Science? I'm not quite sure actually, it's about the earth—the minerals of the earth—not the minerals, the *substance* of the world—the contents of the world, the things there are. I used to think it was mixing things together and making a big bang, but it's a bit different from that now—you have to sort of find out how and *why* things mix together with a big bang, as well as doing it. Physics is a mixture of science and maths.'

(*e*) Boy: IQ 140, social class III, non-manual.
A boy according to his teacher, particularly strong on English studies.

'Well, it's about how things are made up, different things like different elements and different ways different things are made up. It's the way everything is made up and how the earth was formed and things like that. It involves chemicals and engineering and technical developments. It's how men have progressed and what they've invented towards the good of mankind and the way different countries have evolved. It's the *reason* behind a lot of things.'

CATEGORY 2

These responses contained three main points and the concepts used were fundamental to the subject. Newness and novelty were introduced and elementary ideas of control. There was the impression that current learning situations were very much in mind but that the children were trying to generalise from these.

(*a*) Boy: IQ 141, social class III, manual
His performance was good all round at school, and he considered his interests well balanced between the different subjects. He obviously had in mind a special topic, but he implied search for relationships and explanation.

'It's experimenting with many things, finding out more about substances, recording the information; it's exploring different subjects such as animals, finding out how, well, how they work—finding out what happens in different conditions and looking at how different animals live in different environments and the life cycle of fish and things like that. Experimenting with different things, substances or liquids, metals, animals, water, soil and things like that and finding what happens to them in chemicals or gases.'

(b) Girl: IQ 131, social class II
She was most keen on sport but did not reject science as she did mathematics.

'Well, it's finding out about all sorts of things—all about the moon and everything, and doing experiments to see what you have to wear on the moon for protection and what food you have to use, and what—if you lived up there—what kind of housing you'd use—scientists are doing all sorts of things. Science isn't just on one subject, there's different sciences all over the country and different subjects—some plants, houses—some the moon and space. Experiments on animals, guinea pigs and things; sometimes they don't turn out, but some do. Some experiments are all right some not all that much good.'

(c) Boy: IQ 154, social class II
He had exceptional understanding of mechanical functioning and had decided to become an engineer. He invented gadgets for the home. He was quiet and not a talker.

'Science is understanding how things work and as much about them as possible. In science you can find out how a thing is made up—of atoms—and find out how it works and you study the growth and see what happens in its life cycle. You see if you can make something better than it was before.'

(d) Girl: IQ 132, social class II
She was very good at languages at school, but her main interest was science at home.

'You find out about things—ways of travel—plant life—pond life—insects—animals. Experiment and find out about chemicals and things. It's different from other lessons, usually it's about things you didn't know about. It's a study, it helps you to understand the ways of life. It's interesting, and lots of people enjoy it because it describes life for you and makes you realise what it's really like, and it shows people how things came about, why they came about—what made them come about. You can do all sorts of things, like getting a flower and grow it yourself, and measure it every day.'

(e) Boy: IQ 136, social class III, manual
This boy was gifted musically and his interests in and out of school centred around music, though he was able to do well in other things when they were demanded of him.

'It's a study of things of interest and importance. First find out basics—how it works, analyse material what it is made out of. Different kinds of science; science of the universe, chemistry, there's a science of electronics, of mechanics and of elements. The study of things—you have to find out how to make things too, to learn what you're going to make it do—what you need to do, in analysing. Practically all science is based on working with the elements. Radium is the most powerful. You have to learn what you are doing to make it do what you need to do.'

CATEGORY 3

First level generalisations were consigned to this group. There were indications of some awareness of the conscious activity of other persons, but current lessons tended to dominate the thoughts of the children while they struggled to make a more general statement.

(a) Girl: IQ 125, social class III, manual
'It can be sort of hospital science to do with medicine, or I suppose it could be aircraft and rockets and things like computers and whatnot, machines. You need to be able to work things out properly—science with anything really—what they did with bread—how they used to grow the corn and grind it and make it into flour and bake it into bread, and how bread was made. We had some pictures of some great millstones.'

(b) Girl: IQ 133, social class II
'Science is a subject where you learn all different kinds of things about the earth—you learn about oils and fats and all sorts of things and you do experiments which help you to understand what the science is, and you make things and try them out. At school we're doing it about health.'

(c) Boy: IQ 143, social class II
'Studying rocks and plants—animals and all things like that. In science you have different names for metals not just iron—you don't just call it iron, they have letters or numbers for it instead of calling it iron—and you find out how much of each metal is in such and such a rock. The scientists find out what kills animals—how they died—if they don't know, if they're dead, they try to find out and they cut the body open to see if they can find anything that's killed them. Scientists make rockets and design rockets and things and motors—lots of things they design—weapons and things like that.'

(d) Boy: IQ 121, social class III, non-manual
'Science is finding out I'd say. You have to find out for yourself in science, it's not just handed to you on a plate. They say "Do something" and unless you do it, you'll never find out what they wanted you to do, and you've got to find out what you want all by yourself, you see. It is experimenting—oh well—it comes back to the same thing, because if

you don't experiment you'll never find out anything. 'Cause great inventors they find out things—steam engine, they looked at things, and they found out things, and they had to use their eyes a little bit. Use their eyes and their ears so they found out.'

CATEGORY 4

There was little elaboration in the following answers, the children expressed uncertainty and focused on specific things they had done or information picked up at random.

(a) Girl: IQ 118, social class II
'Looking into things—like a thermometer and see how it works. Things, how they work and what they do.'

(b) Girl: IQ 126, social class III manual
'Um, experiments, and testing things. Well, to find out about something you put it under a microscope. . . . Finding out things, like if you get some ink and put it on a special paper, do some other tests, to find out all the colours in it, and er, letting beans grow in blotting paper.'

(c) Boy: IQ 133, social class V
'About the earth—stars, moon—and all the planets, might be electricity—I'm not quite sure. Gravity. How the world spins round. Things about the universe you live in. How all the planets are made.'

CATEGORY 5

These replies were brief and vague, specific but not very meaningful.

(a) Boy: IQ 115, social class III, manual
'Things outside—living things—we've written about nature and flowers and things—we've written about experiments.'

(b) Girl: IQ 113, social class III manual
'When you got to put liquid into tubes and things and you make things.'

What is history?

The responses in this section confirmed the work of other researchers which showed that 11-year-olds clearly connected history with time but their knowledge was limited because their level of conceptual thought was inadequate to encompass the generalisations and abstractions required for the understanding of types and causes of change taking place in a continuous process.

The answers as a whole covered most aspects of history, i.e. political, social, constitutional and biographical references were made, but the children tended to focus on one or other of these areas. The better answers showed that history was an activity associated with historians, that it involved study and resort to evidence. Some managed to convey awareness of the passage of time, the notion of change, the uniqueness of events, the idea of classes of events; others hinted at ideas of exploration, inference and imaginative reconstruction but most were tied to descriptive facts and specific items remembered from school lessons.

CATEGORY 1

(a) Boy: IQ 146, social class III, non-manual
He was keenly interested in history (see p. 92). He was trying to convey its comprehensiveness and general range of applicability.

'What a funny question! Well, I suppose yesterday was history, I think *past* is really history. You can make history by doing something—when you get into trouble you make history! I like recording things, I suppose that's what history is. Geography is sort of history when it's studying the evolution of the earth and things like that. It *was* a load of old dates, wasn't it—well so my mother and teacher say, but you watch it on TV nowadays! I like looking up dates as well. It's not just when battles were and when kings changed, when you make something it's history or when the dodo died out that was history as well. I think history is rather a useful thing to know about because it has all sorts of things crammed into one—because the evolution of man is history.'

(b) Girl: IQ 148, social class II
'Events that have happened before, everything is history, something that happened yesterday is history; it doesn't really go in history books till a long time afterwards. History can go right back to cave men up to within living memory and lots of times in very old history only archaeology can tell us a bit about it. It's a lesson taught at school, also a lot of people find out about it at home; each different country has a different history and history, normally, does one country at a time in the book, and at school we are only taught the history of our own country.'

(c) Girl: IQ 148, social class III, manual
'It's the study of things in the past, usually you've got to find remains of these things that would help to establish what happened and what people did. This is why they excavate where people are buried to find out more about them, and then find out how we developed.'

(d) Boy: IQ 131, social class II
He conveyed awareness of the continuity of time with acknowledgment of change by comparison and causal explanations.

'Well, it's the study of past times, explaining how people lived, how they evolved; how towns and clothes differ from nowadays. I expect in the future they'll be more different.'

(e) Boy: IQ 154, social class II (see Science 1a)
'History is the story of bygone times, of the past, bringing events

together to form a chain reaction and a study of the development of
various things, for instance, science, the development of science through
the ages, how in the early days very little was known of doctoring,
and how it's gradually become so sophisticated, and so much is known
of it now. History is the development of civilisations in other words.'

CATEGORY 2
These answers contained some of the higher level concepts of the subject
but the children did not manage to phrase them in such inclusive
generalisations as in category 1.

(*a*) Boy: IQ 127, social class III, manual
'History is when we learn about things that happened a long time ago
out of the past, and all the people who lived then—their clothes and
transport, and what they were like at that time. History's things about
yesterday—it's from yesterday right back to the beginning.'

(*b*) Girl: IQ 128, social class I
'It's what happened quite a long time ago—things that you know from
various diaries and things, like Pepys's *Diary*. It tells us what went on
quite a long time ago, and how we have improved, and how life was in
those days—how they cut off heads and hung them—they used to think
people were witches, you know, and hanged them.'

(*c*) Boy: IQ 129, social class III, manual
'It's going back in the ages and finding out information about dates and
what happened. About people long ago and finding out what it was like
to live in them days and finding out about all the battles and things like
that. Finding out about creatures which lived long ago, by bones in the
ground, finding out the shapes of the creatures and finding how man
developed, by the shapes of the skulls from apes till they gradually
formed like our skulls.'

(*d*) Girl: IQ 128, social class II
'Finding out about things that have happened before your time or
during your time, but in the past. Like Anne Boleyn and Henry the
Eighth and that—about people like Francis Chichester—they've made
history because they were the first ones to go round the world—and
Francis Drake. There are people who have made records of things that
have happened—and they've put it down in books so we read about it
and get our own ideas.'

(*e*) Boy: IQ 146, social class II
He tried to convey the idea of the passage of time.
'It's things about the past tense—wars—kings that came to the throne,
and special things that happened—it's all about the past tense—right
back to the ice age, coming forwards slowly—cars are invented, and

then trains, after this, more aeroplanes, and coming on, coming more modern jets, and slowly forming into what's now.'

CATEGORY 3

These answers referred to the past in a more global sense and the activity of finding out was more personally orientated to their own learning.

(a) Girl: IQ 131, social class II
'Well, it's sort of learning about people that lived before you do or what's done before in the past or something. The sort of history you do is when something big happens like there's a war or sometimes you have them or kings and queens, people like that, or people who killed a king or if a king gets executed or something. In a sense you could say that what you did last week was a kind of history, but, um, the kind of history you write down is sort of big things that happen.'

(b) Boy: IQ 131, social class III, non-manual
'When you look back into the past. Find out things that went on in the past, like tracing your family tree. Historical events, battles and things like that.'

(c) Girl: IQ 125, social class II
'The study of the past and the people that lived before us, and how they lived, what they looked like, what sort of houses they lived in, what weapons and things they used.'

(d) Boy: IQ 146, social class I
'Finding out about the past. The history of famous people and what they did in their life. Your own history—what has happened to you in the past.'

CATEGORY 4

These answers consisted of associated items without co-ordinating concepts.

(a) Boy: IQ 112, social class III, manual
'Dates, learning about people, ancient kings and queens, things of the past, ancient wars.'

(b) Girl: IQ 108, social class III manual
'Things about the past, things about people that were famous, things that they did and who ruled the country then.'

(c) Girl: IQ 108, social class II
'I think it's when you look back into the past and learn about the Vikings and the Romans and ancient things, anything back into the past—lots of people go deep into ancient pottery.'

CATEGORY 5

These items contained one statement of a vague and confused nature, the time references were simple.

(a) Girl: IQ 107, social class IV
'It's about famous people from quite a long time ago if they've done something brave.'

(b) Boy: IQ 112, social class IV
'It happened long ago; well known things; Bonny Prince Charles getting help from Flora McDonald.'

What is geography?

'Geography is concerned with the study of the surface of the earth and of the natural and physical forces which exert their influences on it, in it and around it. It is concerned with the lives of people who inhabit it and particularly with the relationships which are seen to exist between them and their surroundings. From these things a place derives distinctive character. This is the very core of geographical work' (Gospill 1966).

This geographer's definition of his subject gave a model against which the children's attempts could be judged. The most frequent response from this group of children was that geography involved learning about other countries. Some managed to generalise this idea, others referred to specific topics probably connected with their most recent lessons. The children, who gave the responses rated highly, managed to introduce more inclusive generalisations, a wider range of concepts to include different aspects of the subject, and sometimes the activities of comparing and contrasting data. Physical, human and economic geography are represented, but they were, as expected, expressed in an elementary way.

CATEGORY 1

(a) Girl: IQ 131, Verbal IQ 150+, social class II
This was her favourite subject of study in and out of school. She had a longing to travel.

'Geography is a study of life on the surface of the earth and a study of the surface of the earth, divided into lots of countries.'

(b) Boy: IQ 154, social class II (See Science 1a, History 1e)
'Geography is the study of the shape and the composure of the earth's crust, and its surface, and the wind systems of the world; the prominent landmarks that are featured. In geography—positioning something— the latitude and longitudinal system covering the world enables you to define any position you like, and also to show physical features and the nature of the region in question.'

(c) Girl: IQ 141, social class IV

'It's all about places and people and lands, and what sort of people live in certain countries, and how many people there are and what sort of food they eat—what sort of products their countries grow to send to other countries. How certain lands are different to other lands and what seas surround certain lands, and what minerals are found in certain islands and countries—about certain people and tribes that live in countries and the sort of food they eat and how they dress, and their beliefs and religions, what gods they worship—what religion there is in the country.'

(d) Boy: IQ 149, social class I

'It's the study of places in the world. How they were built up. How the people live in the places, what type of homes they live in and how they differ from other people in different parts of the world, and also the physical properties of the world, for instance, the mountain ranges of the world, the lakes of the world—the rivers. The people who live by them and how they live.'

(e) Boy: IQ 154, social class I

He showed interest in the different point of view achieved from an aerial position which was considered advanced for this age.

'It's about other countries where they are and what the places are like— what the main produces are, how large they are, and whereabouts situated—which continent it's in—it could be what you use in your own country, industry and things like that. It could be a description of the country, what it looks like from the air, the roads, if it has high mountains or if it's all flat; if it's famous for anything, the language the people talk and the sizes of population.'

CATEGORY 2

These answers were above average in the extent of subject matter they included rather than the level of generalization in which they were couched.

(a) Boy: IQ 132, social class II

'Study of the layout of things, of the land and places like Russia, how where the hills are, and where the rivers are and where the sea is, where the mountains are, where the roads are, where the towns and houses and villages and hamlets are—where anything is that's on the ground or under the sea, where the sea stops and begins, how deep it is.'

(b) Boy: IQ 149, social class II

'Well—there's many things to do with geography—learning about physical geography, and the ordinary, country geography—to do with other countries. When I said "physical geography", I mean about—not knowing what things are—if you are going to go around England on a

tour or something, you'll need a certain map to find out what things are
—like a bay or a delta or something—Ordnance Survey reading, and
then again, the ordinary country maps—oil and iron and all that—
sugar beet.'

(c) Girl: IQ 129, social class II
'It may be maps, and different discoveries, and things around us in the
world—and what different places are like, what sort of things were
discovered there, and what sort of imports and exports come from and
go to countries. Other parts of the world and how they live, and what the
surroundings are.'

(d) Girl: IQ 128, social class IV
'Geography is learning about other children and other people in other
lands, trying to compare their way of life with our own. Learning about
things in other countries, their produce say, like oranges and things like
that; the animals abroad, like kangaroos and wallabies—how they are
different from our animals, and how they've changed the way of living
in their country. What sort of houses people have abroad, how they're
different, like in Palestine they have flat roofed houses, whitewashed,
with only one floor, and in some places in Africa, they have little huts,
in other places in Africa there are quite big cities.'

(e) Boy: IQ 145, social class III, manual
'Studying maps or making maps. Looking around the world and at
people in other countries. How they live in America and how different
it is over there to what it is over here. It's making maps and going into
detail—what every city is, say, in Lancs, or studying one town and
finding all the references in it.'

CATEGORY 3
References to other countries were elaborated but dealt with as problems
of 'what' rather than 'how'.

(a) Boy: IQ 127, social class III, non-manual
'Learning about other countries—what they wear and what they eat.
What kind of houses they live in and what are their jobs.'

(b) Boy: IQ 152, social class IV
'It's learning about the world and the countries, and finding out where
they are, and what the people are like—what colour skin they've got
and traditions and ways they incorporate in living in that country.
The main thing about geography is looking at maps and finding out
where places are.'

(c) Girl: IQ 132, social class II
'Geography is a study when you're given something to do like find out
about wool—you find out how it is made, where it came from, and

everything that can be made from it. Finding out all sorts of things like coal and steel and iron, and that they are made into things that are needed. You usually find out information from other lands and do the subject at school.'

(*d*) Girl: IQ 124, social class II
'Learning about the world, about different countries, different towns and if there's anything of real importance going on in certain places. Learning about different types of people in the countries, about their ways of living.'

CATEGORY 4

The contents of recent lessons dominated these answers.

(*a*) Girl: IQ 124, social class IV
'It's all about other places, seas—when you learn where we are and things like that, and like if you're learning about Africa, you learn about where it is, if it's near us or whether there's a famous sea in it, or just something like that. At school we hear about geography on the wireless, but it's quite different from that because we have got a book, we get one every term, and it's got all the programmes that you're going to hear about every week and there is one called 'Oranges from Spain' and it told you all about the oranges from Spain, and how they collect them and wash them and all things like that, and we've just—how they eat them. Well, they've got three different programmes in that—one was on Italy, I can't remember where the other two were, but that's the kind of geography we learn at school.'

(*b*) Boy: IQ 115, social class III, manual
'It's about other countries—the atlas—finding out about things— things what grow in other countries and the animals.'

(*c*) Boy: IQ 124, social class IV
'You get something that's made in the world, and you see, it's put in books—rubber plantations and cotton plantations—that's geography. Geography tells us how—how they make it and how they turn it into cotton. Wool, geography is how they get it off and purify it, and make woollen clothes with strands of wool.'

CATEGORY 5

Short, specific, crudely expressed responses.

(*a*) Girl: IQ 116, social class III, non-manual
'I think it's a thing you have to do from maps.'

(*b*) Boy: IQ 109, social class IV
'It's maps that show you pictures of maps and all round the world what it's like.'

What is mathematics?

This was the most difficult of the definitions as far as the children were concerned. The nature of the subject which deals with abstractions from an individual's actions and transformations on objects rather than abstractions from the properties of objects themselves, defied the generalising power of even the brightest children. What they were left to do was to describe the subject as they had experienced it, the most able children managing to include more aspects of its content than others, or to show that they were aware of wider applications of the subject beyond the classroom.

CATEGORY 1

(a) Girl IQ 132, social class II
This was the nearest a child got to explaining the abstract nature of the subject.

'Learning about figures, and how to know how to work things out, and how to understand how things are made, but there's a lot of things in maths which are possible written down on paper, but *not* when you do it in real life, for instance, if it's written down on paper, if you travel faster than the speed of light, you can travel backwards in time, but it isn't possible really, because if you did that, and you landed in the middle of yesterday, it wouldn't be possible because yesterday you were still here, and you didn't start, so it isn't possible—but it is when it's written down on paper. There are lots of things like that.'

(b) Boy: IQ 154, social class III, manual (see History 1b)
He had a strong bias towards mathematics and science.

'Mathematics is a study of how numbers behave in fact, and you can add them up, subtract, multiply them, and divide them. You can do anything you want with a number, you can do equations by balancing numbers, and algebra uses letters and figures instead of numbers. A study of numbers.'

(c) Girl: IQ 128, social class IV (see Geography 2d)
'I think mathematics is a form of calculating, working out things, puzzling them and trying to find out for yourself without other people helping you. Maths is often adding up, subtraction, division, and multiplication, yet there's modern maths where you get all sorts of things, measurement, weight, capacity, and all things like that. Finding out different things we learn something new every time, keeping it as informal as possible. I think maths should be made more interesting.'

(d) Boy: IQ 154, social class III, manual
He generalised by giving wide limits to the range of applicability.

'Mathematics is arithmetic and other forms of adding, multiplication, division, take away, algebra. It's like adding two and two together—

it's numbers or signs added together to make an end product or something—it can tell you the speed of a rocket—the number of yards in the school playground. It can tell you the gravitational pull, to how high a tree is; it's the adding up and taking away of anything that's what it all boils down to isn't it? Adding and taking away, to show distances, area, or perimeter, height.'

(*e*) Boy: IQ 140, social class III, non-manual (see Science 1*e*)
'It's the way different things are worked out and how problems are worked out, and the way the country keeps itself stable. It's a way of keeping track of time and money and things like that. How things have been worked out and how they became what they are. It's the scientific definition of different things. It's a subject to help you work things out, help different people work things out and how they, well, how they managed to solve different problems. It's a way of measuring things.'

CATEGORY 2
These children managed to recall several aspects of mathematics indicating a range wider than basic processes and skills.

(*a*) Girl: IQ 144, social class II
She viewed the subject in terms of knowledge and understanding.

'I think it's calculating things not for the sake of calculation, but to develop your mind sort of thing. It helps you—adds to your knowledge of figures and symbols and what they represent. Maths is finding out how you work things out not necessarily by being told how, but understanding why you did it.'

(*b*) Boy: IQ 121, social class III, non-manual
The beginning of an awareness of the differences between science and mathematics was shown.

'It's adding two and two together and making four. I'd say it's finding out again. It's being given something to do, and you have to write it out on paper. I'd say mathematics is different from science, because you do science with your hands, more than you do mathematics—with mathematics you do it with your brain, and then you write it down, and then you read it out, but in science you apply to your brain what you see, and then you write about it, by yourself, you don't have a book in front of you.'

(*c*) Girl: IQ 107, social class II
'Mathematics is the study where you've always got to know, and no matter what you do in life—you've always got to have mathematics study behind you. If you are a cashier, you have to know money sums and that; mathematics is a part of anyone's life, so it's good to have the experience behind you. It's the study of numbers and facts, and the

facts are about numbers, and the basic thing in it, in the study about it, is the know-how of the technique to know what you are doing.'

(*d*) Boy: IQ 141, social class III, manual
'It's being able to multiply, divide, add and subtract, and work out problems, know the names of shapes and how to find area, measuring subjects. Maths comes into a lot of subjects—in science and chemistry you work out the different formulas, and sometimes that involves maths—it comes into geography sometimes.'

(*e*) Girl: IQ 154, social class III, manual
'Arithmetic and sums and problems and numbers and drawings—figures put together to mean things, signs and symbols. Way of writing in not so many different letters to bring it down to—four to power of—whatever it was—a way of working out problems using numbers instead of using words.'

CATEGORY 3

The responses described various activities carried out in a lesson.

(*a*) Girl: IQ 125, social class III, manual (see Science 3*a*)
'Well, you couldn't really say it's figures because it's not all figures, you could have mathematics anywhere—say whether that corner is a right-angle or how long that is or how wide it is, and whether these are right-angled triangles or whether they are equilateral triangles—things like that. How wide this is, what the diameter is, what the circumference is—anything, really. You can just have mathematics saying how many people can fit into the church hall or how many people fit in a bus—things like that, you know.'

(*b*) Boy: IQ 129, social class III, manual
'Mathematics is the study of numbers, all different things about numbers. There's a lot of different types of maths. Mathematics can help you in your work in lots of different ways. Certain types of maths help certain types of people in their work.'

(*c*) Girl: IQ 120, social class III, manual
'It's doing sums and finding out how many things there are and how much they weigh and working out how many things you need for people. Finding out how much things cost and adding up money from a till in the shop.'

(*d*) Boy: IQ 132, social class III, manual
'It's really like discovering about numbers, and how much a certain container would hold—it includes volume, capacity, weight and length. It's discovering about those things and learning tables about them.'

CATEGORY 4

The previous category gave examples of children referring to what they did in school, but there was some attempt to indicate that certain activities on the part of the learner were called for. The following responses list the processes involved without relation to the learner or application.

(a) Boy: IQ 121, social class IV
'It's like—to see how you get on at school—they see if you can do hard sums or easy sums. You do problems, times, take away, addition, subtract and divide.'

(b) Girl: IQ 123, social class V
'Numbers added together, objects added. Capacity and weight, the amount of anything.'

(c) Boy: IQ 128, social class IV
'Mathematics is another word for arithmetic, but it isn't arithmetic like sums just adding numbers together, it deals with angles, triangles and shapes and degrees and things like that.'

CATEGORY 5

(a) Boy: IQ 109, social class IV
'It's sums and mental and that, shows you how to count and yer tables so's you can do sums.'

(b) Girl: IQ 109, social class IV
'All kinds of sums, questions and that. You have to know quite a lot of mathematics to go places and see things.'

What is art?

The children found this one of the easiest definitions, they mostly answered with greater confidence, but not necessarily greater knowledge. Few managed to come outside the activities of painting and drawing in which they engaged at home and school to take a more general look at art as a subject. And yet the definitions judged to be of the highest level were remarkably perceptive for young children, they showed insight into the nature of processes within an artist's mind and some sense of standards and skill required for excellence in the field.

CATEGORY 1

The highest level answers expressed something of the aesthetic and psychological aspects of the subject in abstract terms. These were connected if not related functionally to each other. The idea of communication was further abstracted by reference to the nature of symbols.

(a) Girl: IQ 128, social class IV (see Geography 2d, Mathematics 1c)
She was considered gifted in art by her parents and teachers. She was

quite conversant with different schools of art and brought art history books to the interview to represent her main interest.

'I think you can put down art as feeling structures. I think you can construct something out of modern art, you put a few things together to construct something, and then make it into a picture, although most people, older people probably, think that art is doing, drawing something, which it really isn't. I think your mind is constructing something and then putting it on paper and building up from that—sometimes you get a bit of paper and you just start a pattern, and if it resembles something you go on to draw the actual picture—bright colours should be used to show happiness and gaiety, but I think the more dramatic pictures should be in black and white, preferably charcoal.'

(b) Boy: IQ 143, social class II
'Putting your own thoughts on paper. Creating images on paper with your hands and pencil and paints. Putting ideas on paper and creating things with paint. It doesn't necessarily have to be on paper—sculpture is art and an architect has to have an artistic mind, you know, if he wants to make nice buildings. Everybody should be able to appreciate art. Lots of people have artistic minds and everybody is good at drawing except me!'

(c) Girl: IQ 128, social class II
This girl was considered gifted in art by her parents and teachers. She was one of the few who brought drawings and paintings that were freehand efforts that showed appreciation of the use of colour.

'It's something that you put life into so you can see what you mean by it, and something that looks realistic more than—matchstick people. Art is something a person has in mind—they have something in mind and they're just drawing it and something that is original—that they've made up by themselves and nobody else has—something that's different from everyone else's. They have their own ideas instead of copying.'

(d) Boy: IQ 139, social class II
'It's a sort of picture, it could be a model, something to look at something made, created and drawn, shaped, different colours to it, schemes—things in the foreground, in the background, the actual things that are in it, you bring to life, another model, a new world it could be. It's shape and making an object and something very new—if it was in the way of a model, try and make it different—something that's interesting—what would make someone want to look at it—interesting scenery with the sky —or just a picture of something, a sketch of a living thing.'

(e) Boy: IQ 154, social class II (see Science 1b, History 1e, Geography 1b)
'Art is the study of cultural works, particularly paintings and drawing. Colour schemes are a very important part of it, and the idea of collecting

a focal point in the design. Representing things by colour and making a picture *move* even, by the way it's put over, if it looks harsh and sharp, or soft and easy. Art is the portrayal of moods by various tones and colours and designs.'

CATEGORY 2

The responses of the most able definers in this subject began to show a clear differentiation between the psychological activities and philosophic functions which delimit the subject. In this category usually one or the other aspect was focused on. Some children raised the issue of imagination and originality, others saw the communication value of art, a few referred to the aesthetic/expressive nature of the subject.

(*a*) Girl: IQ 137, social class I
This child was acknowledged to be musical and artistic by her parents.

'Art is a way of drawing what you think—painting and, making something that you've seen and like what you've imagined, so that other people can imagine it the same as you do.'

(*b*) Boy: IQ 140, social class III, non-manual (see Science 1*e*, Mathematics 1*e*)
'Art is the different way things are formed and what their shape is—it's a way of describing talent. It's a subject, how artists paint—they have artistic minds, a way of making beautiful things. It's what paintings and music and sculpture is.'

(*c*) Girl: IQ 144, social class II
'Art is a thing when you don't really have to use the part of your brain that makes you have to work hard, a time when you can enjoy yourself more, express yourself more—art—if I said "paint a picture about spring" you could use your imagination about spring. Art is sort of a talent and skill to do it like—cavemen—you can be a sculptor, or anything like that, but it's hard to make people understand what it's about—an old piece of brass with holes through it could mean a lot to a sculptor, but to other people it's just a piece of brass.'

(*d*) Boy: IQ 127, social class III, non-manual
'Sketching and painting—reviewing things you've done, or something you might have seen or just done with a paint brush or a pencil, or anything like that—fingers. Art is sort of describing something—describing something in a picture without words.'

(*e*) Girl: IQ 128, social class II
She executed skilful freehand drawings and complained that people would not believe she had not traced them.

'Just trying to capture a scene—a scene that wouldn't stay for ever so you have to draw it to keep it there. Beautiful and interesting things, nature—not being able to keep it like it is. If you go on holiday and see a beautiful scene, then if you paint it, you can remember what it looks like. Nature—painting the wild life which again won't stand still.'

CATEGORY 3

The majority of children managed to elaborate on at least one major aspect of art. The idea of representation was the most popular, with the allied ideas of the permanent recording of the likenesses of people and objects, and the fact that the subject had a history.

Just emerging in some children was the idea of standards required in the various activities sometimes as skills of the artist or of psychological processes such as 'creating'. Some categorical terms were used such as 'natural'—'abstract'—'old'—'modern'.

(a) Girl: IQ 150, social class II
'It's painting and drawing and designing and patterns. Drawing and painting things—sort of—so that you can see things that are not really there—say you painted a flower one day and it was dead the next—you'd still be able to see it as it was.'

(b) Boy: IQ 125, social class III, non-manual
'It is marking on paper or drawing on paper, things you see or things you have seen and get ideas from in order to make up something, and you keep that in record by drawing it down, writing it down, in a shape and form. If you're copying something from the landscape somewhere, you can remember what it was like if you have to look back at that picture. It stands for something you see it yourself—you see if you can get what you're drawing—art, or a painting—to match the things you're copying, that you've got in your head.'

(c) Boy: IQ 127, social class III, manual
'Art is painting, painting pictures of scenes and people and animals, creating scenes on paper or canvas.'

(d) Girl: IQ 131, social class II
'It's a subject with a lot of interest in it, you can sort of put feeling into the picture. I suppose it's got many different ways of using art— advertising, illustrating books, posters, things like that. It depends which way you use it—it could be sculpture, painting, drawing, could be needlework, sort of craft, modelling aeroplanes and things and designing.'

CATEGORY 4

These responses expressed simple and straightforward ideas on the activities of drawing and painting, the emphasis was on the manual rather than the mental processes involved.

(*a*) Boy: IQ 130, social class III, manual
'Drawing and painting, designing things or copying a picture. You learn how to draw and paint and learn how to blend colours to get a certain colour you want.'

(*b*) Girl: IQ 121, social class II
'A thing in which you draw and paint. You draw pictures of houses and rivers and countrysides.'

(*c*) Boy: IQ 134, social class I
Says he is not creative; he is trying to overcome this by choosing to paint.

'Art is using your hands to make something, it could be a painting, it could be a statue . . . it could be a lot of other things which you use your hands to do.'

CATEGORY 5
These responses were brief and elementary.

(*a*) Girl: IQ 117, social class V
'A thing you do with your hands and a paintbrush and use a paintbox.'

(*b*) Boy: IQ 117, social class II
'It's what we do—like painting.'

What is poetry?
There was as wide a range of responses to this question as there was to the other subjects. The children who seemed to have the clearest general idea of poetry managed to abstract and describe both the psychological and aesthetic aspects. The average response indicated that a conceptual difference between prose and poetry had been made and it was appreciated that poetry had its own form and enjoyment as a recreative or creative activity. The poorest responses focused only on the one specific aspect of rhyming.

CATEGORY 1
These answers attempted to relate both expressive and aesthetic ideas. The children took into account the processes within the poet or his audience and related this to the specific criteria by which poetry is judged.

(*a*) Girl: IQ 144, social class II (see Art 2*c*)
This girl liked writing and had already produced a novel and many poems.

'Poetry is English, one of the things—English with rhyming words and capital letters, and a thought on each line of it—it needn't rhyme at all,

it's shorter than writing because it has more expression in it. I think
that poets have a very hard life, because different people have different
opinions on their poems—it's always hard for people who work at that
sort of thing. Poets are like sculptors—they see what they make a poem
about—can imagine and see something out of the stone.'

(b) Boy: IQ 146, social class III, non-manual (see History 1a)
'It's not just making a thing up which rhymes—it's perhaps describing
something in the best possible way—like saying a river is silvery green—
like that, not saying "a river is like a dinner or a duck" or something
like that. Most olden day poets make things rhyme, but nowadays
they tend to forget about rhyming and get down to describing more.'

(c) Girl: IQ 128, social class IV (see Geography 2d, Maths 1c, Art 1a)
'Thoughts being put into verse—I think that if a person goes down say
to a very poor place, where there are rats going round on the floor, and
people haven't any money to live, and they put that into words and
express feelings like that, and try to get through to others; sometimes the
first time you can't really understand it, and then it grows more deep
as you read it—I don't think poetry necessarily has to rhyme. I prefer
the poetry that doesn't rhyme.'

(d) Boy: IQ 154, social class II (see Science 1b, History 1e, Geography
1b, Art 1e)
'Poetry is similar to art, but this time it's described in words, this again
portrays the mood, a good poem is not necessarily eloquent, but well
phrased, and put over correctly, in the right way, and the mood again is
passed over—it's just an amusing form of composition or speech—a
cultural form of composition or speech.'

(e) Girl: IQ 133, social class II
'Like an art—a way of putting down words till they make a picture of
something, that's a way to express yourself isn't it—sometimes it sounds
very beautiful, but sometimes it can be funny. A lot of beautiful poems
are about nature; some poems rhyme, they don't have to to make a
good poem, words—they have to keep working at the poem until they
have got it exactly right.'

CATEGORY 2

The responses elaborated on the psychological or the philosophical
aspects of the subject. The qualitative use of language was appreciated
and its communicative value. Aesthetically standards were required
and enjoyment was seen as part of poetry's function.

(a) Girl: IQ 137, social class I
'I think poetry is someone expressing the thoughts of the poet—their
thoughts about something in a manner that will in a way rhyme, and
you can enjoy reading it perhaps more than if it were ordinary writing.

I like the way it rhymes and the way it's put together, and the things people write about in poetry, I like nature—poetry about flowers and animals and things like that.'

(*b*) Boy: IQ 140, social class III, manual
'The ability to use words that make a meaning in some sort of form, and that fits together nicely. Setting things out in a distinguishable manner— you know what it *is* and what it *means*.'

(*c*) Girl: IQ 117, social class V
The family believed it had a famous poet in its ancestry.

'It's like a story, but sometimes it rhymes, and sometimes it doesn't. It puts ideas into your head—what it's like. It doesn't sound boring, it says it in a different way; instead of saying, well, "Spring" for instance, if you talk about "Spring" it sounds a bit boring, but when you write a poem about spring, it doesn't sound like that. It sounds—how shall I say it, it's gay, it puts words in your mouth you wouldn't put in your story about it.'

(*d*) Boy: IQ 149, social class I
'It's making out of words into several lines which have a basic beat to each line and the beat does not vary from piece to piece in one poem, it usually has a general pattern of lines. For instance, four to each verse of poetry which is a group of lines. Quite often the poetry has rhyming words at the end of each line which makes it more interesting. Words which originally have been spelt one way have quite often been changed into a poetical sense of the word which is quite often quite different. It must be a bit difficult doing all that writing. The greatest poets have been Shakespeare—who was born in Stratford on Avon, in the fifteenth century—Browning and Keats, and several other good poets. There are several books made up of poetry containing a selection of poems either by one person or by several people. There are nonsense poems, sense poems and also poems which convey to you what things are like. Edward Lear is one of the best known writers of nonsense poems.'

(*e*) Girl: IQ 125, social class III, manual
'Well, it doesn't need to be rhyming, I like it better when it does, but it doesn't need to—just a poetical way of saying anything really—going a long way round. Some people, poets, they don't write in rhymes, they just sort of write in lines and make it sort of sound well together. When you're reading poetry it's different from just reading an ordinary book. You can tell it's poetry—I know it's in lines and all that, but it joins together and it fits and it sounds nice together.'

CATEGORY 3

(*a*) Boy: IQ 129, social class III, manual
'A way of telling a story in a few words. They write about things and it's

more interesting than it would be if you just wrote about it on a piece of paper. Poetry is more interesting. You can write about something like leaves falling off trees. It would look stupid if you just wrote that down on a piece of paper, but poetry makes sense.'

(b) Boy: IQ 132, social class I
'Sort of doing phrases and words which go together—to make up a piece of work that people can read and they like—not necessarily rhyming.'

(c) Boy: IQ 112, social class IV
'Words like a song really, they're sung. They have words that rhyme, and you can get enjoyment from them. You can write poems yourself, you can listen to it.'

(d) Boy: IQ 125, social class III, non-manual
'It is forming words that match, and when you recite and speak it, it sounds nice to listen to, because it matches, and it's interesting to listen to.'

CATEGORY 4

In this category children listed things associated with poetry, i.e. kinds of poems or poets. The reference to meaning (i.e. describing or telling a story) suggested a first level idea on the communicative aspect. Rhythm was introduced as well as rhyme as a component.

(a) Girl: IQ 104, social class II
'Getting a rhythm in words and trying to get words rhyming, and well, making a rhythm.'

(b) Boy: IQ 132, social class III, manual
'It's usually in rhythm, sometimes it doesn't make sense, sometimes it tells a story—nonsense poems—and you learn, with help, how to write your own poems.'

(c) Boy: IQ 140, social class III, non-manual
He was interested in prose but not poetry.
'Lines of writing that kind of rhyme or not, as long as they have a good beat.'

CATEGORY 5

Abstraction of rhyme and tautologous statement.
(a) Boy: IQ 109, social class IV
'Poetry is writing that rhymes.'

(b) Girl: IQ 108, social class III, manual
'Things people put together, words they put together and make a poem.'

Summary

The ways in which the children tackled these questions and the awareness of some of them of the level of intellectual complexity they represent provided clues to personal interests and preferences, previous educational opportunities and degrees of confidence in the grasp of material being learned. As in other tests where there was a heavy reliance on verbal ability, the children in the non-manual social classes had an advantage. However, it was not verbal facility alone that was meant to reveal the more able children, but the more complex conceptual ideas they could express. If more refined techniques of marking could be produced with, for instance, standardised lists of the levels of difficulty to be anticipated for the concepts in different subjects, teachers would be helped in their assessment of the most able pupils who, even at eleven years of age, can show that they are beginning to apprehend what a subject's purposes are rather than what it is about.

13. Case histories

Introduction

It was difficult to know which children to select for presentation in some detail. There was a wealth of data available on each one, and every case history was interesting in that it told a progressive story of the triumphs and successes as well as of the trials and tribulations, of an individual from birth to 11 years of age.

As the results suggested that the most intelligent children had factors associated with health, home and education in their favour it seemed appropriate to present four portraits of successful children. David and Mark stand as examples of the highly intelligent boys doing well in everything at school, and so full of personal interests at home that it was to be wondered at how they fitted everything into their day. Sharon and Paula represent the highly intelligent, lively and active girls.

Edward's was a different story because, though perhaps the cleverest of all the children interviewed, he was in some ways in difficulty. He revealed some of the signs of maladjustment that are sometimes quoted as typical of gifted children, such as manual clumsiness, unsociability, erratic behaviour. But there was evidence in his case which demonstrated how careful one must be about attributing difficulties solely to exceptional intelligence.

John was chosen to represent those children who have least opportunity of being identified as gifted. It was fortunate that his mother, when given the opportunity, brought him to our notice. The unanswerable question must remain in our minds as to how many such children remained undiscovered in our whole national cohort.

DAVID

Identified as 'gifted' on attainments at 7 years of age. (Group 5) Wechsler Intelligence Test: Full scale IQ 149, Verbal 155, Performance, 129.
Reading test at 11 years   Top 1 per cent of age group
Mathematics test at 11 years   Top 1 per cent of age group
Favourite subjects: science, mathematics, music (no subject boring)

Interests: science, painting, drawing, reading, collecting, music, pets, sports, clubs, TV.

Not interested in: making things, inventing games.

Social class II

At birth

David was a firstborn child; all the circumstances of his birth were normal. His father was a research engineer and his mother had been a technical assistant. Both parents went to grammar school and left at sixteen, but went on to further education later.

David was described as being slow to sit up, walk and talk as a baby and to have been shy and fearful of new situations as a little boy.

At 7 years of age

David cried himself to sleep for 2 weeks before starting school at 5, but once there all signs of distress disappeared. He made good progress and was rated at 7 by his teachers as in the top 5 per cent of his age group in oral ability, awareness of the world, reading, creative skills and number work. He was completely at home with adults and children. He had a series of throat ailments throughout his infant school career but was cured of these by 7.

David had a brother two years younger than himself.

At 11 years of age

INTERVIEWER'S REPORT

David was very tall and of strong physique for his age. He was most attractive in looks and manner. He was relaxed during the inerview, he enjoyed it and carried it along co-operatively. He made a quick start on anything mathematical, and was able to do the whole difficult logic test. He was slower on tests concerning words, but he had a sensitivity to sounds and meanings and a fluency that enabled him to talk his way round things he found difficult. He seemed mature in almost every way except for expressed irritation with his younger brother.

His awareness of himself in the interview situation and his occasional references to this were surprising for the degree of objectivity with which he could view himself and others. His tremendous enthusiasm for his interests and his willingness to elaborate on every fact and idea made his one of the most rewarding interviews, it could have lasted for many more hours than was allowed.

SCHOOL REPORT

David was rated in the top 5 per cent of his age group on general knowledge, use of books, mathematics and oral ability. His teachers considered him exceptional in natural science and saw him as a boy who needed the challenge of difficult work. They made special provision for him by giving him an 'enriched' curriculum and individual attention. He had no adjustment problems.

PARENT'S INTERVIEW

INTERVIEWER: Could you tell me something about David, what's he like, what sort of a person is he?

MOTHER: He's rather sensitive, takes things to heart rather a lot. He worries about new things even now when he has learned to cope more. I know he'll worry when he changes schools, will he know where to go, what will he have to take and so on. He gives the appearance of being very confident but I do not think he is underneath. When he was playing the recorder at a school concert, he was very worried. Other people thought how confident he looked. It's us and the people who are close to him, like his teacher, who notice it now. I think his self-confidence has been bolstered up because most of the things he has set out to do he has achieved. If he'd been a slow child, a sense of failure could have really hurt. He likes to do things well—I suppose all children do. When he did this double jump of class last year he worked and worked and worked to make up. When he first came here he was behind the others and got very tired until he caught up. He's mad if he can't do things. He can't stand a lot of teasing either, he takes it from the family but he's not keen from outsiders. He's good company now, he's past the real childhood stage and you can talk to him as a person, as opposed to a child. He's old enough to understand things. You don't have to talk down to him or play down to him in games. He's self-contained, he doesn't need other people's companionship, he enjoys it if he's got it, but it doesn't worry him if he hasn't.

INTERVIEWER: Tell me something about his interests.

MOTHER: He's not easily bored, he likes books so he doesn't need company. He has a chemistry set and enjoys doing experiments. He's good with his hands and terribly awkward at the same time. My husband bought him a Meccano before he started school, I thought he was too young but he could make things. He reads a lot about chemistry and gardening at the moment. He's read practically every one of Gerald Durrell and Peter Scott's books. He's a keen member of the children's section of the Royal Ornithological Society. He's good at things he's particularly interested in because he has a wide knowledge. For years he's been interested in ornithology, between us we have a lot of general knowledge of the countryside but he's teaching me about birds now. He is able, he seems to have powers of concentration because he's interested, not because he's got a flair for a thing. He can spend hours concentrating on one thing whereas other children would get fed up.

INTERVIEWER: Does he enjoy school?

MOTHER: Yes. Before he started he cried himself to sleep for a fortnight, but there's not been a sign of this since. It was the fear of the unknown. It's a good school, it has expanded a lot in the last few years. They have a well-qualified and good staff. There are high standards, I think, and a wide cross-section of children.

INTERVIEWER: What kind of secondary school would you like him to go to?

MOTHER: We're hoping he'll pass the eleven-plus and go to grammar school. We want him to be able to go on and do what he wants to do. To do the things he wants now means university and I think that still means grammar school.

INTERVIEWER: Do you think he is highly intelligent or gifted?

MOTHER: He's very intelligent. He has enormous powers of concentration which have brought him to the top. In the past I've never thought of him as being out of the ordinary though the impression other people give is that he is so clever. I don't think he has that extra flair but he has powers of concentration and memory. He's consistently at the top of the class, that doesn't mean anything out of the ordinary when people are good in ways he isn't. I wouldn't want him to get big-headed. I don't think he's any brighter than a lot of the children at school are. I think he'll make the eleven-plus. He's widely read. You just don't know what is ability and what is acquired do you? For instance, when he started stamp collecting he learned quite a lot about geography. He has a tremendous interest and I do think it has got him a long way. It's given him a good general knowledge. Again, when he has asked things and I've felt he could find out for himself, I've let him. It helps them to try to find out. What's ability and what's knowledge, I don't know.

INTERVIEWER: Have you thought what kind of work you would like him to do?

MOTHER: Well, there'll be no persuasion from either of us. He's interested in natural history but it's something we don't know much about. We would give him complete choice. I'd like to think he has a happy home life eventually.

DAVID'S INTERVIEW

INTERVIEWER: Tell me about your interests.

DAVID: Oil painting. I haven't done very many. I've only got about twenty colours and bits of canvas, but that's what I use. I've always been interested in birds, it's probably one of my favourite hobbies and I've got used to the colorations of some of these. Of course, the duck's my favourite group and this is one of the birds that is commonly seen where I live. (*He shows a painting.*)

It's a shelduck that one. There was one on the dub a little while ago— which is the pond, sorry, you know, you go along and say, 'Have you seen the dub' and nobody knows what you mean! (*He shows another painting.*) Shelducks again and a tufted duck which is very similar, but then I wasn't very good at drawing birds, I had only just started, you see, and I'd got only this one method—wings straight down. There, I've got the wings coming over like that, one slightly down as if it's gliding.

I can get several different methods, if you look at it slightly sideways on you can see the wings are just slightly too wide. I didn't look at it sideways when I was doing it, I just did it from memory. Just to check on the colouring I had to look in my identification book.

INTERVIEWER: Who taught you oil painting?

DAVID: Nobody. First of all I always liked drawing and painting birds since I was little, if I liked them I liked drawing them. So, I decided that I would try and get myself an oil painting set. Well, I was lucky because one of my uncles was out with us and my brother said how much he liked this pencil case, and I was very lucky because he got that and so I had my choice.

INTERVIEWER: How did you become interested in birds?

DAVID: It was in 1964 I think, for a Xmas present I got some books of birds, Dad knew a little and Mum was learning so they started me on it. Now, I already enjoyed reading an awful lot so I got the idea about a few birds, and between books and Mum and Dad I began to learn.

INTERVIEWER: You know a lot about birds?

DAVID: Quite a bit. Yes, I should think I know quite a bit. Put it this way, if anyone wants to know anything in our school about birds he just comes straight to me.

INTERVIEWER: Do you learn biology at school?

DAVID: Well, we don't do biology on the whole. I'd like to do this, I'd awfully like it. We do a little bit, the trouble is I know it mostly. We do science, but we don't do that type of science, our headmaster usually sticks to more basic experiments before we go on to more specialised subjects. Now I'm at the top of the school and I'll be going to a different school next year, I hope to be able to do biology when I go to my new school.

INTERVIEWER: What else have you brought to talk about?

DAVID: Silver, I'm very interested. This is a pocket watch which I thought you might like to see. I think I worked it out at 1759 by the silver mark, I'm not sure, but we're pretty certain it's eighteenth century.

This other one I think is Victorian. This bit should open to show the workings but I've never managed to open it. This doesn't work now, but there's a beautiful silver marking there. I'll see if I can remember what it is. That is Sterling silver, isn't it? Tiger's face, that is London and B I can't remember what that—I think it might have been 1759 or something like that. Beautiful isn't it? I love just looking at the time.

INTERVIEWER: I'm glad you brought them along.

DAVID: It's awfully difficult to know. You think you are going to have a formal interview with somebody. I hadn't an idea what an interview was like really. I've seen people being interviewed on the television and

'Sorry we've got no time now'—and that's that. Anyhow, what else have I got. I've got my stamp album. This has got mainly Great Britain. If you'd like to look all the way through them.

INTERVIEWER: Where did you get them all from?

DAVID: Now then, this is very hard because I just can't remember where I got some of them from. I bought some from a dealer. I got several others from several other different places. Now, these dates aren't very accurate. I used a simplified catalogue and now I've got a British Commonwealth catalogue which is not simplified in the slightest and has got all the proper dates to the nearest day, so they're not at all accurate. Some of these are rather valuable actually, I was rather surprised. That one there is worth about £3 believe it or not.

INTERVIEWER: Any more interests?

DAVID: I've got a lot of interests. I've got some stones which I've collected—very nice ones. These are my best. That has some beautiful crystals and quartz in it. I found this, this Easter, on top of a place—Allan Crag—it's one of the mountains. I like going walking. All the family go walking an awful lot. We found it—there was a lot of snow in the winter and it was awfully snowy and we found this deposit. There are some beautiful crystals. There is a nice perfect one just in there, do you see? It is six-pointed. They are all quartz. That's called milky quartz when it's not transparent. They are called rock crystal if they are transparent. I found a fossil on the beach one day when I was out. I split it open so that it can be seen better. If you look—these, in my experience of geology, I think are pretty certain to be the stems of lilies which used to grow. Then, I think there's little bits of shell and things which makes me think it's about one hundred and fifty to two hundred million years—just roughly that. In other words—I cannot remember the era—I think—I just cannot remember the name of the time that it was—I used to know all the eras but—that was the time when we were some kind of tepid area all around here; it was fairly warm and there were a lot of shells and things in the sea and it was shallow water all over Britain as it were, and that was out by the coast. I'm interested in anything to do with natural sciences. I like astronomy especially. I've got a telescope which I managed to get. It's only a small one, but it does for me to look at some of the stars. I've not really gone to town on it because I haven't really got very much money to spend. I'm trying to save up with one of my friends who has got pretty well exactly the same interests as me, to buy a telescope which has got a power somewhere in the two hundred area which is not a lot, but it costs about £20. I can't at the moment see the day when we are going to have it.

INTERVIEWER: Do you like sports?

DAVID: I like some sports. I think most people like football best, but it's not so with me. I have got four favourite sports. One which I like watching, but I've never played to tell you the truth—it sounds silly—but I like Rugby—that's the one and I watch several matches. I watch all the internationals on television. Swimming—well I have lessons every Thursday night. There's three or four of us in a group. It's a little bath and it's for half an hour. That's swimming. Then there's tennis. I enjoy playing that on the courts at the green. I worked up from not being able to play at all to a pretty good standard I suppose. Cricket—I always go up to the local cricket ground because they've got a couple of nets.

INTERVIEWER: Who shares your interests?

DAVID: Well, um, I usually do a lot of my interests with two of my friends—one's Peter and one's Paul. With Paul I usually do biology—astronomy I usually do with Paul; geology I do with Paul. So, I do most of the things with Paul. As for cricket, I usually do that by myself—of course I go to cricket practice every Tuesday and Thursday night at the club.

INTERVIEWER: You lead a very busy life.

DAVID: Busy—yes, it is a bit difficult, because you are always switching over from one subject to another. You are playing cricket and suddenly you see a bird which you haven't got on your list and it's a bit difficult then to know what to do!

INTERVIEWER: Where does school fit into all this?

DAVID: Well, I like school to give me a general background. It brings up the English and mathematics and some of the pieces of science which I don't know, so that it just gives me a general background to work on. Of course, I enjoy writing from notes on what I've seen. I didn't bring any along, I'm afraid. I've got so many things in my bedroom. I buy so many books all the time that my bedroom is overflowing with books. I enjoy reading books on sailing round the world and I buy reference books for birds, animals, stones and the lot. There's a nice series out—have you seen them? They are little books about so big and they've got a coloured cover and they're full of pictures all the way through. There's astronomy, rocks and minerals, birds—several.

INTERVIEWER: Maths and science are your favourite subjects?

DAVID: Well, of the ones we do at school, I should say quite possibly, yes. I enjoy doing English, especially with our teacher now, she's very good. She is a very good teacher in the fact that she tries to do it properly. She has even taken it as far as giving us points of controversy. Then we work out which side we want to be on—either we want it or we don't want the point and then we have a debate and we vote and everything, which is very interesting because the first one that we had which I think was last week—we shall be having another one tomorrow—I was doing the speaking and the girl was speaking as well as me, and the trouble is she took all of the class except for one of them from our side. We were debating whether children should be paid to go to school. At first it was split about half and half and we were definitely against the motion for several reasons. It was very interesting just to stand up and do your talking, and it's marvellous fun.

INTERVIEWER: Do you get class places at school?

DAVID: We don't, but we do get star prizes. Well, last year I didn't do exactly very well because he just didn't give us things. I'm not brilliant, shall we put it that way at some of the things the head teacher likes giving more stars for than anything else. Paul, one of my friends at school and myself, we're good especially, this is what the teacher says, at maths and science and he hardly ever gives stars for them. I got a couple for English, but he gave more for general studies.

INTERVIEWER: Have you a good school library?

DAVID: Well, there's three or four good books but once—you see you can take them out once a week—(it's a bit difficult that, because every time I say something, I suddenly realise that you don't know about it, so I have to explain it)—the school library has got three or four good books and you get them out and when you've read those, you get a bit bored with them.

INTERVIEWER: What do you want to be when you grow up?

DAVID: It's awfully hard to say because I always think of new things, but really, I think that I'd enjoy perhaps to start off with, keeper at a zoo or something like that, and work my way up in the field of biology. In fact, in time, study geology and astronomy and all the others of my interest. I suppose, do you know Peter Scott? Well, he does pretty well everything I'd like to do, except that I've got a few things that he doesn't do. I haven't been to his place, but that's one of the places I want to go.

INTERVIEWER: What kind of a person are you?

DAVID: Well, I picture myself really as a person who wants to know about things. I seem to want to know about everything. It is rather hard to say exactly what I'm like. It's a tough question to ask. It'd be best to ask a parent but they don't know everything. I think I like not to have people around me who make things a bit nonsensy and play around. This is always me—I want my own bedroom to keep to myself. My brother, he still enjoys playing with toys like Leggo. I mean, they're constructive, but myself, I'd much rather settle down to read a book and I read for long periods at night. I usually leave as much place as possible in the day for enjoying any good books I'm reading. I think I've got a great love for animals. I'm against anybody who really likes to hunt them and kill them, that's one point I'm really against. I always enjoy science.

Summary

David had much in his favour from home and school. He made sensible judgments about himself and others and was already powerful in obtaining what he wanted from life. He conveyed the impression that he had himself well in hand, and if he had not planned his future in detail at least he knew the main direction in which he wanted to go.

MARK

Identified as 'gifted' on attainments at 7 years of age (Group 4) Wechsler Intelligence Test: Full scale IQ 154+, Verbal 154+, Performance 154+

Reading test at 11 years   Top 1 per cent of age group

Mathematics test at 11 years   Top 1 per cent of age group

Favourite subjects: mathematics, science, sports (found no subject boring)

Interests: science, reading, sports, music, inventing games, collecting, making things, playing outside.

Not interested in: drawing, painting, belonging to clubs.

Social class: II

At birth

Mark was the firstborn child of young parents in their twenties. He was a normal baby in every way. His father, who came from a working-class home, was working as a factory supervisor. He hated school and left at the earliest opportunity at the age of fourteen; he gained promotion quickly and all the time felt ambitious to achieve more. Mark's mother came from a similar social background, but stayed at school until she was sixteen. She started a professional training but discontinued it when she married, though she continued working in a clerical capacity until near the birth of her baby.

At 7 years of age

Mark was continuing to be a healthy child. By this time he had a brother and a sister. His parents had improved their circumstances by going into business for themselves, something Mr M wanted to do very much. ('I couldn't get out of the factory gates fast enough.') Mark started school at four and a half years of age and was said to settle down quickly within the first month. His progress was rapid and at seven his teacher recorded, 'This particular child is so bright that he is in a class above his age group.' He was considered to be in the top 5 per cent in relation to all children of seven in oral ability, awareness of the world, reading, creative skills and number work. It was noted that he frequently preferred to do things on his own rather than with others and sometimes seemed to be restless and inclined to worry, but in social adjustment to adults and children he was considered normal.

At 11 years of age

INTERVIEWER'S REPORT

Mark was a very handsome boy of average height and weight. He held himself upright, perhaps a little stiffly, and when talking took a stance somewhat like a lecturer about to address a large meeting, which made him appear rather formal in behaviour. There seemed no need to spend time easing him into the situation, he was ready for anything and asked intelligent questions about the survey and its outcome.

He was a boy who could not be hurried, he seemed to have his own pace for everything and whether he was answering a straightforward question or eating a biscuit he did it in his own time, unmoved by pressure from outside to hurry or slow down. It was not necessary to suggest break periods, he decided for himself when he wanted to stop and when he wanted to begin again.

He tackled everything with interest, and had exceptional powers of concentration, once he started to do something or say something he went on until it was completed, it seemed that he could not do anything casually. He made jokes and appreciated jokes but did not laugh openly: he would give a controlled smile and a look of acknowledgment at the interviewer.

He spoke slowly and deliberately as if reflecting on each phrase.

SCHOOL REPORT

Mark was promoted to a grammar school one year early. He was put into the first year 'A' stream.

He was rated in the top 5 per cent of his age group for general knowledge, use of books and oral ability, but one grade lower for mathematics. He was considered 'outstanding' in poetry.

His teachers described him as 'Enthusiastic about everything', but inclined to be 'concerned with his own importance and sometimes extremely serious'. His score on Stott's Social Adjustment Guide was 10, showing some 'unsettledness'.

PARENT'S INTERVIEW

INTERVIEWER: Does he enjoy school?

FATHER: He absolutely adores it. He moved to the high school last September, he's a high flier. They couldn't teach him any more at primary school. I can certainly say he received every attention there, he's enjoyed every teacher he's had. One made, what I consider, a most startling statement, 'If I'm not careful I find him running the class and I come second!' I put it down to inexperience. He was one term in that, class and then moved up. He's always been eighteen months to two years younger than his friends. Physically this made it a struggle for him; physical status is very important to a youngster.

He enjoys everything hugely, nothing doesn't interest him intensely. We were a little apprehensive when we moved to the secondary school, he was so young, but he didn't seem to be particularly perturbed at all. After his first term last Christmas his average was 80 per cent on all subjects, so obviously he's not disturbed at all. The advantage of the high school is that there are different teachers for different subjects. He still finds it confusing but it gives him a chance to progress at his own individual rate. I don't like all this streaming business, I think it tends to set a child; on the other hand I'm very pleased for my son that he gets the best advantage to bash on at his own rate. He's in the top class, it seems to be a sort of exclusive club where he gets the best of everything. The rights and wrongs of this I won't go into, but he enjoys it.

There's a wide gap between juniors and high school. I was a bit appalled at the gap between what they're expected to do there and at the high school. His friend who went up with him struggled and was very bewildered by it, but he's settled down. It was more a spur to my son. There's his physical age, I used to be a bit of a sportsman locally myself, he tried tremendously hard to get into the rugger side, he was a terrible failure, he's not that way inclined. We've coached him in cricket as much as possible and he's useful at it, and he seems to have made the first eleven cricket team. One teacher said he's full of his own importance in class, he shouts the loudest, he feels he's *got* to shout to make himself heard, to come up to their level. If he does well in cricket it will prove to him that it doesn't matter being younger. He usually enjoys PE. It's most important that children should be allowed to progress at their own rate, it leads to happy children not out of their depth. The variety of subjects covered at that school is quite remarkable, the facilities are first-class for any hobby such as drama; the teachers are quite dedicated there to helping the children.

INTERVIEWER: What are his interests at home? Does he get bored easily?

FATHER: He gets bored during the holidays, he thinks they are a waste of time. Like most bright children he thinks he's got to be occupied every minute of every hour of every day.

He likes all sports, cricket, football and, to a lesser degree, swimming. The thing he's least interested in is art, but he will sit for hours in his own bedroom working out maths problems, he loves drawing graphs, charting the progress of various things. His interests cover almost everything, he has an intense interest in just about everything that goes on.

He occasionally helps me at work but he likes all the glamour jobs, the chores, it's virtually impossible to get him to do. I usually end up saying, 'For goodness sake go.'

He's very absent-minded, he's dependent on his mother anticipating what he needs. He's more of a hindrance than a help in the house.

He likes reading, he'd read a toffee paper, anything from Biggles to the most serious subjects. He gets himself lost in geographical books, he tries to understand biographies, he likes to understand why they were trying to achieve certain things in their lives. He still has comics every week, anything that comes to hand.

INTERVIEWER: What sort of person is he?

FATHER: He's favourably optimistic about things, he's inclined to be temperamental, occasionally difficult from his mother's point of view. He will argue right down to the last minutest detail, to the last and finest point. He drives his mother frantic at times. He has a marked lack of urgency whenever it's required, he leaves twenty minutes to go three miles to school, he wouldn't worry, something would save him. He can be extremely rude and he can be extremely thoughtful on occasions. He's most generous. His ego! He knows he's good, he's got bags of confidence. He's quiet and well spoken. There have been several occasions where he's had to stand up before an audience, and he's quite unmoved. He gets very passionate about things he's interested in, his team lost the cup final, he worked himself up all the week to Saturday afternoon, it fermented inside him, and when they lost he folded up. He went to bed, he didn't want to speak. It was amusing from our point of view, but we understood it from his.

He very rarely lies, on the very few occasions he did he was full of remorse afterwards. He's open, that's one of his good points. He detests cruelty of any sort.

INTERVIEWER: Have you thought what kind of work he might do?

FATHER: He appears to be academically biased rather than engineering and technical subjects. As long as he's prepared to go on we will back him to university if possible. I'm sure whatever he does do he will go fairly near the top.

MARK'S INTERVIEW

INTERVIEWER: Tell me about your interests.

MARK: Swimming's really my interest, and drama. I'm quite good at drama, I played quite a part in the school play. Then there's cricket, I'm doing quite well in the first year squad. And there's violining, playing the fiddle, I don't play in the orchestra, I'm only learning. I make a few kits, plastic model kits, and I've got a kit I had in two stages, it's an electronic kit. I had the basic kit, that's number eight for Xmas, and Dad promised me if I could do well with it I could have the second kit for my birthday.

INTERVIEWER: What is it about?

MARK: Well, it makes electronic gadgets, like a burglar alarm; it's got a little resistor, the resistance of which alters if you catch light on it; if, say, you put a book on it, while it was attached to the circuit and then you lifted the book up, because of the light falling on it you make the circuit whistle and then you'd know that the book had been picked up. And you can use this, say, on a door, make a little hole at the top of a door and put it in and when the door was opened the light would fall on it, you know, it's a sort of electronic bell. It was with the second kit; with the first you could make an elementary morse set with just one earphone; it was just a one way tapper, and you can make with the second kit a two way morse tapper with loud speakers; and even an electronic organ—it doesn't work very well though—very difficult—as you press the metal key down it completes a certain part of the circuit, according to which part, that creates a pitched whistle. I've made an intercom, I listen to the radio at night the odd time, and television, perhaps a football match that sort of thing, and it's been quite successful.

INTERVIEWER: What about art?

MARK: I do quite well in art lessons. I don't do it very much at home, not really.

INTERVIEWER: Do you collect anything?

MARK: I've got a small collection of coins, a lot brought back by relatives who've been abroad; we find some in the till, we found a Chinese coin in the till once, somebody thought it was a penny, it was a ten cash coin, that's where we get the word cash from apparently. I've got about forty coins, some old British including an 1806, I keep that specially it's worth about a pound now. Then I collect stamps, I don't find all that much time for putting them in but I've got a lot on the waiting list.

INTERVIEWER: Which school do you go to?

MARK: I'm at the high school at the moment, since last September. I'm under age. When I was in the infants' school, well, I had about half a term's start, with a few other children; well, I was sent up to the junior department a year early, and then in my second class I was put back where I should be 'cos it was thought I couldn't cope with being the year ahead, but I was ahead of the rest of the class really in my own year; and then I was put up to the top class a year before time with another lad and then I went up to the high school.

INTERVIEWER: What is your favourite subject at school?

MARK: Well, I like them all really. The one I'm not keen on is religious knowledge; for one thing we have it last period on a Thursday which is a bit boring and the teacher doesn't care one toss if you're not learning it, he doesn't teach the sort of teaching that drives it into you. I enjoy most of the lessons, I prefer maths and science. I particularly like the maths as the maths teacher we have puts it across so enjoyably, he may be un-orthodox but he teaches us quite well, he gets across to us and we *enjoy* the lessons. I am jolly good at maths, I came fifth in the form at the end of the first term.

I'm not particularly good at the crafts, metalwork and woodwork, although the art teacher thinks quite a lot of me.

INTERVIEWER: How much do you like writing things down on paper?

MARK: I don't like that quite so much, you know, as actually *doing* something or *making* something; not so much as mathematics 'cos when we do put that down I feel I've made something.

INTERVIEWER: How much do you use books?

MARK: Well, I do read quite a lot, I've got seventy-odd books, it's touching on eighty at times when they're all in the bookcase. I've got quite a lot of Enid Blyton books—not the Noddy sort—the ones like the *Secret Mountain*, that sort of thing and *The Boy Next Door*. I've got five or six of those and I've got quite a lot of the Biggles books by Captain W. E. Johns and I have read some of these other books about space. I've got one very nice book which I had as a present it's quite fascinating, the story of speed, how travel's developed right up to the space ship from running.

INTERVIEWER: Do you think you read more than other children?

MARK: Well, I won't say that, but I would think I do read rather better than other children in my class because—well, to recall one incident at the primary school, well the infant part of it in my last but one class I think it was, I was the only child in a class of forty who could read.

INTERVIEWER: What kind of a person are you?

MARK: That's a difficult question! Well, being underage I do get . . . I don't compare quite so well with children I live with, you know, although in certain games I do catch up with them and in some things overtake them, like in maths, that sort of thing; but no, I don't think I'm put out by the fact that I *am* underage, like my friend is, he's older than me, he's not so much underage and he's completely put out by the fact. I'm not going in for any school sports (athletic events) I won't make it, but I've made the cricket squad and I feel I'm up on level terms with the other children. I'm not rough in my ways, quite quiet really, just like other children around, apart from being underage.

INTERVIEWER: Is there anything you'd like to change about yourself?

MARK: Well, if I could I'd like to be a bit more wholehearted about football. I go in for football a bit delicately, I'd like to change that a bit and feel on equal terms with everybody when I barged in. I'd like to be as strong as the other lads, that sort of thing, it's about the only thing I'm really lacking in, I think . . . physically.

INTERVIEWER: What do you want to be when you grow up?

MARK: I don't really know, I'd like to go into a job, perhaps scientific or one which involved mathematics, but I wouldn't like to be stuck up in an office all day. I would like to go to a college or university after I leave school, of my own accord . . . or, like I say, something I'm interested in, maths–science something like that.

INTERVIEWER: Are you looking forward to being grown up?

MARK: I don't know, I'll be sorry not to be a child, but there again I'll have to wait and see when I'm grown up what it's like.

INTERVIEWER: You're 11 now, you've lived quite a few years, what do you think about life?

MARK: I think it's a bit mixed up, and it can turn around on a pinhead, it changes all of a sudden, like when my sister was taken into hospital, and my grandad died, these sort of things upset me quite a lot and they did change me.

Summary

Mark was doing exceptionally well all round, at home, at school and in his own estimation. He had every support from home and plenty of encouragement from school.

The one thing that was a source of unease to him was the fact of being 'underage'. He referred to this time and time again. He was not as well developed physically for his age as he was intellectually. He was in an 'A' stream with children who were twelve to eighteen months older so that competition was keen for him especially in sports and PE. His teachers needed to be very much aware of his individual circumstances if he were not to be under-estimated in relation to his age. The following extracts from the sentence completion test revealed further his anxiety:

> 'Other children . . . sometimes leave me out of things as I am underage.'
> 'My greatest worry is . . . that being underage will make me left out of school activities, although I compare quite well with the other boys in my form.'
> 'My greatest fear is . . . that because of me not having very many friends of my own age at home I will feel alone and left out of life in the village.'

The fact that he scored 10 on the Stott's Social Adjustment Guide also revealed his teachers' awareness of some 'unsettledness'. He appeared to be over demanding which could well be so because as one of the youngest and smallest in the class he felt himself to be in a highly competitive situation and had to strive to draw attention to himself. He was well aware of his teachers' views as a sentence completion showed:

> 'My teachers think I am . . . rather concerned that I am important, very good at the subject they teach me, and some think I'm just another pupil in IA.'

The overall picture was one of an exceptionally able boy of strong personality with a wide range of abilities and interests which were likely to lead him on to the university and a professional career.

SHARON

Identified as gifted on the Draw-a-man test at seven years old (Group 1) Wechsler Intelligence Test: Full scale IQ 154, Verbal 152, Performance 149.
Reading test at 11 years   Top 4 per cent of age group
Mathematics test at 11 years   Top 4 per cent of age group
Favourite subjects: all (none boring)
Interests: science, making things, reading, inventing games, sports, clubs.
Not interested in: collecting, writing stories.
Social class: II

At birth

Sharon was the third child to be born of parents who managed their own general store. Events surrounding the birth were normal and the baby was strong and quick in development. Her parents wanted 'better things for the children than we had—a bedroom of their own, something to interest them at weekends—the opportunity to compare our way of life with other countries—and to be individuals, not part of the crowd—that's important'.

At 7 years of age

Sharon was rated in the top 5 per cent of her age group for everything. She settled down quickly at school and made rapid progress, always being noted for her sociability.

At 11 years of age

INTERVIEWER'S REPORT:

Sharon was tall and rather plump. She was vivacious and lively from the start. She brought bags full of the evidence of her interests; a model zoo, soft toys designed by herself and beautifully made, and puppets also showing a high standard of sewing skill and sense of design. She was fully confident and mature, happier when making spontaneous conversation than doing tests, but nevertheless co-operative. She showed no focused academic interest yet. She would tackle anything and seemed avid for new experience. She expressed a wish to be a boy so that she could join in football and other masculine sports activities. Her thoughts turned more readily to marriage and motherhood than career choice. She summed up adults quickly and managed to accommodate her behaviour to them. She had to make an adjustment to her present teacher whom she saw as not very skilled at her job.

SCHOOL REPORT

Sharon was in the top 5 per cent of her age group in all subjects. She was described as 'enthusiastic, frank and confident'. Her only fault was that, in being exceptional all-round herself, she could sometimes be intolerant of those who were slower.

PARENTS' INTERVIEW

INTERVIEWER: What is it you most enjoy about Sharon?
MOTHER: She's always been a child to amuse herself, when she was ever so tiny she'd sit in the playpen for hours with a few toys and she didn't need people around her, you'd know she was all right. She's a bit argumentative at times, sometimes thinks what *she's* doing at the time is more important than anything else.
FATHER: She's so affectionate and demonstrative, she comes up and flings her arms around you for the smallest thing, she expresses it. She's

very very open but inclined to be bossy with a crowd—probably wants to dominate. She doesn't get steamed up over anything, I've never seen her really angry about anything. She's a leader, I wish in a way she wasn't quite so bossy with other children, there's an aura probably round her—the others feel compelled to follow. She's confident in what she's doing.

INTERVIEWER: How does she get on with school work?

FATHER: She copes very well, but I'd say she could do better. We've no complaints about the school, the teachers' standards are very good, they cover a wide field in what they do. We think she's capable of doing the utmost with the limited scope at present available, it's a question of putting children of mixed ability in one class—it's awfully difficult to do justice to each extreme end. She is at one extreme and at the other there's a child who couldn't read or count. When she's finished her work she's told to help the other child—I don't think it's right—in our opinion it's better to stream for ability. There are 'top' tables within the class but in the class teacher's view it's a nightmare to keep all the children going all the time.

MOTHER: Somebody's got to be top, you've got to introduce a competitive spirit. We want her to go to grammar school because the teachers are better qualified there, they seem to have got to a higher standard. It's probably prejudice but it takes a long time to die.

INTERVIEWER: How long do you want her to stay at school?

MOTHER: Till 18—it depends what she wants to do, if A levels will be an advantage she'll try to get them. She'll go to university if it serves some useful purpose for the subject she has chosen, if it's a question of just going to university for the sake of not starting work she won't go. If it's just to study English and not know what she intends to do after I'd have second thoughts about letting her go.

INTERVIEWER: Have you though what kind of work you'd like her to do?

MOTHER: I can't quite see what way her interest lies carreer-wise, providing she's doing something really useful to herself it wouldn't matter. She's a leader, she has the capabilities to be a teacher. We are ambitious that they should *progress*—not just highly paid, it's got to have worth to the person doing the job. Obviously we'd like her to have a better education than we had, with her ability, under the present system she should get the education she deserves.

SHARON'S INTERVIEW

INTERVIEWER: Tell me about your interests.

SHARON: I love making things . . . and animals. I've got four hamsters, and there's the dog which is a sort of family animal and then there's Gyp, the rabbit, and Waffles, the guinea pig . . . I had a few mice. I used to have a terrapin and a slow worm and a lizard.

INTERVIEWER: Do you look after them?

SHARON: Yes, the hamsters—there's Harry who's father of about fifty, some of whom have died—not all at once though—there's Tiny, she's the daughter of Harry and some relation to Freddie, who's also the son of Harry but they're not brother and sister. I kept . . . actually in the first litter Becky was the mother, she died though . . . there were three like Harry, five like Becky, which was a sort of tawny colour, you know, golden hamster, and one which was Freddie who was a cream one and we haven't the faintest idea what he took after . . . I kept one of the little cream ones, the cream one which was Frisky and one of the golden females.

INTERVIEWER: What about your other interests?

SHARON: Reading . . . I love it. I like adventure books.

INTERVIEWER: How many books have you of your own?

SHARON: I should think somewhere over a hundred easily. I've got the Mystery series and the B . . . series, that's not a very long one, and the S . . . series that's not a very long one either.

INTERVIEWER: Do you read books for information?

SHARON: Yes, sometimes, mostly animal books . . . when I'm in the library I sort of, if I can find a book on animals or things like that I look at it.

INTERVIEWER: Do you belong to any clubs?

SHARON: Yes, a youth club, it's not registered yet because I'm only 11, so you see you can't be registered until everybody's over 13. I enjoy going out with somebody, really, in the evening. We're doing something, my friend and I, we've started putting on puppet plays, string puppets, we make them ourselves. I got a book from the library and this sort of started us off and this year we're going to do the Sleeping Beauty. I've got rather a good idea for the magic scene . . . any time there's a change the lights go out and we just switch over puppets. What I've got to do is the coach, I'm going to draw a coach and four. We've already made the dress for Sleeping Beauty Two. Sleeping Beauty One is almost finished except she needs hands and a wire hoop in her dress.

INTERVIEWER: Do you like doing things with your family, or do you prefer to do them on your own?

SHARON: Well, I think I like doing things by myself, mainly. I built a hut, my brother helped me carry the wood over because it was in enormous big bits which I had sort of sawed up slightly, and Mum helped me put the roof on, but I did most of it.

INTERVIEWER: What are your favourite subjects at school?

SHARON: Games, PE and crafts.

INTERVIEWER: Which subjects do you like least?

SHARON: English, especially spelling tests. I loathe spelling tests because they're so easy. I like things much more difficult.

INTERVIEWER: What is your idea of a 'good' teacher, one who helps children to get on?

SHARON: One that's friendly with the class, I think. Miss G was a popular teacher, she taught us well which is one thing, but she gave us things which were right for us. She used to take us to a farm or a town, and we could sort of do what we wanted—well practically all we wanted. We had to go round in a group sort of thing, but we enjoyed it because we were able to look at things and you were out in the air not shut up in a stuffy classroom.

INTERVIEWER: What do you want to be when you grow up?

SHARON: An air hostess, because you visit all different places and meet a lot of people. I think you have to write to somebody and have to have an interview and if you're accepted you have to have training.

INTERVIEWER: What does mother want you to be?

SHARON: She hasn't got any ideas . . . she says to me she hasn't got any ideas because she thinks I should make up my own mind.

INTERVIEWER: What kind of person are you?

SHARON: Usually truthful, untidy, tomboyish . . . I suppose, clever.

INTERVIEWER: What do other children like about you?

SHARON: I suppose . . . friendliness.

INTERVIEWER: And anything they might dislike?

SHARON: Um, I think they might think I boast a lot, well, some of them do, I know.

Summary

Sharon took everything in her stride, she did well at school and was full of home interests. Her bias was not strongly academic at that moment. She had artistic flair which she cultivated on her own initiative. The direction of her future career was not clear yet. With such diverse abilities she would have a wide range from which to choose. She stood out as a fortunate child who had faced no serious setbacks in her life to date. Her temperament was an easy one which gained her quick acceptance.

PAULA

Identified as 'gifted' on Attainments at 7 years of age (Group 4)
Wechsler Intelligence Test: Full Scale IQ 154+, Verbal 155, Performance 146.
Reading test at 11 years   Top 2 per cent of age group
Mathematics test at 11 years   Top 5 per cent of age group
Favourite subjects: all (none boring)
Interests: Reading, sport, playing outside.
Not interested in: painting, chess.
Social class: III manual

At birth

Paula was a healthy first baby. Her father was a factory worker and her mother a shop assistant. Both parents had happy childhoods, but knew the difficulties of financial insecurity. They determined to give their children openly expressed affection and a secure home. They left school at fifteen years of age but continued to educate themselves at night classes.

At 7 years of age

Paula made a quick start at school and by seven was considered in the top 5 per cent of her age group on all subjects. She had one sister.

At 11 years of age

INTERVIEWER'S REPORT

Paula was one of the most mature looking children seen. She looked especially grown-up in facial features and expression. Her ability to laugh at herself and her own ideas was rather unusual for mostly the very intelligent children seemed to be serious about their own purposes.

She was a child who was completely absorbed in school and school work, it obviously had provided the outlet for her abilities. Reading was her dominant interest.

SCHOOL REPORT

Paula was rated in the top 5 per cent of her age group for mathematics and the top 6–30 per cent for general knowledge, use of books and oral ability. Her teacher said: 'If not quite outstanding her work in both mathematical and creative writing spheres is very good. She is very friendly and a good natured child who can be both serious and humorous when the occasion merits it. The most serious weakness, which she is overcoming, is an inability to take second place. She does not like to be beaten, but is overcoming this.'

There were no indications of any social adjustment problems on the Stott scale.

PARENT'S INTERVIEW

INTERVIEWER: Does she enjoy school?

MOTHER: She loves school. On the whole we're quite happy with it— it's a comprehensive school. There's a tendency to merge good and bad; they don't push enough children in front. There's no way of knowing whether she's progressing as well as she did. We know she's still doing very well, but now she has an A pass (80–100) in her report card, before she had 98 per cent. I spoke to the teacher recently about it, I think it's better from a personal point of view if she's still in a competitive atmosphere. They were streamed in her previous school. At first when she came to this school, she wasn't too happy. In the other school she collected all the prizes, that was good from her point of view. When she

moved to this school she felt she had missed her prizes. This Head
doesn't believe in prizes. To him this is a personal attitude; he just
doesn't believe in it. Both of us would prefer a more competitive atmosphere. She thrives on competition—she wants to be top. She blossoms
under pressure; she really comes to the fore under strain. It's a different
type of education from what we're used to. You don't seem to be able
to accept it. The results speak for themselves, she seems to me far in
advance of a child of her age. She converses about subjects far and away
above her. She seems to be in advance of everybody. When I go to the
PTA I'm told this. She's good at maths and creative writing, she has the
ability to put down on paper what she's thinking about. She loves
maths. She comes home and sits doing these for days. It is a challenge
to conquer. She reads a lot, she's a great reader she can tackle anything.
Several teachers have said she's a joy to teach—a teacher's dream. She's
really interested, no matter what the subject is. One teacher at the PTA
said she just had to see me again to say what a joy it was to teach her.
Teachers seem to like her, she's a likeable nature. It's not just academic
subjects she's good at. She knits her own jumpers. She could write her
name and address long before she went to school. She always wanted to,
we did teach her. She's quite artistic—she draws and makes things.
She's not terribly interested in music—we had to take her off the violin
in the school orchestra—she cried and cried, she wasn't interested. The
teacher said it was a pity, she was doing so well.

INTERVIEWER: What type of secondary school would you like her to
go to?

MOTHER: Grammar school. But the choice is very limited as far as we
are concerned. Our area has the comprehensive system. We would have
chosen grammar school. I would tend to push her academic interest—
a greater percentage go to university. It's essential at school to mix with
children who want to go to university. The parent has to keep reminding
the child that they want to do something better when they're mixing
with children who all they want to do is to get out and earn money. For
different children—different things. It's important for her to find out
the subject she really excels in and decide what she's going to be and
keep at that. I think one reason the grammar school is better is that
they're more aware of social problems and modern insights into modern
history and modern problems, whereas these older schools tend to plug
away at 1066. The grammar school has a good scientific background.

INTERVIEWER: Could you tell me something about her—what sort of
person is she?

MOTHER: She's very obliging, quite a good nature, better than she used
to be. Two years ago she was very withdrawn and very reserved. We
said she worked too hard at school, there was nothing we could do.
Now she's mastered things she can relax. She's got a sense of humour,
she can talk and hold her own. She's quite witty. We've always encouraged them to talk. She's a very grateful child, she appreciates it

if you buy her anything. I think she's an awfully good, intelligent child. Never a day passes but she tells you that she loves you. It's a great thing to see her and her sister playing together—they very, very rarely disagree.

INTERVIEWER: Is she easygoing, or inclined to find life difficult?

MOTHER: Quite easygoing, but some time ago I used to think there were problems inside her life. She was moody and used to cry a bit. She couldn't explain it to us. Now in this past couple of years this has gone. She doesn't need people, she does not like being fussed over. She used to be apt to cry when people fussed over her.

INTERVIEWER: Have you thought what kind of work you would like her to do?

MOTHER: I think she'll be a teacher. She has great patience and she enjoys showing children how to do things. Her father thinks she'll do something mathematical or possibly something in science. He doesn't think that teaching is good enough for her.

PAULA'S INTERVIEW

INTERVIEWER: How much do you like school?

PAULA: I enjoy everything.

INTERVIEWER: What is your favourite subject?

PAULA: Oh, nothing really, I don't think I have any preference for subjects in school. I enjoy doing projects—I did one on our country and I not only enjoyed that but I did another one about the President. I like to go and work on my own; I like looking up facts about all these people, it's quite difficult to find some information.

INTERVIEWER: How much do you enjoy reading?

PAULA: I enjoy reading books quite a lot.

INTERVIEWER: Do you read more than most children?

PAULA: Well, according to my friends I seem to, I do really enjoy reading that's one of the things I enjoy most. I've read all the paperbacks and all the Enid Blyton books in the school library and I can't get any more and there was none in the public library the last few times I've been up.

INTERVIEWER: Do you choose to read information books?

PAULA: Yes, quite often I do. We've got a big encyclopaedia in the house and I hear something on the news—something someone's talking about and I read it—Mother says I don't know what I'd do without my encyclopaedia.

INTERVIEWER: Tell me about your other interests.

PAULA: I write to my pen-pal quite often, she's in France, and I go to see football matches and I sometimes go to the baths, and I play netball in the school team often going away to play. Finally I took an awful interest in sketching or drawing all over the place but it went off again. I knitted myself a cardigan and jumper.

INTERVIEWER: Do you collect anything?

PAULA: Yes, I collect stamps. I was really getting quite a good collection but in the last couple of weeks I haven't really been bothering.

INTERVIEWER: Tell me about your friends, and the things you like to do together.

PAULA: Well, I've got all the girls in the class. We've all started clubs. I hate it if I'm in anything if I'm just one of a crowd. I like to be up in a committee or something like that.

INTERVIEWER: Have you a best friend?

PAULA: Yes—I've always liked her.

INTERVIEWER: What does a 'friend' mean to you?

PAULA: A person you go about with, a person you like, a person who sticks up for you in arguments.

INTERVIEWER: What are the other members of your family interested in?

PAULA: Well, my sister's been trying to get through to the netball team this year and I've been trying to help her, there's a type of ring in the garden up on the wall—we use that as a shooting stand and I give her tips on how to play. My dad, oh, he's football mad—we all go on Saturday. My mum, she goes to the Women's Institute, they voted her president, she's mad about it. My dad goes to the Union, he used to be chairman or something.

INTERVIEWER: What do you want to be when you grow up?

PAULA: Earlier I wanted to be a vet but it's just a fit you take.

INTERVIEWER: What else have you considered?

PAULA: I've taken an awful fancy to be a cowboy a wee while ago— my teacher she'll say—what do you want to be this week! (laughs).

INTERVIEWER: What kind of a person are you?

PAULA: Well, quite fiery tempered at times, but I try to calm it down. I used to get up in the morning, couldn't look at anyone—but I just lie in bed now and say—you don't get up until you're going to behave yourself!

INTERVIEWER: What do your friends like about you?

PAULA: I don't know—they like I can laugh at a joke and we usually agree instead of just arguing—I just try to avoid an argument.

INTERVIEWER: What might they dislike about you?

PAULA: I don't like being bossed around, I hate being bossed around— I like to be the one doing the bossing around!

INTERVIEWER: Do you ever think about serious things, grown-up things?

PAULA: No I don't usually, if I'm on my own I just sit and think about friends and things that have been happening.

INTERVIEWER: Politics, religion?

PAULA: Yes, specially when I did the project on President Kennedy. I seemed to think about politics a lot then during that election.

INTERVIEWER: Did anything puzzle you?

PAULA : Yes, why some of the parties had certain ideas on race relations, that always used to puzzle me, because we're all people really—why couldn't they get on together, all the people of the world. I always seem to think we're silly that people of different religions can't get on together as well, especially Catholics and Protestants because they're both Christians, it's stupid to fight over that, they're not really thinking about it as religion—just as a thing. I think they should think about religion as religion and not something to fight over.

INTERVIEWER : Are you looking forward to being grown up?

PAULA : No. I don't want to think about being grown up—too much responsibility, as a wee bairn you can enjoy things without having to worry about what'll happen.

Summary

Paula showed clearly how school had satisfied her intellectual interests. She was almost wholly orientated towards traditional school subjects in her interests and without stimulation from teachers in this respect might well have been a less happy child. Her parents were ambitious and encouraged an attitude of competitiveness in an academic setting, they looked to the school to foster their daughter's abilities, though in the final resort teaching as a career was not thought good enough for her. Her fine sense of humour ensured her a welcome in most groups and her personal qualities and social maturity suggested that she would be one of their leaders.

EDWARD

Identified as gifted on attainments at 7 years of age (Group 5)
Wechsler Intelligence Test: Full Scale IQ 154, Verbal 155, Performance 150.
Reading test at 11 years   Top 1 per cent of age group
Mathematics test at 11 years   Top 1 per cent of age group
Favourite subjects: art, craft, science.
Boring subjects: history and geography.
Interests: making things, drawing, reading, science.
Not interested in: painting, sports, writing, music, collecting, inventing games and keeping pets.
Social class: III manual

At birth

Edward was a first child, he was 'at risk' at birth because his mother was under 20 and of small stature, but there were no perinatal complications. His father was a mechanic and his mother had been a clerk.

At 7 years of age

Edward showed his exceptional ability very quickly in his first school. The teachers rated him in the top 5 per cent oral ability, awareness of the world and reading, and in the top 6–30 per cent in number work. The head teacher wrote: 'A very intelligent child who is lefthanded and has difficulty in doing written work, handwork and art. He has difficulty in sitting still and his exercise books quickly become untidy and dog-eared. He is aware of this and makes an effort to improve. He loves to talk at great length, usually about cars and he can be a nuisance in this respect as he seems to wish to be constantly the centre of attention'.

His mother said, 'The first school he went to the teachers petted him, he could read before he went. They took him everywhere, even to teachers' meetings. He didn't associate with the children there and it became a set pattern.'

He was found to be short-sighted and slightly deaf when physically examined in the first follow-up of the birthweek children at seven years of age.

There were two younger children in the family at this time.

At 11 years of age

INTERVIEWER'S REPORT

Edward was a slightly built impish-looking boy. He had a large mouth and protruding ears, he himself said that he would like to change his face because, 'It doesn't look nice'. One was aware of his difference from most children of his age as soon as he spoke. His phraseology was complex and arresting in style; steady, deliberate and always elaborated to make his meaning clear. He had a great sense of humour and recounted school escapades with dramatic enjoyment. He told one story to illustrate how he triggered off disturbance in class without intention:
TEACHER: An ape's brain is 750 cc—a man's brain is 1500 cc.
EDWARD (*seriously*): That means I have a brain like a family saloon car!
ANOTHER BOY: You *are* a saloon car, I'll pull your ears to see if you work.

He had terrific concentration; he seemed to be able to mobilise interest for any topic under discussion and did not like to let it go until it had been fully explored. The interview could have lasted longer: he showed no sign of fatigue after 3 hours.

SCHOOL REPORT

He received top ratings in all areas. The head teacher reported, 'He is of outstanding ability in regard to scientific knowledge and oral ability. He is a powerful person not acceptable to other children. His weakness is that he will not listen to other people's arguments, he is too full of his own importance'. He was marked as having poor control of his hands and poor physical co-ordination (see his birth history, above). His Stott score was exceptionally high (35) indicating 'maladjustment'.

PARENT'S INTERVIEW

INTERVIEWER: Does he enjoy school or not?

MOTHER: He does, it's a new school with modern ideas. I don't think he mixes with other children very well. He gets on far better with adults than children. He's always been like this so we don't take much notice.

INTERVIEWER: How does he get on with school work?

MOTHER: Very well. He's no good at music—using his hands, games. He's very good at arithmetic—exceptional in reading—far above standard for his age. He reads books on electronics and car engines etc. He's much more interested in them than in Biggles. His conversation is very good—he's been able to speak fluently since he was eighteen months old. His conversation has always been very adult so he doesn't get on with other children because he talks above them. They don't like it at all—he has been put upon physically by other children. He's an outcast at school. He's lived with this all his life, providing he can interest the staff of the school that's all he cares about.

The teacher said he'd sit him in the corner with a pile of motor magazines and get on with the rest of the class. He does chatter too much to the teacher at school—he's always asking questions when he should be doing his work. Everything has to have a long answer. He would rather spend the day discussing than getting down to work because he can't write very well. Six months ago the head teacher suggested that he was very narrow-minded, only interested in car engines, boats etc., and not in wider things. We thought this unfair— he knows an awful lot about general things. He sits and reads encyclo- paedias at home quite happily. Anything he reads goes in and he tends to speak quoting from books, which is why he sounds so adult. He reads quickly, he can scan a page and pick out the relevant facts. I think the Head is a bit narrow-minded—he caters for the normal run of children. My son is a waste of time to him—he's a child who will get in the way— he asks too many questions.

INTERVIEWER: What type of secondary school would you like him to go to?

MOTHER: Grammar school. Perhaps at grammar school he'd keep his mouth shut and listen a bit more—not be so big-headed with children there that are as clever or cleverer than he is. In secondary schools they should treat children more like adults. He likes to be treated as an adult. At grammar school they have a wider range of subjects and outside school activities.

INTERVIEWER: Is he a busy child or does he often get bored?

MOTHER: Yes, he does get bored. He likes to go out on his bicycle— do jigsaw puzzles and read. He reads all day and every day, all the time.

He does sometimes try to do some design—he's quite interested in design but as I say he's not very good with his hands, drawing and everything. They don't usually end up as he intended them. He gets a bit disgruntled with those. He does technical drawings, things like that. He reads them up so he knows how it's all done and he does try to do them himself. I think he feels he would like to invent something but he's never yet succeeded. He belongs to a judo club. When we first moved, the children used to take it out of him physically so we thought he'll never really be a lot of good, he can't fight or anything, so we started him at the judo club and we're carrying on. Actually he's got on quite well. We were surprised because he's not good at games at all. I don't think the other children even know that he does this. He usually gets beaten up on the way home from school—we're quite used to it and so is he now.

INTERVIEWER: What is he like, what sort of person is he?

MOTHER: To me he hasn't any commonsense—this annoys me. Speaking to people outside he has good mastery but he is not practical in the home. It's a lack of commonsense—he can't clean his shoes properly, he can't even tie his tie properly or comb his hair properly—it's another of these things that infuriates me as a mother. I'd like him to come home covered in mud—if he does it's because he's done something stupid, not something boyish. He has no boyish activities, his father would like him to play football that he was interested in as a boy. He tries but it doesn't last. He's different from either of us.

INTERVIEWER: Can you say what it is you most enjoy about him, what pleases you most?

MOTHER: Really the fact that he's a lot cleverer than I was at his age. The fact that he's got the potential to do something with his life—that would make any parent proud. I can trust him to do the shopping—he's got good manners—he's a good citizen. I don't think he will get on very well in the man's world except in the academic world.

INTERVIEWER: Have you thought what kind of work you would like him to do?

MOTHER: No, but something academic. I see him more amongst professionals. I'd like him to be a doctor but he's shown a leaning towards the law.

EDWARD'S INTERVIEW

INTERVIEWER: How much do you like school?

EDWARD: Quite a lot actually, my favourite subjects are art and craft and reading. I'm not really stuck on history or geography. Well I sometimes like English and I do like maths sometimes, it depends what sums and equations I'm doing. Science I like, practical science that is, history and geography are out, I don't like those at all. Art and crafts, I'm very interested in, although I'm no good at it. Foreign languages,

I know a tiny bit of French, and I'd like to learn privately Russian. Music I'm interested in although I can't sing; PE games I'm no good at them and I'm described as a weakling by my fellow classmates, well, I don't mind that. Religious instruction I'm quite interested in, and project work, I like to do my own projects on my own.

INTERVIEWER: Are you allowed to do your own projects?

EDWARD: Yes, we can do private study in groups or on your own, and I prefer to do it on my own. I'm doing a project on electronics, and you see my Aunty and Uncle sent me a great thick book with about 230 pages all about transistors, diodes, everything to do with electronics, so I'm quite happy. They said there are a lot of books that were too young for me, and a lot too old for me, and nothing in my age, so they bought me one that was slightly too old for me, and I was going to grow into that.

INTERVIEWER: You are enjoying it—tell me a bit about it.

EDWARD: Yes, well it's all about the study of how electrons which are fractions of atoms, so that's something really small, behave in a way and with certain components such as resistors and transistors; these have made the tape recorder possible and things like this. There's capacitors, which let the electricity pass through, least they stop the electricity until the electricity has large enough voltage to pass right through the capacitor—and this is on a car's trafficator system, the blinker-light system, there is a capacitor used.

INTERVIEWER: What is your favourite subject?

EDWARD: Oh, I like woodwork, I have just a natural love of woodwork—balsa woodwork, at the moment I'm working on an aircraft, and I remember I got into tearing trouble about 2 weeks ago because I had a piece of wood that long, that wide and that high and I made an extreme mess of it and reduced it to that size.

INTERVIEWER: Why do you dislike history?

EDWARD: I'm just not interested in history and people being beheaded, I'm interested in up-to-date and in the future—history is all dead, history won't come again except the things like the ice age, there might be another of those, scientifically, but I'm more interested in what we are doing now and what we will be doing, such as men landing on the moon, I like learning more about this.

INTERVIEWER: Are you exceptionally good at anything at school?

EDWARD: I wouldn't like to say that really—if you don't mind me saying, I am exceptionally good at reading, in fact I'm always sloping off and finding a book and burying my head in it, I must have something in the region of 150 books at home and must have read my way through about 75 of them, that's in the course of about a year.

INTERVIEWER: Anything else you know you are very good at?

EDWARD: Generally, dictation, composition, comprehension and use of the language. They said so in my report, I usually get A's and B's for that, A is excellent and B is good.

INTERVIEWER: How many schools have you been to?

EDWARD: Four.

INTERVIEWER: Tell me about the one you've enjoyed the most.

EDWARD: Well, that would really be unfair seeing as I'd been to A . . . school the longest, but now, let's see, it's swaying between A . . . school and D . . .. I liked A . . . school for its teachers, and my friends there, they were my kind of people.

INTERVIEWER: What are your kind of people?

EDWARD: Well, people who recognise a decent idea, and they'll go along with it and say, 'Well, this has some potential so we try this out', but the people who aren't my kind of people such as the people at my school often say, 'Oh no, your ideas are too far-fetched'—I mean you couldn't build a hovercraft—and I know that I could.

INTERVIEWER: What is your idea of a 'good' teacher, one that helps children to get on?

EDWARD: Someone who will give choice of what you want to do and let you do it your own way, and will occasionally crack jokes but makes you work, and that is my opinion of a good teacher.

INTERVIEWER: What is your idea of a teacher who does not help children to get on?

EDWARD: Someone who is exceptionally strict, and exceptionally stern, a real old square, never cracking jokes at all about anything, who doesn't really like children much, and I think to be a good teacher you must like children.

INTERVIEWER: Tell me about your friends.

EDWARD: My only true friend is Matthew.

INTERVIEWER: What do you mean by a true friend?

EDWARD: Someone who is decent and considerate and will listen, someone who will understand.

INTERVIEWER: What sort of things do you like doing together?

EDWARD: Well, we like talking on practical subjects such as the Apollo 9, we say now how could we make this a safer project, how could we make it a lot safer, to get the astronauts back if one of the main propulsion rocket fails, and we think well we could carry extra fuel, and keep all the retro rockets reversed and still firing. [*Note*. This interview was carried out a year before the Apollo XIII trip.]

INTERVIEWER: What things do you dislike in some children?

EDWARD: Fighting. I know that sounds stupid for a boy but quite honestly I'm not thrilled by violence, I'm not interested in violence. This is mainly why they don't like me, they don't like Matthew either because he won't fight—neither will I.

INTERVIEWER: Do you visit each other's houses?

EDWARD: Rarely.

INTERVIEWER: Do you live a long way away?

EDWARD: No, about 100 yards away from each other actually, but we are very seldom granted permission to go out.

INTERVIEWER: Why is this?

EDWARD: I don't know, but I think it's something to do with the fact that I am sometimes late home, but we of course are allowed a decent modicum of freedom, I mean I am allowed to go into town—whereas my younger sisters aren't—on my own, and I've been allowed to go into the library.

INTERVIEWER: You belong to the Public Library?

EDWARD: Yes, and in fact it's quite obvious that I would join sooner or later because of my interest in reading. I read *really* fast.

INTERVIEWER: Have you any other interests besides reading and science?

EDWARD: Cars, and things to do with cars.

INTERVIEWER: When did this interest start?

EDWARD: About the age of 4, I believe it started when I found I could only draw cars, I'm not much good at drawing.

INTERVIEWER: Who helps you with this interest?

EDWARD: Nobody, it's my own interest.

INTERVIEWER: Are there any hobbies or interests you would like to have but haven't had the opportunity?

EDWARD: Hovercraft, I've been for four different rides on hovercraft and I'm jolly interested in them.

INTERVIEWER: Is there any special hobby your parents would like you to have?

EDWARD: Probably stamp-collecting or bird watching, or boring things like that.

INTERVIEWER: What kind of a person are you?

EDWARD: I don't approve of cheating. I don't like collecting in case I don't get the set. I'm scientifically-minded. I don't like writing things down. I like closely guarded secrets. I feel a lot older than I really am. I like to feel grown-up. I'd like to have a job of my own and money to buy books and cars.

INTERVIEWER: Do you ever think about serious things?

EDWARD: I don't know about God, that's not proved—I puzzle about it sometimes but I don't know.

INTERVIEWER: Do you ask grown-ups?

EDWARD: No, I don't ask about things like that, I puzzle for myself.

INTERVIEWER: You've lived 11 years. What do you think about life?

EDWARD: There's more to it than having a good time. We should all do the hard things as well as the easy things. It's wonderful, full of wonderful things like us—we have such highly developed brains.

Summary

Edward might be taken to represent the stereotype of a 'gifted' child; he talked like a 'professor', he was not popular with his peers, he was clumsy and unworldly, an irritant to his teachers and parents. However, he was unique in this study group. He was perhaps the most academically able child of all those seen and one of the most interesting to interview.

He had not been equally well received by the schools he had attended; one spoiled him by making him a teacher's pet, perhaps setting up a permanent pattern of difficulty in relation to his peers; another resented his power as a person in some way and could not welcome his kind of ability. However, one group of teachers managed to provide a setting in which he felt at home and satisfied, they were his 'kind of people'. They did not rate him at 7 years of age as 'maladjusted' on the Stott social adjustment guide, only as 'unsettled' (score 12). The main problem he posed in class was his need for adult conversation. Should this be regarded as a fault?

Edward received encouragement from his parents though they found him different from themselves and hard to understand. They had done what they could to prepare him for the situations he met and were proud of his abilities, but perhaps not tolerant enough of his idiosyncrasies.

Edward resented being treated as a child by the local librarian, he was not allowed at 11 years of age to use the adult section to which he needed access. He was aware of his own problems and objective about the efforts of adults to control him.

His case showed how important is the relationship between parents and teachers. Someone of his ability needed to have special consideration and provision in school to satisfy in him what adults only can give. A small country school with few members of staff might well have difficulty in catering for someone of his talents.

JOHN

Identified as 'gifted' by parents' letter (Group 7)
Wechsler Intelligence Test: Full scale IQ 143, Verbal 131, Performance 147
Reading test at 11 years   Top 25 per cent of age group
Mathematics test at 11 years   Top 18 per cent of age group
Favourite subjects: craft, art, science, games
Boring subject: music
Interests: making things, painting, drawing, science, playing outside
Not interested in: collecting, writing, music and clubs
Social class IV

At birth

John was a firstborn child. His birth was prolonged and for the first month of his life he suffered from convulsions. His father worked on an assembly line in a factory and his mother also worked in a factory before marriage.

At 7 years of age

When the record from his teachers when he was 7 was consulted, it was found that he was considered *below* average in oral ability, reading, number work and awareness of the world, although his results on the test of reading and that of arithmetic suggested he achieved more than appeared (21/30 reading score 8/10 arithmetic). From the Stott social adjustment guide, some clues are obtained about his behaviour; he was reported to be shy, wanting adult interest but could not put himself forward, could not concentrate for long, was too restless ever to work alone; however, he was a good mixer with other children, never fought and was liked. He was also reported to be attractive, well-dressed and healthy.

At 11 years of age

INTERVIEWER'S REPORT

He brought with him a drawing of a complicated electrical experiment he had invented consisting of batteries and wires, etc. He was very co-operative in the tests, quick, competent and insightful on scientific, spatial and non-verbal material. His drawings showed originality. He was slow and deliberate on verbal questions, his answers were restricted but generally to the point. His chief interest was inventing things and he was very definite about this, he wanted to be an inventor 'to invent things that move'. His standard of English was low, spelling and sentence construction weak.

SCHOOL REPORT

His teachers rated him as in the middle 40 per cent of the age group for general knowledge, use of books, oral ability and mathematics. His test scores indicated higher achievement and so did the fact that he was in an 'A' stream class (there were forty-five children in it). No answers were given to the open questions about future school and job performance, nor to the personality questions on virtues and faults. He had a low Stott score so there was no indication of 'unsettledness' or 'maladjustment'.

PARENT'S INTERVIEW

MOTHER: He's a very quiet child. Well-mannered—it just seems to be natural although I keep him to it. He's got feeling for others.
INTERVIEWER: Can you say what it is you most enjoy about him?
MOTHER: He's a good child, he doesn't give much trouble.
INTERVIEWER: How does he react to being punished or corrected?
MOTHER: He gets very upset if he's shouted at for something serious, when his report was not so good. We said, 'How has this happened,

you're slipping?' He got very upset. He said he'd tried and he didn't know what had happened. If he knows he's done his best and it's not up to scratch he gets upset.

INTERVIEWER: Is there anything that really worries you about him?

MOTHER: Sometimes I think he hasn't as much confidence as I think he should have—just with children of his own age—he can stick up for himself if anyone picks on him, but he'd sooner forget it and not trouble.

INTERVIEWER: Does he enjoy school? What is the school like? What do you think about it?

MOTHER: Oh! yes—quite enjoys it. It seems all right, I don't seem to have too much confidence in it.

INTERVIEWER: How does he get on with school work?

MOTHER: It's very easy for him. The headmaster said he was about average. English is not as easy to him as arithmetic. He doesn't seem to do so much painting and drawing in primary school as he'll get at secondary. He does the sketching and painting for the school paper—he's very interested. There's no science rooms in the primary school so he can't practice—he's got a microscope I bought him the Christmas before last, a small one. He loves watching things, but not at school. I think he gets a bit bored at school.

INTERVIEWER: What type of school would you like John to go to?

MOTHER: Secondary modern, but if his ability is better he would go to a selective school. At first he was keen to go to a selective school. Now he's changed his mind. I suppose because of his friends. They don't have woodwork at grammar school and they have a lab in the secondary modern; I don't know much about the grammar type, but he's got just as much a chance, if he's got any ability, of it coming out in secondary modern as they are now.

INTERVIEWER: What sort of things does he like to do in his own time?

MOTHER: Since nine years of age his main interest is to potter around at home with a hammer and nails. He made a table—very rough—his dad helps sometimes with difficult bits of Leggo or inventions. He loves his microscope and drawing and printing. He likes to play out like other boys.

INTERVIEWER: It's early yet, but have you thought what kind of work you would like him to do?

MOTHER: No, I haven't because it would only be something he was interested in. He's always drawing—perhaps he should be a draughtsman, follow it up; only once he said he wanted to be an architect. I don't know if he really knew what it was, I said 'You've got a long way to go!'

INTERVIEWER: What sort of things does he read?

MOTHER: Comics, encyclopaedia he's got, he's always looking that up. Not the daily papers at all, not news.

INTERVIEWER: Where does he get books from?

MOTHER: I buy them, not the public library.

JOHN'S INTERVIEW

(The efforts of the interviewer to encourage John have been omitted, only questions immediately preceding his responses are quoted.)

INTERVIEWER: How much do you like school?
JOHN: Don't like it much . . . not very keen on school.
INTERVIEWER: Which subjects do you find interesting at school?
JOHN: Science, art, crafts . . . games . . . that's all.
INTERVIEWER: Which subjects do you find boring?
JOHN: Music.
INTERVIEWER: What about the others? (*He has a list in front of him. No response.*) English?
JOHN: It's all right.
INTERVIEWER: Mathematics?
JOHN: Not very much.
INTERVIEWER: What is your favourite subject?
JOHN: Crafts.
INTERVIEWER: Can you say what has made it your favourite subject?
JOHN: I like making things.
INTERVIEWER: How much do you like getting things down on paper?
JOHN: Not very much.
INTERVIEWER: What are your interests, tell me about them.
JOHN: Inventing things . . . drawing . . . painting.
INTERVIEWER: Anything else? Tell me some more about your hobbies. (*No response.*) Do you ever invent games?
JOHN: Yes—invented one.
INTERVIEWER: Tell me about it.
JOHN: I forget.
INTERVIEWER: Do you ever write stories or poems at home?
JOHN: No . . . only at school . . . don't like writing them.
INTERVIEWER: How did your interest in inventing things start? (*No response.*) What do you invent? Tell me a bit about it.
JOHN: I like inventing things that move . . . I like seeing things that move, you see, so I make them meself . . . I like seeing things that work so I make some meself.
INTERVIEWER: Is there anything you would like to do as a hobby but haven't had the chance?
JOHN: Invent a computer . . . or a robot.
INTERVIEWER: How much do you use books?
JOHN: Use them a lot in school.
INTERVIEWER: Tell me the names of some books you've read recently, say in the last month.
JOHN: Don't think I've read any.
INTERVIEWER: How many books have you of your own?
JOHN: None . . . reading books, just reading books? I've got an encyclopaedia and atlases.

INTERVIEWER: What are the other members of your family interested in?

JOHN: My brother and father are interested in football.

INTERVIEWER: Anything else, and what about your mother?

JOHN: I don't know.

INTERVIEWER: What kind of person are you?

JOHN: Person who likes inventing things.

INTERVIEWER: What do other children like about you?

JOHN: I can draw good.

INTERVIEWER: What do you want to be when you grow up?

JOHN: An inventor.

INTERVIEWER: How does a person become an inventor?

JOHN: Start when he's young.

INTERVIEWER: You've lived 11 years now, what do you think about life?

JOHN: Interesting.

INTERVIEWER: Have you ever puzzled about something because you couldn't decide whether it was real or not real?

JOHN: . . . yes . . . drawings that can be seen from two angles.

(An interesting answer, but no further elaboration evoked. His definitions of different subjects were just as brief and sporadic.)

Summary

In the specially selected gifted group John did well. His IQ and high scores on divergent thinking tests put him in the top fifteen boys. He performed on achievement tests at an above average, but not superior level. His shyness may have been due to his difficulty with verbal expression or vice versa, but these two things go together and seemed to be preventing him from revealing more of himself in school. Although his teachers rated him as only average, he was in an 'A' stream, he received no special help of any kind though it was obvious that he needed it in English. As one of forty-five in a class he was unlikely to get the individual instruction he needed to improve his spelling. He had a keen interest in science and was supported by a mother who did the best she could for him, but he needed more active help in pursuing his ideas about inventing and more contact with books if his interests were not to wane for lack of stimulation.

Perhaps John should have the last word. His essay showed the difficulty he had with spelling and sentence structure, but he had ambition and a positive outlook for his future life.

His approach to the essay was rather original, only thirty-two children used a story form for their answer. He conveyed his interest in science and awareness of its special approach, he saw himself as a professor and managed to include reference to the satisfaction and pleasure of inventing.

'Imagine that you are now 25 years old. Write about the life you are leading, your interests, your home life and your work at the age of 25.'

I start out from the house at seven o'clock, my work is fifty miles away and I go by car. My car is a rover and I get to work about twenty to nine. My work is in a Laborty and my name is proffesser J. I work mostly with the microscope looking at backtria and other things like it. Today I am going to try to find or make something to cure a sertian germ. I use lots of diverent things, mixing them toether and - writing down each time I add another sustence what it is, and how much I use.

Every time I add somthing to it I test it whith germs by puting them in it puting them and the subsence under a microscope and then looking at it for a few mintes and when it does not work I sterile it and add another subsence, I then do the same as I did to the one before. Just before I have my lunch I find somthing, after a while, evrything is - still. I then eat my lunch firly quily but when I came back I found it only knocked them out for a bit but the next subsance realy killed the germs and I whent home very pleased with myself.

Conclusion

14. Discussion and recommendations

Problems of identification

This study of gifted children presented a formidable challenge. It raised problems of selection and testing of a most difficult kind for which there were no conventional solutions: one could only choose those which seemed most appropriate at the time. The identification of 'giftedness' by such means might have resulted in a cancelling out of excellence by the disparity of results on such a variety of criteria of selection and of tests. It might have proved, too, that the children were superior to the questions and tasks presented, too sophisticated to co-operate and clever enough to confound the interviewers' purposes.

Bridges (1969) in his recent book brought out into the open once again the fantastic ideas that still surround our notions of 'genius', 'gifted', 'intellectual' children. His students hesitated about offering to work with such children, for they felt inadequate to deal with superior talents and daunted by the thought of them. They are not alone in their doubts: many teachers are similarly disturbed when they are confronted with an exceptional pupil, and some parents also share these feelings when they are told, or observe, that their child is exceptionally able or talented. One says: 'Yes, she is very intelligent, but she's a *normal* girl'; another says: 'The teacher says he's a gifted boy but he's not peculiar in any way'. Both are trying to inhibit the ideas of abnormality and strangeness that are sometimes associated with exceptional talent.

Most people seem to think of themselves as 'average' and 'normal' if they can manage their affairs satisfactorily, because for the most part they associate with others like themselves. The idea that others are a little cleverer, a little better endowed can be accepted, but if that idea has to stretch to some who are a great deal cleverer and much better endowed, this widened gap can lead to inadequate and uncomfortable feeling. The idea of the unknown is challenging in any sphere and 'exceptional', 'superior' and 'genius-like' children can certainly come into this category. For one thing, there are relatively so few of them that most parents and teachers do not get regular enough experience with them to form realistic ideas about the possible general features of their

198

thinking and behaviour. For another, there is so much more that is common to any group of children that it is difficult to select those features to attend to that differentiate 'exceptions' from the rest.

The difficulty lies in the fact that a category like 'gifted' is a disjunctive concept, individual children may stand out from their peers by reason of their advanced skill in a sport, or their advanced ability in mathematics, or music or language, and though each one is alike in terms of the 'standing out from' or 'advancement over' his peers, they may have no other defining attributes in common. Yet all studies focused on 'giftedness' search for common attributes. When these are found the danger is that they may be used to predict from class membership to the properties of the members in an absolute way instead of a probabilistic way. For instance, because it has been found that children of high IQ (over 140) tend to be heavier or healthier than others it is likely that those outstanding in sport, where physical fitness is at a premium, will be of high intelligence, but it is not necessarily so. The relationships between what is common to some children who come into the gifted category and what is specific to some others are complex. There are no simple conjunctive definitions as yet on which action in the applied field of education could be confidently based.

Musical precocity in young children seems to stand out more clearly than that in other subjects. Perhaps this is because in our culture comparatively few people are musically literate, and in education it tends to come low on the list of priorities, so that anyone with any talent at all is noticeable. Perhaps it is that the judgment of promise in music is not left to general class teachers but is made by experts in music who seem clear about the perceptual and conceptual criteria upon which to judge ability. There are many experts outside the confines of school who are vocationally committed to fostering talent and to teaching skills and knowledge in music. Individual instrumental lessons with a local teacher give children an opportunity to cultivate musical interests; some children revolt, some flourish, but at least the opportunity is available to those whose parents see its value and can pay for it.

There is no such out-of-school evaluation and education available in any comparable sense for other subjects. Opportunities for children in sport, particularly in football, swimming and tennis, are increasing in some areas where coaches are seeking young talent, but mathematicians, scientists, historians, geographers, artists, etc. have no such nationwide private teaching system as music although a few local clubs of one kind and another are being provided.

Primary school children are usually deemed gifted in mathematics if they can encompass the school syllabus and gain high marks in a test standardised for their age group. Are mathematicians satisfied with this description of talent in their field, or, like the musicians, have they criteria of perceptual and conceptual skills by which they would rather judge children's performance? And what does an historian accept as a gifted child in his subject? Until we have a much clearer knowledge of the developmental logic, as distinct from the academic structure, of various subjects in which we are evaluating children, we are unable to make precise judgments about ability at an early age. It is probably more useful to be guided by tests of reasoning or intelligence which, by their method of construction and general assumptions about the nature of thinking, obtain a sample of several abilities which have been shown to have predictive value over a range of different content. But it has to be remembered that exceptionally high scores in such tests do not necessarily mean that the children will stand out in any particular traditional school subject.

The Plowden (1967) and Donnison (1970) reports raised the difficulty of deciding what proportion of the population should be classed as 'gifted'. They drew attention to the fact that definitions range from 5 per cent to 0·5 per cent or even less (IQ 125+ to 140+). The Donnison committee defined giftedness as the top 2 per cent (IQ 130+) in their analysis, noting the decrease in reliability of tests at the extremes of their distributions. Factors of interest, motivation and personality were quoted as determining the degree, manner and slant of achievement. Educational opportunity, amount and quality of teaching and social variables could be added to their list. 'Thus to ensure that all those who are likely to achieve highly in later life were included, one might have to cast the net so widely as to include a majority who would not be classed as gifted by anybody' (Donnison 1970).

The present study group

The children who were identified as 'gifted' were selected on multiple criteria. Although some of the criterion subgroups differed in range of intelligence, the children as a whole were well above average, 48 per cent having IQs over two standard deviations above the mean, 37 per cent having IQs between one and two standard deviations above the mean and only 15 per cent in the average range. The group showed above average all-round ability at 7 years of age and continued to do so at 11.

The children who were selected on superiority in one specific area tended to obtain IQs in the top 2 per cent of the Wechsler scale. Although they showed considerable promise in mathematics, science, story and poetry writing, sport, etc., their performances were relative to other children of their age. No child was sufficiently forward in any one area for his products to be judged on equal terms with those of adults. That is why in studying the children as a group, the intelligence quotient was resorted to as giving the best categorical unit of analysis.

Performance in school

There were thirteen children quite outstanding on the Wechsler scale in that they obtained a maximum score of 150+. Nine (70 per cent) were placed by their teachers in the highest category (top 5 per cent) on at least one of the four areas rated (general knowledge, mathematics, use of books, oral ability); the other four children were rated in the second category above average (top 6–30 per cent). In the 140 IQ group nineteen children (50 per cent) had one rating at least in the highest category, and only one child was considered only average in all four areas. It follows that although one or two individuals might have been underestimated or underfunctioning in school, the majority of the very intelligent children were assessed as above average in most respects. The rating scale was a coarse grading and every child came from a different school with a complexity of variables operating on the teachers' judgments: in these circumstances this result seems satisfactory in doing justice to the children as a group. It might be said, however, that there are indications that teachers are not differentiating finely enough the abilities of their pupils at the top end of the scale.

Among those with the highest Wechsler IQ scores was a majority of boys who were marked by their high performance in mathematics and their keen interest in science both at home and at school. Yet on another intelligence test the girls excelled. A group test (second follow-up of the cohort) showed the girls changing rank order with the boys. Although the boys changed rank they were still well above average. The differences could lie in the type of test given, one an individual test, the other a group test. The individual test was shortened (four subtests verbal, four subtests non-verbal) and it was given at the end of a long session which perhaps was more fatiguing to the girls than the boys. There may have been something in the fact that the individual testers were women. Perhaps the girls responded better in their known school situation where they were seen as high achievers. The differences could lie in the tests themselves: one oral, one pencil and paper; one standardised on American children; one on British children; one with practical things to do, the other relying more on visual and reading skills. Whatever the reasons, these results reaffirm that for reliable estimates of children's abilities by standardised tests, more than one test and one kind of test are necessary, particularly at this top end of the scale when finer discriminations of ability are required.

It was no surprise to find that there was not more overlap between the groups selected on different criteria; this could have been predicted statistically. It only confirms that, if selection of a gifted group has to be made, multiple criteria should be employed or some children of high general or specific abilities will be overlooked. Burt (1962a) suggests that the focus should be on each individual child as a whole and not merely on his intellectual capacity. He advised selection not only by formal standardised tests, particularly those administered individually, but also by continued observations of the experienced teacher during his daily contacts with each pupil in the classroom and outside it. The results of this study show the need to add to the list the opinions of parents and even of the children themselves. Many able children know and accept that they are clever in some way and can express this without conceit. It may be important that their judgments should be affirmed.

The children in the present study showed that on the whole they were satisfied with the provision made for them at school and so were their parents. The children expressed considerable appreciation of teachers who by sheer teaching skill held their interest and stretched their powers of learning to a satisfying level. They were all achieving reasonable standards in the main skills of basic subjects or literacy which standardised tests of attainment measure, but beyond these many children were having an extension of their all round abilities by being introduced to a wide range of subject matters and activities which are available to people in our culture. These are, for some children, already forming the bases for well-defined interests and these in turn are the bases for the beginning of vocational choice to which the children, even at the age of 11 are turning their thoughts. It is the excitement of knowledge in special areas and a glimpse of their future possibilities that is important at the junior stage, the practical necessity of choosing a job is not urgent upon them as it will be in later adolescence.

'Excitement' seems an appropriate word to use here because children of this age like the idea of adventure and indeed search for it in their literature, and the brightest children are already aware of adventure in ideas. Many of them gain delight from collecting and ordering and classifying objects and information, searching for the unusual, hoping to find the unique, already well beyond the amorphous amassing stage of average 11-year-olds. Others gain pleasure from the use of words and try their skills out in writing a novel, or more difficult still, a poem involving the exploration of abstract ideas. It is this anticipation that more is yet to come from the use of the thinking skills they know they possess that adults need to cultivate. Each teacher a child meets may have his or her own areas of special interest and pleasure in knowledge, but no one teacher or perhaps even one school (especially a small school) can cover the variety of subject matter that able primary children can encompass. Where middle schools are being established, it has to be accepted that the overall level of knowledge possessed by general subject teachers will no longer satisfy the intellectual level which the most able children can reach. Therefore, as recommended in the Plowden report, ways of involving many teachers and other adults in children's education must be sought.

Dullness and repetition are unlikely to be avoided altogether during the educative process. Bright children who so clearly see that life has its ups and downs can tolerate the boredom of it along with the rest, but to be held exclusively to that feeling could only be personally damaging in that it leads to the avoidance of effort in the pursuit of knowledge.

Special care for the underprivileged

Most of the children studied received excellent stimulus at home for their intellectual growth, from parents who take them out and about, who share their own interests and provide equipment and books for the children to pursue theirs. There are, however, a few children who are caught in limiting circumstances, financial, social or educational, and who are not recognised as highly able. They are doing averagely well, but circumstances are not forwarding them in the main area or areas of their immediate strivings for knowledge and skills. These children can be found and assisted only by awareness on someone's part of the very high degree of their general ability, their home circumstances and school setting and who can form a relationship with each child that is of a kind to allow him to express his personal interests and hopes. Head teachers would seem to be the people who have the opportunity to take this overview of each child. They have access to records, the immediate duty to consult parents and the right to ask for consultation with advisers, inspectors, educational psychologists and others who may serve a local education authority. Since the 1944 Education Act stressed the responsibility of LEAs for handicapped, including maladjusted, children, great progress has been made in diagnosis and educational provision of many kinds. The agencies involved in the assessment of individual children in these categories perhaps are not yet employed sufficiently in the assessment of children who are 'exceptional' by reason of their cleverness. It would be unfortunate if they were to be considered 'handicapped' for they are in quite a different category, as the positive personality descriptions and the superior scores on the social adjustment scale of the study's children have shown. But some are in need of more intricate assessment than can be made by one class teacher.

Intelligence and 'creativity'

Nothing was gained in this group by separating the 'intelligent' from the 'creative' children on test results. It was clear that the children in the top IQ range were able to do well on all types of test. In the final analysis, creative work needs to be under the constraint of evaluation, so both aspects of thought are likely to be highly developed in those who are to make their mark as outstanding in adult life. The complexity of the problems of convergent and divergent thinking is beginning to emerge in psychology and the results of research to date only leave educators with reminders to observe the individual styles of problem solving that children reveal and to provide educational settings that give opportunity for the exploratory aspect of the sciences and the expressive aspect of the arts as well as the impressive of both.

The American literature on creativity needs to be read with caution by English teachers. It has to be remembered that most American schools use a strict grade system with a compulsory syllabus which does not encourage the search for differentiation of and provision for individual talents. In this country the search for promising children for scholarship places has always been a feature of the educational system and methods have been devised and revised to assist teachers in the problem of selection. It has been accepted that there are above average children and efforts have been made to help them to do well in those subjects on which they were to be judged. It has been held by many primary teachers that the pressures associated with selection for different types of secondary school at eleven-plus prevented a wide range of subjects getting equal attention on the time table. Teachers have sometimes considered it too risky to experiment with new syllabuses or methods of teaching and classroom organisations which take into account different rates of development among children of similar age and variation of abilities within individual children. But restrictions of selection are diminishing as comprehensive secondary education is being developed, and many junior schools are now able to be more adventurous in range of subject matter and teaching procedures, as adventurous at least as size of classes, suitability of building and interest and skills of teachers will allow.

It was perhaps to be expected that there would be different results in USA from in Britain on some kinds of tests. The consistent policy of the Department of Education and Science here has been to encourage diversity and experiment, and freedom has been given to teachers to make the best use of their skills and circumstances. The simulation exercises in creativity recommended by Torrance (1961) and De Bono (1969) need critical evaluation against what our best primary schools achieve through their flexible approaches to the curriculum.

Thought and language

One of the outstanding features of the most able children studied here and elsewhere is the volume of information they are able to obtain and retain. They have detailed knowledge of a wide range of subject matter. Sometimes the word 'magpie-like' is used to describe the facility with which such children appear to amass facts, but the information is not as randomly collected as might appear, the children become emotionally committed to an idea or topic and spare no efforts in their searches to encompass what is to be known about it. The importance of books in relation to intelligence has been reaffirmed in this study: ownership of books, access to books, encouragement to search in books are all features associated with the cleverest children. This emphasises the better verbal ability and conversational facility which marks so many of them and earns them comments on confidence and sociability. However, the work of Lovell and Shields (1967) and this study show that there is more to be investigated in the apparently high verbal content of gifted children's minds and their underlying thinking structures. Few 11-year-olds even with intelligence quotients over 140 appear to be able to reason at the level of formal operations in Piaget's sense of the term. More information about the areas of knowledge where it might be possible for such children to be superior is needed, and it must be considered whether acceleration in one or two areas is worth sacrificing to the enrichment of mind that variety and detail on a broad front in concrete operational thinking can bring.

The study included children selected on non-verbal criteria and extra numbers from social classes IV and V were added, but the sample remained skewed in the middle-class direction. The results show that the children of above average intelligence from working-class homes managed to hold their own in basic school subjects between 7 and 11 years of age. They did less well on tests with a high verbal content, though equally well as others from the middle class when performance and non-verbal tests were employed. There is some affirmation of previous studies that have shown such children to possess adequate language structures though they perhaps use them infrequently. This suggests that it is the content of ideas that is limited, perhaps because they do not engage enough in activities and conversation that demand a high level of conceptual thought and language.

The case for non-segregation

The results of the study indicate that criticisms of the failure of teachers to identify and provide for the most able children are probably being made on a few extreme cases since the majority of such children were found to be known and catered for satisfactorily. This is not to deny that schools and teaching skills could be improved. Some children throughout the intelligence range are being understimulated, unrecognised in one or another aspect of their potential, but it seems that general improvement throughout the educational system is as likely to improve the lot of able children as segregating them permanently for different treatment. There was no clear case of a child in difficulty simply by reason of his degree of brightness: change of school, physical handicap, limited parental ambition, uninspiring school situations were other variables operating against some children, but each one presented his own pattern of interaction. It would be difficult to justify special treatment for any one IQ group when the associated limiting factors are equally distressing for those in other IQ groups.

'Acceleration' by grouping able children with those older than themselves was one method used to cater for half the number of children in this study. This form of provision must involve long-term planning for a child's career in the primary school. If it means that eventually 2 years have to be spent in the final class it can cause distress to some children who feel resentful when their older friends move on to secondary school while they have to stay behind to join again their age group. There is also the problem of the repetition of work which has a frustrating effect on those who probably mastered it quickly the first time.

The Plowden (1967) and Donnison (1970) reports recommend that special arrangements be made for individuals or groups by means of enriched courses allowing the most able pupils to explore subjects in greater detail, both in and out of school.

There seems a strong case for an overview of each gifted child's life circumstances and this is indeed the right of every child. 'Giftedness' in the definition of general or specific ability would be one aspect among many that would be considered in making educational decisions about a child. Enrichment of curriculum and the challenge of children of high intellectual level will present teachers with problems, but our educational system allows for and encourages flexible solutions to such problems. It has to be remembered that if one of the solutions were to be to withdraw the children of highest intelligence for education separate from others, they would no longer be gifted in relation to the group that was formed, a few would become very superior, but the rest would statistically fall into 'average' and 'below average' categories, and such children might not have the opportunity to form realistic ideas about themselves in relation to a more normal population. Many who were outstanding in leadership in a normal setting might, in the segregated situation, be deprived of the experience of learning to understand and co-operate with companions of less able intellect who, nevertheless, have equal value as persons and equal rights as members of the group.

The risk of nervous strain

In all the tested items the only one on which the more intelligent children showed themselves to be at a disadvantage was concerned with their tendency to 'worry' and to find life somewhat difficult. This was observed by parents; the children themselves were positive about welcoming life and making the most of it. Perhaps, however, adults should be alerted to the degree of strain that might have to be associated with high achievement if it were forced rather than cultivated. Seventy per cent of the gifted children expressed negative attitudes, fears and symptoms of nervousness on the item in the sentence completion test which began 'Tests and examinations . . . .'. There was no greater welcome for the competitiveness which can be associated with high academic achievements from the exceptionally intelligent than the rest.

Points that call for greater awareness

Teachers could be reminded by this study of a probable tendency to overestimate girls, which means paying closer attention to promising boys, ensuring that activities provided cover their special interests particularly in the sciences and manipulative skills, where reading and writing need not play such a large part in assessment. Special attention, too, can be drawn to children who, because of social circumstances, need more help than others from teachers to possess and have access to books. Lastly, the quiet and shy children, who though they did not appear to be overlooked by teachers in this study, always need special encouragement to find an avenue of expression through which they can reveal their talents.

Parents in this study have shown a tendency to undervalue the abilities of their bright girls. They also need, especially if they are well-educated themselves, to be more aware of the range of ability in the population at large so that they do not judge their children on the evidence of the behaviour of a narrow social band.

There are cultural stereotypes of what is appropriate masculine or feminine behaviour which may be limiting to the development of some children. The highly intelligent are able to rise above these restrictions.

Everyone needs to be conscious of the range of meanings subsumed under the term 'gifted' in our society and the word should be qualified by specific description when it is used. We should not be surprised if unevenness in development and behaviour is found in a child of high general intelligence: it is as typical of children in that category as it is in any other IQ group. If some 'average' children are expected to show variations—physical, social and emotional—within their development, so also should some intellectually superior children, for even if exceptional in the intellectual aspect at 11 years old they are still more like children than adults and need to be judged within that context. Gifted children, on whatever criteria they are selected, stand or fall by the quality of education they receive. Their successful development is dependent on their being with adults who are informed about child development and methods of assessment of human potential, knowledgeable about subject matter and skilled in stimulating, instructing and guiding children's efforts to understand the world. The best educators, parents and teachers, are those who are able to enjoy human beings in the stage of childhood and yet are quick to appreciate and encourage their thrusts into adult thought and behaviour whenever they appear.

Bibliography

Abbreviations used: *Brit. J. Ed. Psychol: British Journal of Educational Psychology;*
N.F.E.R.: National Foundation for Educational Research.

ANDERSON, C. C. and CROPLEY, A. J. (1966) 'Some correlates of originality', *Australian Journal of Psychology*, **18** (3), 218–27.

ANDERSON, H. H., ed. (1959) *Creativity and its Cultivation.* New York, Haysen & Row.

ARMSTRONG, H. S. (1967) Wastage of ability amongst the intellectually gifted *Brit. J. Ed. Psychol.*, **37**, no. 2, 257–9.

AUSUBEL, D. P. (1966) 'The use of advance organisers in the learning and retention of meaningful verbal material', in Rosenblith and Allinsmith, *Causes of Behaviour*, **11**, Allyn & Bacon, 1966.

BABARIK, P. (1966) 'Preference for subordinating or superordinating and creativity in engineers, scientists, designers and artists', *Perceptual and Motor Skills*, 23 Jan. pp. 271–8.

BARBE, W. B. (1955) 'Characteristics of Gifted children', *Educational Administration and Supervision*, **41**, no. 4, 207–17.

BARBE, W. B. (1956) 'A study of the family background of the gifted', *Journal of Educational Psychology*, **47**, pp. 302–9.

BARKER-LUNN, J. C. (1970) *Streaming in the Primary School.* N.F.E.R.

BARRON, F. (1955) 'The disposition towards originality', *Journal of Abnormal Social Psychology*, **51**, 478–85.

BARRON, F. (1958) 'Psychology of the imagination', *Scientific American*, **199**, no. 50, 151.

BARRON, F. (1963) *Creativity and Psychological Health.* Princeton, N.J., Van Nostrand.

BARRON, F. (1965) *The Psychology of Creativity in New Directions in Psychology*, vol. ii. New York, Holt, Rinehart & Winston.

BARRON, F. and TAYLOR, C. W. (1963) *Scientific Creativity: its recognition and development.* New York, Wiley.

BARRON, F. and WELSH, G. S. (1952) 'Artistic perception as a factor in personality style: its measurement by a picture preference test', *J. Psychol.* **33**, 199–203.

BEREDAY, G. Z. F. and LAUWERYS, J. A. eds. (1962) *Yearbook of Education*, New York, Harcourt, Brace & Warter.

BERNSTEIN, B. (1960) Language and Social Class, *British Journal of Sociology*, **2**, 271–6.

BRANCH, M. and CASH, A. (1966) *Gifted Children.* Souvenir Press.

BRIDGES, S. A. (1969) *Gifted Children and the Brentwood Experiment.* Pitman.

BRITTAIN, M. (1968) 'Comparative study of the use of W.I.S.C. and St-Binet with 8-year-old children, *Brit. J. Ed. Psychol.*, **38**, pt. I, 103–4.

BURNS, C. L. C. (1949) 'Maladjusted children of high intelligence', *Brit. J. Ed. Psychol.*, **19**, 137–41.

BURT, C. (1911) 'Experimental tests of higher mental processes', *Journal of Experimental Pediatrics*, **1**, 93.

BURT, C. (1945) 'The Reliability of Teachers' assessments of their Pupils', *Brit. J. Ed. Psychol.*, **15**, 80–93.

BURT, C. (1959) 'General ability and special aptitudes', *Educational Research*, **1**, 3–16.
BURT, C. (1961) 'The gifted child', *British Journal of Statistical Psychology*, **14**, 123–39.
BURT, C. (1962a) 'The gifted child', in *Year Book of Education*. London, Evans, General introduction.
BURT, C. (1962b) Review of Getzels and Jackson, *Brit. J. Ed. Psychol.*, **32**, 292.
BURT, C. (1963) 'Is intelligence distributed normally?', *British Journal of Statistical Psychology*, **16**, 175.
BURT, C. (1967) 'Critique of gifted children by Branch and Cash', *Brit. J. Ed. Psychol.* Pt. I, **37**, 143.
BURT, C. (1968) 'Mental capacity and its antics', *Bulletin of the British Psychological Society*, **21**, 70.
BURT, C. (1968) 'What are we doing for the highly gifted?', Association of Educational Psychologists, *Newsletter* no. 10, p. 2.
BURT, C. (1968) *Creativity in the Classroom*. Assoc. of Educ. Psychologists.
BURT, C. (1970) Foreword to Pringle (1970).
BUTCHER, H. J. and HASAN, P. (1966) 'Creativity and intelligence. (Replication of Getzels and Jackson)', *Brit. J. Psychol.*, **52**, nos. 1–2, 129.
BUTCHER, H. J. (1968) *Human Intelligence; its Nature and Assessment*. Methuen.
BUTLER, N. R. and ALBERMAN, E. (1969) *Perinatal Problems*. Livingstone.
BUTLER, N. R. and BONHAM, D. G. (1963) *Perinatal Mortality*. Livingstone.
CATTELL, R. B. (1945a) 'Personality traits associated with abilities: I, Intelligence and drawing', *Educational and Psychological Measurement*, **5**, 131–46.
CATTELL, R. B. (1945b) 'Personality traits associated with abilities: II, Verbal and Mathematical', *Journal of Educational Psychology*, **4**, 36, 475–86.
CATTELL, R. B. (1945c) The description of personality: III, Principles and findings in a factor analysis, *American Journal of Psychology*, III, 69–90.
CATTELL, R. B. and DREVDAHL, J. E. (1955) 'Comparison of eminent researchers, teachers, administrators and general population', *British Journal of Psychology*, **46**, 248.
CATTELL, R. B. and DREVDAHL, J. E. (1958) 'Personality and creativity in artists and writers', *Journal of Clinical Psychology*, **14**, 107–11.
CHAZAN, M. (1959) 'Maladjusted children in grammar schools', *Brit. J. Ed. Psychol.* **29**, no. 3, 198–206.
CHAZAN, M. (1968) 'Inconsequential behaviour in school children', *Brit. J. Ed. Psychol.*, **38**, no. 1, 5–9.
CHORNESS, M. H. and NOTTELMANN, D. A. (1956) *The Predictability of Creative Expression in Teaching*. Air Force Personnel and Training Research Centre, Texas.
COLTHAM, J. B. (1960) 'Junior school children's understanding of some terms commonly used in the teaching of history', Ph.D. thesis, Univ. of Manchester.
CONVERSE, H. D. and HUGHES, H. H. (1962) 'Characteristics of the gifted: case for a sequel to Terman's study', *Exceptional Child*, **29**, 179–83.
CRELLIN, E., PRINGLE, M. L. K. and WEST, P. (1971) *Born Illegitimate*. N.F.E.R.
CROPLEY, A. J. (1966) 'Creativity and intelligence', *Brit. J. Ed. Psychol.*, **36**, no. 3, 259–66.
CROPLEY, A. J. (1967) *Creativity*. Longmans.
CROSS, P. G., CATTELL, R. B. and BUTCHER, H. J. (1967) The Personality Pattern of Creative Artists. *Brit. J. Ed. Psychol.*, **27**, no. 3, 292.
COX, CATHERINE (1926) *Genetic Studies of Genius II. The Early Mental Trends of 300 Geniuses*. Stanford University Press.
DATTA, L. E. (1967) 'Birth order and early scientific attainment', *Perceptual and Motor Skills*, **24**, no. 1, 157–8.
DAVIE, R., BUTLER, N. R. and GOLDSTEIN, H. (1972) *From Birth to Seven*. Longman.
DAVIS, F. B. and LESSER, G. (1960) The Identification of Gifted Elementary School Children with Exceptional Scientific talent. *Hunter College Educational Journal*, Chicago.
DAVIS, F. B., LESSER, G. S. and FRENCH, E. (1960) *Identification and Class Behaviour of Gifted Elementary School Children*. The Gifted Student Co-op Research Mono. U.S. Govt. Printing Office no. 2, 19–32.
DE BONO, E. (1969) *Lateral Thinking*. Penguin.

DE CECCO, J. P. (1967) *The Psychology of Language, Thought and Instruction*. Holt, Rinehart and Winston.

DE HAAN, R. F. and HAVIGHURST, R. J. (1957) *Educating Gifted Children*. Univ. of Chicago Press.

DEPARTMENT OF EDUCATION AND SCIENCE (1968) Educating Gifted Children. *Reports on Education*, no. 48.

D'HEURLE, A., MELLINGER, J. C. and HAGGARD, E. A. (1959) 'Personality, intellectual and achievement patterns in gifted children', *Psychological Monographs, General and Applied*. American Psychological Association, **73**, no. 13, 483.

DE MILLE, R. and MERRIFIELD, P. R. (1962) 'Creativity and intelligence', *Educational and Psychological Measurement*, **22**, 803–8.

DONNISON REPORT (1970) Public Schools Commission, *Report on Independent Day Schools and Direct Grant Grammar Schools*. H.M.S.O.

DOUGLAS, J. W. B. (1964) *The Home and the School*. MacGibbon & Kee.

DREVDAHL, J. E. (1964) 'Some developmental and environmental factors in creativity', In C. W. Taylor, *Widening Horizons in Creativity*. Wiley.

EINDHOVEN, J. E. and VINACKE, W. E. (1952) 'Creative processes in painting', *Journal of General Psychology*, **47**, 139–64.

EDWARDS, M. P. and TYLER, L. E. (1965) 'Intelligence, creativity and achievement in a non-selective public junior high school', *Journal of Educational Psychology*, **56**, 96–99.

ELLIS, HAVELOCK (1904) *A Study of British Genius*. Hurst & Blackett.

FLOUD, J. E., HALSEY, A. H. and MARTIN, F. M. (1957) *Social Class and Educational Opportunity*. Heinemann.

FRASER, E. (1959) *Home Environment and the School*. Univ. of London Press for Scottish Council for Educational Research.

FREEMAN, J., BUTCHER, H. J. and CHRISTIE, T. (1968) *Creativity—a selected review of research*. Society for Research in Higher Education.

FRENCH, J. L. (1964) *Educating the Gifted*. Holt, Rinehart & Winston.

GALTON, FRANCIS (1892) Hereditary Genius, 2nd edn. Macmillan.

GETZELS, J. W. and JACKSON, P. W. (1960) *The Study of Giftedness*. Co-operative Research Monogr. U.S. Govt. Press, no. 2.

GETZELS, J. W. and JACKSON, P. W. (1962) *Creativity and Intelligence*. Wiley.

GALLAGHER, J. J. (1966) 'Sex differences in expressive thought of gifted children in the classroom', *Personnel and Guidance Journal*, **45**, no. 3, 248–53.

GALLAGHER, J. and LUCITO, L. (1960) 'Intellectual patterns of highly gifted children on the W.I.S.C.', *Peabody Journal of Education*, **38**, 131–6.

GHISELIN, B., ed. (1952) *The Creative Process*. University of California Press.

GOERTZEL, G., VIC, H. and MILDRED, G. (1962) *Cradles of Eminence*. Little, Brown & Co.

GOLANN, S. E. (1963) 'Psychological study of creativity', *Psychological Bulletin*, **60**, 548–65.

GOLANN, S. E. (1962) 'The creativity motive', *Journal of Personality*, **30**, 588–600.

GOLD, M. J. (1965) *Education of the Intellectually Gifted*. Columbus, Ohio. Charles E. Menill Booty.

GOLDBERG, M. L. and PASSOW, A. H. (1962) 'The talented youth: a progress report', *Exceptional Children*, **28**, 223–31.

GOLDBERG, M. L., RAPH, J. B. and PASSOW, H. A. (1966) *Bright Under-Achievers*. New York, Teachers' College Press.

GOLDMAN, R. (1964) 'The Minnesota tests of creative thinking', *Educational Research*, **7**, no. 1, 3.

GOODENOUGH, FLORENCE (1926) *Measurement of Intelligence by Drawings*. New York, World Book Co.

GOODENOUGH, F. L. and HARRIS, D. B. (1950) 'Studies in the psychology of children's drawings', *Psychological Bulletin*, **47**, 369–433.

GOODENOUGH, FLORENCE (1956) *Exceptional Children*. Appleton-Century-Crofts.

GOSPILL, G. H. (1966) *The Teaching of Geography*. Macmillan.

GOUGH, H. G. (1946) 'Relationship of socio-economic status and personality and achievement', *British Journal of Educational Psychology*, **37**, 527–540.

GOUGH, H. G. (1961) 'Techniques for identifying the creative research scientist', Mackinson, ed., *The Creative Person*. Berkeley, Calif.

GOWAN, J. C. (1955) 'The under-achieving gifted child: a problem for everyone', *Exceptional Children*, **21**, 248–9.

GOWAN, J. C. (1957) 'Dynamics of the under-achievement of gifted students', *Exceptional Children*, **24**, 98–107.

GOWAN, J. C. (1961) *An Annotated Bibliography on the Academically Talented Student*. N.E.A. Project, Washington D.C.

GOWAN, J. C. and GOWAN, M. S. (1955) 'The gifted child—an annotated Bibliography', *California Journal of Educational Research*, **6**, 72–94.

GOWAN, J. C., DEMOS, G. D. and TORRANCE, E. P. (1967) *Creativity: Its educational implications*. Wiley.

GRUBER, H. E., TERRELL, S. and WERTHEIMER, M. eds. (1962) *Contemporary Approaches to Creative Thinking*. New York, Athendor Press.

GUILFORD, J. P. (1957) 'Creative abilities in the arts', Psychological Review, **64**, 110–18.

GUILFORD, J. P. (1959a) 'Three faces of intellect', *American Psychologist*, **14**, 469–79.

GUILFORD, J. P. (1959b) 'Traits of creativity', in H. H. Anderson, ed. *Creativity and its Cultivation*. Harper and Row.

GUILFORD, J. P. (1967) 'Creativity: yesterday, today and tomorrow', *Journal of Creative Behavior*, **1**, no. 1, 3–14.

GUILFORD, J. P., FRICK, J. W., CHRISTENSEN, P. R. and MERRIFIELD, P. R. E. (1959) 'A factor analytic study of creative thinking', *Educational and Psychological Measurement*, **19**, 469–96.

GUILFORD, J. P., WILSON, R. C. and CHRISTENSEN, P. R. (1952) *A Factor Analytic Study of Creative Thinking*. University of California Press.

HADDON, F. A. and LYTTON, H. (1968) Teaching approach and the development of divergent thinking abilities in primary schools. *Brit. J. Ed. Psychol.* **38**, 171–80.

HALLAM, P. N. (1966) 'Logical thinking in history', *Educational Review*, 1966.

HALSEY, A. H. ed. (1961) *Ability and Educational Opportunity*. Organisation for Economic Co-operation and Development.

HALSEY, A. H., MARTIN, F. M. and FLOUD, J. E. (1957) *Social Class and Education Opportunity*. Heinemann.

HAMMER, E. F. (1961) *Creativity*, Random House.

HARRIS, D. B. (1963) *Children's Drawings as Measures of Intellectual Maturity: a revision and extension of the Goodenough Draw-a-Man test*. Harcourt Brace & World.

HASAN, P. (1965) 'Creativity and intelligence', B. Ed thesis, Edinburgh.

HASAN, P. and BUTCHER, H. J. (1966) 'Creativity and intelligence: a partial replication with Scottish children of Getzels and Jackson's study', *British Journal of Psychology*, **57**, 129–35.

HEIM, A. W. (1954) *The Appraisal of Intelligence*. Methuen.

HILDRETH, G. M. (1938) 'Characteristics of young gifted children', *Journal of Genetic Psychology*, **53**, 287–311.

HILDRETH, G. M. (1966) *Introduction to the Gifted*. McGraw-Hill.

HIMELSTEIN, P. and TRAPP, E. P., eds (1962) *Readings on the Exceptional Child*. Methuen.

HOLLINGWORTH, L. S. (1926) *Gifted Children: their nature and nurture*. Macmillan, NY.

HOLLINGWORTH, L. S. (1942) *Children above 180 IQ. Stanford-Binet: Origin and Development*. World Book Co.

HOLLINGWORTH, L. S. and COBB, M. V. (1928) 'Children clustering at 165 IQ. and children clustering at 145 IQ. compared for three years in achievement', in *Yearbook Nat. Soc. Stud. Educ.*, **27**, no. 11, 3–33.

HUDSON, L. (1962) 'Intelligence, divergence, and potential originality', *Nature, Lond.* **196**, 601–2.

HUDSON, L. (1963a) 'Personality and Scientific Aptitude', *Nature, Lond.* **189**, 913–14.

HUDSON, L. (1963b) 'The relation of psychological test scores to academic bias', *Brit. J. Ed. Psychol.* **33**, 120.

HUDSON, L. (1966) *Contrary Imaginations.* Methuen.

HYDSON, L. (1968) *Frames of Mind.* Methuen.

HUTCHINSON, M. and YOUNG, C. (1962) *Educating the Intelligent.* Penguin Books.

JACKSON, B. (1964) *Streaming.* Routledge & Kegan Paul.

JACKSON, B. and MARSDEN, D. (1962) *Education and the Working Class.* London Institute of Community Studies, Report No. 6.

JERSILD, A. T. and TASCH, R. J. (1949) *Children's Interests and what they suggest for Education.* Columbia University Press.

JONES, G. H. (1960) 'Relationship between personality and scholastic attainment', *Bulletin of the British Psychological Society*, **40**, 42.

KEMP, L. C. D. (1955) 'Environment, and other characteristics determining attainments in primary schools', *Brit. J. Ed. Psychol.* **25**, 67–77.

KIRK, S. A. (1962) *Educating Exceptional Children.* Houghton Mifflin.

KIRK, S. A. and WINER, B. B. (1966) *Behavioural Research on exceptional Children.* Council for Exceptional Children. Washington.

KOHN, M. L. (1959) 'Social class and the exercise of parental authority', *American Sociological Review*, pp. 352–66.

LAWTON, DENNIS (1968) *Social Class, Language and Education.* Routledge & Kegan Paul.

LEWIS, W. D. (1941) 'A comparative study of the personalities, interests and home backgrounds of gifted children of superior and inferior educational achievement', *Journal of Genetic Psychology*, **59**, 207.

LEWIS, W. D. (1943) 'Some characteristics of very superior children', *J. of Genetic Psychology*, **62**, 301–9.

LIEBERMAN, J. N. (1965) 'Playfulness and divergent thinking: an investigation of their relationship at the kindergarten level', *Journal of Genetic Psychology*, **107**, 219.

LIGHTFOOT, G. P. (1951) 'Personality characteristics of bright and dull children', *Contributions to Education*, no. 969. Bureau of Publications, Teachers College, Columbia University.

LITTLEJOHN, M. T. (1967) 'Creativity and masculinity-femininity in ninth graders', *Perceptual and Motor Skills*, **25**, 737–43.

LOBAN, W. D. (1963) *The Language of Elementary School Children.* N.C.T.E. Res. Rep No. 1 Champaign, Illinois.

LOVELL, K. and SHIELDS, J. B. (1967) 'Some aspects of a study of the gifted child', *Brit. J. Ed. Psychol.*, **37**, 201–9.

LYNN, R. (1959) Two personality characteristics related to academic achievement', *British Journal of Educational Psychology*, **29**, 213–16.

LYNN, R. and GORDON, L. E. (1961) 'The relation of neuroticism and extroversion to intelligence and educational attainment', *British Journal of Educational Psychology*, **31**, 194–202.

McCLELLAND, D. C., ed. (1958) *Talent and Society*, Von Nostrand Co.

McCLELLAND, D. C. (1962) 'On the psychodynamics of creative physical scientists', In Gruber *et al.* (1962).

McCLELLAND, D. C., ATKINSON, J. W., CLARK, R. A. and LOWELL, E. L. (1953) *The Achievement Motive.* Appleton-Century-Crofts.

MACKINNON, D. W. (1960) 'The highly effective individual', *Teacher's College Record*, **61**, 367–8.

MACKINNON, D. W. (1961) 'Personality correlates of creativity: a study of American architects', *Proc. XIVth International Conference of Applied Psychology.*

MACKINNON, D. W. (1962) 'The nature and nurture of creative talent', *American Psychologist*, **17**, 484–95.

MACKLER, B. and SHONTZ, P. C. (1967) 'Characteristics of responses to tests of creativity', *Journal of Clinical Psychology*, **33**, 1.

MADAUS, G. P. (1967) 'Divergent thinking and intelligence', *Journal of Educational Measurement*, **4**, 4, 227–35.

MALTZMAN, I. ed. (1960) 'Experimental studies in the training of originality', *Psychological Monographs*, **64**, 493.

MALTZMAN, I. (1960) 'On the training of originality', *Psychological Review*, **67**, 229–42.

MARSH, R. W. (1964) 'A statistical re-analysis of Getzels and Jackson's Data', *Brit. J. Ed. Psychol.*, **34**, 91–3.

MARTINSON, R. A. and LESSINGER, L. M. (1961) 'Problems in the identification of intellectually gifted pupils', *Exceptional Children*, **26**, 3–38.

MEDNICK, S. (1962) 'The associative basis of the creative process', *Psychological Review*, **69**, 220–32.

MERRIFIELD, P. R. and DE MILLE (1962) 'Creativity and intelligence', *Educational Psychological Measurement XXII*, **22**, 803–8.

MILES, CATHERINE (1946) 'Gifted children', in L. Carmichael, ed., *Manual of Child Psychology*, Ch. 16. Wiley.

MILLER, VERA (1962) 'Creativity and Intelligence in the arts', *Education*, **82**, 488–95.

MUSGRAVE, P. W. (1965) *The Sociology of Education*. Methuen.

NEWSON, J. and NEWSON, E. (1963) *Patterns of Infant Care in an Urban Community*. Allen & Unwin; Penguin Books.

NEWSON, J. and NEWSON, E. (1968) *Four Years Old in an Urban Community*. Allen & Unwin.

NORMAN, R. D. (1966) 'The interpersonal values of parents of achieving and non-achieving gifted children', *Journal of Psychology*, **64**, no. 1, 49–57.

OGILVIE, E. (1973) *Gifted Children in Primary Schools*, Schools Council.

OXFORDSHIRE EDUCATION COMMITTEE STEERING COMMITTEE (1967) *Exceptionally Gifted Children*.

PARKYN, G. W. (1948) *Children of High Intelligence: a New Zealand Study*. N.Z. Council for Educational Research N.Y. Oxford University Press.

PASSOW, A. H. and GOLDBERG, M. L. (1962) 'The talented youth project: a progress report', *Exceptional Children*, **28**, 223–31.

PASSOW, A. H. and GOLDBERG, M. L. (1963) 'Study of underachieving gifted', in *Educating the Academically Able*. N.Y. McKay. Ch. 7.

PATRICK, C. (1935) 'Creative thought in poets', *Archives of Psychology*, **26**, 73.

PATRICK, C. (1937) 'Creative thought in artists', *Journal of Psychology*, **4**, 35.

PHILLIPS, C. J. and BANNON, W. J. (1968) 'The Stanford-Binet Form LM. 3rd Revision: a Local English study of norms concurrent validity and social differences', *Brit. J. Ed. Psychol.*, **38**, no. 2.

PLOWDEN REPORT (1967) *Children and their Primary Schools*. H.M.S.O.

PRINGLE, M. L. K. (1957) 'The study of exceptional children', *International Review of Education*, **23**, 200.

PRINGLE, M. L. K. (1965) *Investment in Children: a symposium on positive child care and constructive education*. Longmans.

PRINGLE, M. L. K. (1966) *Social Learning and its Measurement*. Longmans.

PRINGLE, M. L. K. (1970) *Able Misfits*. Longman.

PRINGLE, M. L. K. (1971) *Deprivation and Education*, 2nd edn., Longman.

PRINGLE, M. L. K. and EDWARDS, J. B. (1964) Some moral concepts and judgments of junior school children. *British Journal of Social and Clinical Psychology*, **3**, 196–215.

PRINGLE, M. L. K. and PICKUP, K. T. (1963) 'The reliability and validity of the Goodenough Draw-a-man test; a pilot longitudinal study', *Brit. J. Ed. Psychol.* 1963, **37**, 29.

PRINGLE, M. L. K., BUTLER, N. R. and DAVIE, R. (1966) *11,000 Seven-Year-Olds*. Longmans.

ROBBINS REPORT (1963) *Higher Education*, H.M.S.O.

ROE, ANNE (1951) 'Psychological study of eminent biologists', *Psychological Monographs*, **64**, no. 331.

ROE, ANNE (1951) 'Psychological study of eminent physical scientists', *Genet. Psychol. Monogr.* **43**, 121.

ROE, ANNE (1951) 'A study of imagery in research scientists', *Journal of Personality*, **19**, 459.

Roe, Anne (1952) 'What is the gifted individual like?', *Scientific American*, **187**, no. 5, 21–5.

Roe, Anne (1953) *The Making of a Scientist*. Dodd, Mead & Co.

Roe, Anne (1953) 'A psychological study of eminent psychologists and anthropologists and a comparison with biological and physical scientists', *Psychological Monographs*, **67**, no. 352.

Roe, Anne (1956) *The Psychology of Occupations*. Wiley.

Roe, Anne (1957) 'Early determinants of vocational choice', *Journal of Counselling Psychology*, **4**, no. 3, 212–17.

Rushton, J. (1966) 'Relationship between personality, character and scholastic success in 11 year old children, *Brit. J. Ed. Psychol.*, **36**, 179–91

Savage, R. D. (1966) 'Personality factors and academic attainment in junior school children', *Brit. J. Ed. Psychol.* **35**, 90–2.

Schachter, S. (1963) 'Birth order, eminence and higher education', *American Sociological Review*, 28, 757–68.

Schools Council (1968) *Enquiry 1 : Young School Leavers*. H.M.S.O.

Seglow, J., Pringle, M. L. K. and Wedge, P. (1972) *Growing Up Adopted*, N.F.E.R.

Shaw, M. C. and McCuen, J. T. (1960) 'The onset of academic under-achievement in bright children', *Journal of Educational Psychology*, **51**, 103–7.

Shields, J. B. (1968) *The Gifted Child*. N.F.E.R.

Smith, D. C. (1962) *Personal and Social Adjustment of Gifted Adolescents*. N.E.A. Council for Exceptional Children. Research Monograph no. 4 Nat. Ed. Ass. Washington D.C.

Smith I. McFarlane (1964) *Spacial Ability : its educational and social significance*. University of London Press.

Spearman, C. (1931) *The Creative Mind*. Nisbet.

Springer, K. J. and Weisberg, P. S. (1961) 'Environmental factors in creative function: a study of gifted children', *Archives of General Psychiatry*, **5**, 554–64.

Stefflre, B. and Bonsall, M. (1955) 'The temperament of gifted children', *California Journal of Educational Measurement*, **6**, 195–9.

Stein, M. L. and Heinze, S. J. (1960) *Creativity and the Individual*. Free Press of Glencoe.

Stewart, L. H. (1959) 'Occupational level scale of children's interests', *Educational and Psychological Measurement*, **19**, 401–10.

Stott, D. H. (1963) *The Social Adjustment of Children. Manual to the Bristol Social-Adjustment Guides*. University of London Press.

Strumfer, D. J. W. and Mienie, C. J. P. (1968) 'A validation of the Harris-Goodenough Tests', *Brit. J. Psychol.*, **38**, Part 1, 96.

Sultan, E. E. (1962) 'A factorial study in the domain of creative thinking', *Brit. J. Ed. Psychol.*, **32**, 78–82.

Sumption, M. R. and Luecking, E. M. (1960) *Education of the Gifted*. New York, Ronald Press.

Sunday Times (1968) 'Success before Six', 10 and 17 March; also 26 November 1967.

Tanner, J. M. (1961) *Education and Physical Growth*. University of London Press.

Taylor, C. W. (1967) 'Questioning and creating: a model for curriculum reform', *Journal of Creative Behaviour*, **1**, no. 1, 22–23.

Taylor, C. W., ed. (1964) *Widening Horizons in Creativity*. Wiley.

Taylor, C. W. ed. (1964) *Creativity : progress and potential*. McGraw-Hill.

Taylor, C. W. and Barron, F. (1963) *Scientific Creativity : its recognition and development*. Wiley.

Taylor, P. H. (1962) 'Children's evaluation of the characteristics of the good teacher', *Brit. J. Ed. Psychol.* **32**, 258–66.

Telford, C. W. and Sawrey, J. M. (1967) *The Exceptional Individual*. Prentice-Hall.

Tempest, N. 'Leverhulme project on education of gifted children', (unpublished).

Terman, L. M. (1906) 'Genius and stupidity', *Pedagogical Seminary*, **13**, 307–73.

Terman, L. M. (1925) *Mental and Physical Traits of a Thousand Gifted Children*, vol. I. *Genetic Studies of Genius*. Stanford University Press.

TERMAN, L. M. (1954) 'The discovering and encouragement of exceptional talent'. *American Psychologist*, **9**, no. 6, 221–30; also in W. B. Barbe, ed. *Psychology and Education of the Gifted*.

TERMAN, L. M. and ODEN, M. H. (1947) *The Gifted Child Grows Up*. *Genetic Studies of Genius*, vol. 4, Stanford University Press.

TERMAN, L. M., BURKS, B. S. and JENSEN, D. W. F. (1930) *The Promise of Youth*. *Genetic Studies of Genius*, vol. 3. Stanford University Press.

TERMAN, L. M. and ODEN, M. H. (1959) *The Gifted Group at Mid-Life*. *Genetic Studies of Genius*, vol. 5, Stanford University Press.

THOM, D. A. and NEWELL, N. (1945) 'Hazards of the high I.Q.', *Mental Hygiene*, **29**, 61–77.

THORNDIKE, R. L. (1948) 'An evaluation of the adult intellectual status of Terman's Gifted Children', *Journal of Genetic Psychology*, **72**, 17–27.

THORNDIKE, R. L. (1963) 'Some methodological issues in the study of creativity', *Proceedings of 1962 International Conference on Testing Problems*. (E.T.S. Princeton). N.Y.

THORNDIKE, R. L. (1963) 'The measurement of creativity', *Teachers College Record*, **64**, 423–4.

THOULESS, R. H. (1969) *Map of Educational Research*. N.F.E.R.

TORRANCE, E. P. (1959) *Explorations in Creative Thinking in the Early School Years*. Research Memorandum, University of Minnesota.

TORRANCE, E. P. (1961) 'Priming creative thinking in the primary grades', *Elementary School Journal*, **62**, 34–41.

TORRANCE, E. P. (1962) *Guiding Creative Talent*. Prentice-Hall.

TORRANCE, E. P. (1963) *Education and the Creative Potential*. University of Minnesota Press.

TORRANCE, E. P. (1965a) *Gifted Children in the Classroom*. Macmillan.

TORRANCE, E. P. (1965b) *Rewarding creative Behaviour*. Prentice-Hall.

TORRANCE, E. P. (1966) *Torrance tests of creative thinking. Norms—Technical Manual* (+ directions for tests). Princeton, Personnel Press.

TORRANCE, E. P. and DAUW, D. C. (1966) 'Attitude patterns of creatively gifted High School seniors', *Gifted Child Quarterly*, **10**, no. 2, 48–52.

TORRANCE, E. P., GOWAN, J. C. and DEMOS, G. D. (1967) *Creativity: its educational implications*. Wiley.

TRAPP, E. P. and HIMELSTEIN, P. eds. (1962) *Readings on the Exceptional Child*. Methuen.

TYLER, L. E. (1955) 'The development of vocational interests: The organization of likes and dislikes in 10 year old children', *Journal of Genetic Psychology*, **36**, 33–44.

VERNON, P. E. (1964) 'Creativity and intelligence', *Educational Research*, **6**, no. 3, 163.

VERNON, P. E. (1967) 'Psychological studies of creativity', *Journal of Clinical Psychology and Psychiatry*, **8**.

VERNON, R. E. (1967) A *Cross-cultural Study of Creativity tests with 11-year-old Boys. New research in education*. N.F.E.R.

VERNON, P. E. (1969) *Intelligence and Cultural Environment*. Methuen.

VERNON, P. E. (1970) *Creativity*. Penguin Books.

VINACKE, W. E. and EINDHOVER, J. (1952) 'Creative processes in painting', *Journal of General Psychology*, **47**, 139–64.

WALL, W. D. (1960) 'Highly Intelligent Children. The Psychology of the Gifted', *Educational Research II*, no. 2, 101–10 (pt. I); II, no. 3, 207–16 (pt 2).

WALLACH, M. A. and KOGAN, N. (1965) *Modes of Thinking in Young Children*. Holt, Rinehart & Winston.

WALLAS, G. (1926) *The Art of Thought*. Watts.

WARBURTON, F. W. (1961) 'The measurement of personality I', *Educational research*, **4**, no. 1, 2–17.

WARD, J. (1968) 'An oblique factorization of Wallach and Kogan's "Creativity" correlations', *Brit. J. Ed. Psychol.*, **37**, no. 3, 380.

WHITE, J. P. (1968) 'Creativity and education: a philosophical analysis', *British Journal of Educational Studies*, **16**, no. 2.

WIENER, N. (1953) *Ex-prodigy: My childhood and youth.* Sumion & Schuster.

WISEMAN, S. (1964) *Education and Environment.* Manchester University Press.

WISEMAN, S. ed. (1967) *Intelligence and Ability.* Penguin Books.

WITTY, P. A. (1927) 'The play behaviour of fifty gifted children', *Journal of Educational Psychology*, **18**, 259–65.

WITTY, P. A. (1940) 'A genetic study of 50 gifted children', *Yearbook of the National Society for the Study of Education.*

WITTY, P. A. (1951) *The Gifted Child.* Heath.

WITTY, P. A. (1958) 'Who are the gifted? Education for the Gifted'. *Yearbook of the National Society for the Study of Education.*

WRAGG, M. (1968) 'The leisure activities of boys and girls', *Educational Research*, *N.F.E.R.*, **10**, no. 2, Feb. 1968.

YAMAMOTO, K. (1964) 'Threshold of intelligence in academic achievements of highly creative students', *Journal of Exp. Education*, **32**, 401–4.

YAMAMOTO, K. (1965) 'Multiple achievement battery and repeated measurements: a postscript to three studies on creative thinking', *Psychological Reports*, **16**, 367–75.

YAMAMOTO, K. (1965) 'Validation of tests of Creative Thinking, a review of some studies', *Exceptional Children*, **31**, 281–90.

YAMAMOTO, K. and FRENZEL, B. A. (1966) 'An exploratory component analysis on the Minnesota Tests of Creative Thinking', *California Journal of Educational Research*, **17**, no. 5, 220–9.

YULE, W., LOCKYER, L. and NOONE, A. (1967) 'The reliability and validity of the Goodenough Harris Drawing test', *Brit. J. Ed. Psychol.*, **28**, no. 1, 110.

Subject index